Management Education in Canada

Management Education in Canada: Historical Reflections offers a fresh and critical look at the evolution of management education in Canada. Nearly 25 years after the seminal work *Capitalizing Knowledge* by Barbara Austin, this edited collection revisits and expands upon the debates that shaped the field, while introducing new perspectives and overlooked histories.

Featuring ten scholarly essays from leading academics, this volume explores a range of critical and historiographic approaches to management education, highlighting the ways in which history is written, privileged, and, at times, neglected. Through a variety of themes, including the gendered experiences of female Ph.D. graduates, Africentric and Indigenous leadership approaches, and the role of globalization in shaping management curricula, the book prompts readers to reflect on the past, present, and future of management education in Canada. Chapters cover topics such as the influence of the Administrative Sciences Association of Canada, the underrepresentation of French-language business education, and the critical interrogation of management textbooks. Together, these chapters offer a rich and comprehensive analysis of the cultural, institutional, and intellectual forces shaping the discipline.

This volume will engage scholars, educators, and students in business schools, faculties of management, and those interested in the broader history of higher education, as well as anyone seeking to understand the historical development of management education in Canada. It is an essential contribution to the ongoing conversation about what management education has been and what it could become.

Kristin S. Williams is the Director of the FC Manning School of Business and an Associate Professor in Management at Acadia University.

Albert J. Mills is Professor Emeritus of Management at Saint Mary's University.

Heidi Weigand is Assistant Professor at Dalhousie University in Halifax, Nova Scotia.

Routledge Advances in Management Learning and Education
Series Editors – Mikael Holmqvist and Alan Irwin

The role of managers in society is significant and not without controversy. A key aspect in understanding contemporary management is the education of its practitioners. This series brings together scholars from around the globe to examine and analyse the development of management education from various perspectives.

Elite Business Schools
Education and Consecration in Neoliberal Society
Mikael Holmqvist

The Future of Management Education
Martin R. Fellenz, Sabine Hoidn and Mairead Brady

Self-Organised Schools
Educational Leadership and Innovative Learning Environments
Alberto F. De Toni and Stefano De Marchi

The Business School Curriculum Debate
Scientific Legitimacy versus Practical Relevance
Alexander Styhre

Universities in the Neoliberal Era
Ideologies, Discourses and Management Practices
Edited by Mats Benner and Mikael Holmqvist

Management Education in Canada
Historical Reflections
Edited by Kristin S. Williams, Albert J. Mills and Heidi Weigand

Management Education in Canada

Historical Reflections

Edited by Kristin S. Williams,
Albert J. Mills and Heidi Weigand

NEW YORK AND LONDON

First published 2025
by Routledge
605 Third Avenue, New York, NY 10158

and by Routledge
4 Park Square, Milton Park, Abingdon, Oxon, OX14 4RN

Routledge is an imprint of the Taylor & Francis Group, an informa business

© 2025 selection and editorial matter, Kristin S. Williams, Albert J. Mills and Heidi Weigand; individual chapters, the contributors

The right of Kristin S. Williams, Albert J. Mills and Heidi Weigand to be identified as the authors of the editorial material, and of the authors for their individual chapters, has been asserted in accordance with sections 77 and 78 of the Copyright, Designs and Patents Act 1988.

All rights reserved. No part of this book may be reprinted or reproduced or utilised in any form or by any electronic, mechanical, or other means, now known or hereafter invented, including photocopying and recording, or in any information storage or retrieval system, without permission in writing from the publishers.

Trademark notice: Product or corporate names may be trademarks or registered trademarks, and are used only for identification and explanation without intent to infringe.

ISBN: 9781041009993 (hbk)
ISBN: 9781041010029 (pbk)
ISBN: 9781003612612 (ebk)

DOI: 10.4324/9781003612612

Typeset in Times New Roman
by Newgen Publishing UK

We dedicate this volume to Professor Emerita Barbara Austin who inspired us to continue her work.

Contents

List of Contributors	ix
Acknowledgements	xvii

    Introduction   1
    KRISTIN S. WILLIAMS, ALBERT J. MILLS, AND HEIDI WEIGAND

1 Textbooks as Reflections of Who We Are!   9
    TERRANCE G. WEATHERBEE

2 Making History: Identity Work within a Business School   35
    KRISTIN S. WILLIAMS AND CHANTELLE FALCONER

3 The Administrative Sciences Association of Canada and the Development of Management Studies: 1979–2009   65
    KRISTENE E. COLLER AND HEIDI WEIGAND

4 French Language as a Missing Context in Histories of 'Doing' Business Education in Canada   92
    NICHOLOUS M. DEAL AND RENÉ ARSENEAULT

5 Globalization of Management Education: Business Theory, Competency Model, and the Role of Canadian Business Schools   116
    VISHWANATH BABA AND SHAMSUD D. CHOWDHURY

6 NIKANA'LULKWIK (Leadership)   138
    JEFF WARD, KRISTIN S. WILLIAMS, AND HEIDI WEIGAND

7	The Ubuntu Mindset: Learning to Manage and Lead Better Together, the Africentric Way GEORGE FREMPONG AND RAAVEE KADAM	156
8	Embracing "SANKOFA" at Dalhousie University HEIDI WEIGAND, BINOD SUNDARARAJAN, AND KRISTIN S. WILLIAMS	176
9	From Past to Present: Tracing the Development of Canadian Doctoral Programs in Business CHRISTOPHER M. HARTT, NICHOLOUS M. DEAL, AND ELLEN C. SHAFFNER	196
10	Gendered Experiences: A Dialogic Co-Creation with One of the First Female PhD in Business Graduates in Canada KRISTIN S. WILLIAMS AND LOUISE HESLOP	218
	Index	*243*

Contributors

René Arseneault, Ph.D., is Assistant Professor of Human Resources in the Management Department at Université Laval. Dr. Arseneault was born in a bilingual environment and spent most of his professional life living abroad exploring cultural differences. He has over eight years of international living and working experience, is multilingual, and takes pleasure in learning about cultural diversity. His research focuses primarily on cross-cultural differences in the workplace including areas such as recruitment and selection, diversity management, and personality differences. Working at various post-secondary institutions, Dr. Arseneault has taught recruitment and selection, human resource management, and organizational behaviour, including a non-credited course in French through La Cité.

Vishwanath Baba, Ph.D., joined the DeGroote School of Business in January 2000 as Dean and Professor of Management. Prior to coming to McMaster, Dr. Baba was Professor of Management at Concordia University in Montreal where he held the positions of Chairman of Management and Associate Dean of Graduate Studies. He is currently Editor-in-Chief of the *International Journal of Comparative Management* and was until recently Editor-in-Chief of the *Canadian Journal of Administrative Sciences*. He has been the co-editor of the *International Journal of Comparative Sociology*. He also sits on the editorial boards of several management journals. As a mechanical engineer by training, Dr. Baba obtained his Ph.D. in organizational behaviour from the University of British Columbia in Canada. He is active in management research and has published widely in influential journals in management. He has a keen professional interest in management development and training in the developing world and has been a regular consultant to the Canadian International Development Agency, the Swedish International Development Agency, and the International Development Research Centre of Canada. In addition, Dr. Baba has offered a variety of workshops on the management of mental health for professional audiences in health care, transportation, education, and energy sectors in Canada and abroad. He currently teaches Management Theory at the doctoral level at McMaster University.

Shamsud D. Chowdhury, Ph.D., is Professor of strategy and competitiveness at the Rowe School of Business, Dalhousie University. He received his MBA and Ph.D. degrees from the University of Kentucky. Shamsud is an inaugural fellow of the Administrative Sciences Association of Canada (ASAC). Over the past 30 years, he served ASAC in many capacities such as its Annual Conference Program Chair, Annual Conference Doctoral Consortium Chair, and Board of Directors. He serves on the editorial review board of the *Canadian Journal of Administrative Sciences* and *Metamorphosis: A Journal of Management Research*. Shamsud's research has generated presentations at conferences in North America and overseas and appeared in journals such as *Business Horizons*, *Canadian Journal of Administrative Science*s, *Journal of Business Research*, *International Journal of Human Resource Management*, *Journal of Engineering and Technology Management*, *Journal of Management*, *Journal of Management Studies*, and *Long-Range Planning*. Over the years, he has held visiting appointments at Riga Technical University (Latvia), Helsinki School of Economics (Finland), Warsaw School of Economics (Poland), ESSEC Business School (France), and Bielefeld University (Germany). On behalf of the Canadian International Development Agency (CIDA) and the erstwhile Canadian Consortium of Management Schools (CCMS), Shamsud also actively participated in the development and delivery of strategic management courses for Executive MBA programmes at Riga Technical University and the Warsaw School of Economics.

Kristene E. Coller, Ph.D. With a passion for understanding how we come to know what we know, Kristene studies the neglect of Canadian management thought and its implications to scholarship and management and organization studies. As a lecturer for Mount Royal University, the University of Lethbridge (Calgary Campus), and Saint Mary's University (Calgary), Kristene incorporates her interest in management and organization studies into her classes and challenges students to think about the context in which management theories were developed and how this can impact their own knowledge. Kristene writes on a variety of topics including ANTi-History, management history, management and organization studies, health care, workplace health promotion, and the imposter syndrome.

Nicholous M. Deal, Ph.D., is Assistant Professor in the Department of Business and Tourism at Mount Saint Vincent University in Halifax, Canada. His doctoral dissertation focused on the development of a historical style of management research and writing involving individual performativity from within social networks: ANTi-Microhistory. He has published research on historical method, intersectionality, management education, and employee relations. Nick currently serves as Associate Editor for *Qualitative Research in Organizations and Management* journal and handles the social media as an editor for the *Journal of Management History*. His academic service includes Past Chair of the Business History Division of the Administrative Sciences Association of Canada and elected member of the executive representing graduate students and early career academics in the Management History Division of the Academy of Management.

Chantelle Falconer, Ph.D. (University of Toronto), is a socio-cultural anthropologist with a research interest in gender, political ecology, policy, and development. Broadly, her research has focused on how people experience and make meaning in their lives. She is interested in better understanding how people negotiate, rework, or even contest processes that impinge on their everyday lives, places of work, communities, and environments. Her research is grounded in qualitative, ethnographic enquiry, with field sites in Latin America and North America. In the past Chantelle has conducted research with organic farmers, schoolteachers, anti-mining activists, migrants and refugees, and professionals in the field of gender-based violence prevention. In her current role as Research Facilitator at Dalhousie University, Chantelle supports research and grant development in the Faculty of Management.

George Frempong, Ph.D., is the inaugural Director of Research at the Delmore "Buddy" Daye Learning Institute (DBDLI), a unique Non-for-Profit Organization in Nova Scotia, Canada, with expertise in Africentric research. Over the past five years, he has provided exemplary leadership for the institute, developing Ubuntu-inspired vision and collaboration, leading to several transformative research initiatives. Dr. Frempong received his Ph.D. in Curriculum and Instruction, and his M.A. in Mathematics Education, both from the University of British Columbia, Vancouver. Prior to obtaining these advanced degrees, he earned a B.Sc. in Physics from the University of Science and Technology in Ghana. Over the past three decades, he has worked as a classroom teacher, university Professor, and researcher with publications and related citations in accredited journals that have provided an understanding of how education systems should function to provide opportunities for all learners to succeed. Through research grants from Mitacs, SSHRC, USAID, and Endowment funds, his research work has made a significant policy impact on education systems across Canada and Africa. His current research explores how education paradigms with the Ubuntu mindset should inform the development of inclusive education systems. Publications related to this work include "Frempong, G., & Kadam, R. (2022). Educational Paradigm with Ubuntu Mindset: Implications for Sustainable Development Goals in Education. In D. Ortega-Sánchez (Ed.), *Active Learning – Research and Practice for STEAM and Social Sciences Education*. IntechOpen". Dr. Frempong is a passionate advocate of participatory action research,

xii   *List of Contributors*

working and researching with vulnerable communities to support development initiatives.

Christopher M. Hartt, Ph.D., is Professor of Management at Dalhousie University's Faculty of Agriculture. Chris grew up in Dartmouth in an economically challenged area but benefitted from a strong family who prize education. After 22 years (post-MBA) of managing and being an entrepreneur during which he often wondered if his co-workers, colleagues, and employees learned anything in University, Chris decided he should try to make a difference and enrolled in the Sobey Ph.D. at age 47. During that time, he developed Non-Corporeal Actant Theory (NCA Theory). Bringing together Critical Sensemaking Theory with Actor–Network Theory in qualitative methods education with insights which came from Homi Bhabha, NCA Theory could begin to discover what is behind what seem to be irrational choices and possibly predict them. Key to further enlightenment was work with Indigenous Scholars to connect the symmetry of actors (Actor–Network Theory) with symbiosis of place (an idea consistent with many Indigenous traditions). This work is crystallized in the edited book: *Connecting Values to Action: Non-Corporeal Actants and Choice*.

Louise Heslop, Ph.D., is Distinguished Research Professor and Professor Emerita at the Sprott School of Business, Carleton University. Previously, she was on the faculty of the University of Guelph and worked at Statistics Canada as a Senior Social Science Researcher. She has held senior administrative positions at Carleton University, including Director, Associate Dean of Graduate Studies, and Ph.D. Program Director in Sprott, and Associate Dean of Social Sciences. Her research and professional interests focus on marketing and business strategy emphasizing consumer decision making, especially place, brand, and labelling cue use. She has been identified as one of the most published authors of research in country image and branding. Her research interests also involve food marketing, including consumer acceptance of new technologies, domestic vs. international food selection, food promotion to children, and wine marketing. She has authored, co-authored, or edited over 200 publications and received almost $1 million in research funding. She has taught, presented guest and keynote lectures, and conducted research in over 20 countries. She has received numerous best paper awards, three University Research Achievement Awards, a Graduate Mentor Award, and best teaching award. She has consulted to several government departments, served on various national industry associations and boards, and been a member of the executive of the Administrative Sciences Association of Canada and the Canadian Consortium of Management Deans. She is an active participant in her community and has served on many national, provincial, and local not-for-profit and government-appointed associations, boards, and committees.

List of Contributors xiii

Raavee Kadam, Ph.D., is Postdoctoral Fellow at Saint Mary's University, Halifax. As a practitioner turned academic, she completed her doctoral degree in Business Management from BITS Pilani Dubai Campus. She holds a Bachelor of Engineering in Information Technology and a Master of Business Administration in Systems from the University of Pune. Prior to commencing her Ph.D., she worked in the IT industry in various capacities as Project Lead, SAP HCM Consultant, and Software Engineer. Her doctoral thesis focused on Cultural Intelligence (CQ) as a critical capability for employees working in multicultural environments, and she continues to expand the nomological network of CQ by studying its impact on various individual, team, and organizational outcomes. Apart from CQ, her research also focuses on topics such as cross-cultural and intra-national differences, intersectionality, Indigenous knowledge systems, management education, and entrepreneurship. Her postdoctoral research with the Delmore "Buddy" Daye Learning Institute investigates the adoption of an intersectionality framework to design evidence-driven strategies for improving the learning outcomes of African Nova Scotian students. The project aims to inform educational policy development and provide insights on two aspects: closing the achievement gap and informing inclusive education practices for African Nova Scotian learners. Raavee has taught at business schools in the United Arab Emirates and is a Certified Online Educator from the Hamdan Bin Mohammed Smart University (HBMSU), Dubai. She champions a data-driven approach to addressing equity, diversity, and inclusion in educational systems to ensure no learner is left behind.

Albert J. Mills, Ph.D., is Professor Emeritus of Management at Saint Mary's University. He is also 0.2 Professor of Management Innovation at the University of Eastern Finland. He is currently Co-Chair of the International Board for International Critical Management Studies and has previously served as President of the Administrative Sciences Association of Canada (ASAC); President of the Atlantic Schools of Business (ASB); Divisional Chair of the Critical Management Studies Division of the Academy of Management (AoM); Member at Large of the Management History Division of the AoM; and Archivist of the AoM Women in Management Division. His central research interests revolve around discriminatory practices, historiography, intersectionality, ANTi-History, and Critical Sensemaking. He is the co-editor of *Qualitative Research in Organizations and Management* and the author/editor of 30 books and 20 Special Issues of scholarly journals as well as over 250 journal articles and book chapters.

Ellen C. Shaffner, Ph.D., is Assistant Professor in the Department of Communication Studies at Mount Saint Vincent University in Halifax, Nova Scotia. She holds a Ph.D. in management from Saint Mary's University and currently teaches in the areas of communication management, organizational communication, and public relations. Her research is primarily focused on bringing together organizational history and intersectionality to surface narratives of less-privileged individuals and groups in organizations over time. Her doctoral dissertation, *Toward Intersectional History*, offered a theoretical and methodological approach for incorporating intersectionality into historical research on organizations. In addition to this focus, Ellen's research interests extend to the study of history, diversity, and success in the public relations field; inclusive pedagogy in management and business education; and current and historical organizational communication practices. Ellen has published work in *Organization* and the *Journal of Management History* and presented at conferences around the world, including the Academy of Management. She served as the executive of the Business History division of the Administrative Sciences Association of Canada from 2020–2023, is an executive member of the Atlantic Schools of Business, and co-organized the 2023 Atlantic Schools of Business conference in Halifax, Nova Scotia. Ellen is also highly committed to her students and their professional and personal success and is active in student affairs, advising, and events within her department. In recognition of her teaching excellence and service to students, Ellen was the recipient of the Mount Saint Vincent University Early Career Teaching Award in 2022.

Binod Sundararajan, Ph.D., is Professor of Management at Rowe School of Business, Dalhousie University, Canada and currently serving as the Interim Director of the Rowe School of Business. He teaches Corporate Communication, Business Communication, Managing People, Sustainable Leadership, and Doing Business in Emerging Markets. He has published (as lead author) a course book titled *Lean, Ethical Business Communication* by Oxford University Press. Holding a Ph.D. in Communication and Rhetoric, with undergraduate and Master's degrees in Electrical Engineering, Dr. Sundararajan has diverse research interests that lie in Organizational, Professional, and Business Communication, Leadership Communication, Business Ethics, Technologically Mediated Communication, Social Network Analysis, and Organizational Diversity and has published several peer-reviewed articles in journals, conference proceedings, and book chapters and presented at national and international conferences. He is also currently the lead author of an in-progress textbook on Cross-cultural Business and Financial Practices, Palgrave-MacMillan Publishers.

Jeff Ward has been referred to as a Mi'kmaq knowledge keeper and sharer. He is a leader in the White Eagle Sundance, a Lodge keeper, drum keeper and maker, and a conductor of ceremonies, talking circles and justice circles, with over 30 years of experience. Jeff is the Director of Community Culture and Heritage for Wagmatcook First Nation. He has vast experience and knowledge in the field of culture, management, and administration. He is the former Director of Operations for Metepenagiag Mi'kmaq Nation and the former General Manager for Membertou First Nation. Growing up, Jeff was always involved in community events and has been a leader in their planning, coordination, and participation. When it became time to pursue post-secondary education, the Bachelor of Arts Community Studies programme at Cape Breton University was a natural fit. Currently, he is working on his Master's degree. As a public figure, Jeff has been dancing, drumming, and performing his way into people's hearts since he was a child. He is currently a member of Kun'tewiktuk Singers, Sons of Membertou & Thunder Eagle Singers. He most recently performed at the 100th Anniversary of Vimy Ridge in France. He also Emcee's numerous First Nation Pow-Wows in the Atlantic region and eastern USA Jeff has been a keynote speaker and Emcee for a variety of conferences, including MLSN Justice forum, Reform on Social Security AFN and the latest being the MMIWG Commission of Murdered and Missing Indigenous Women's & Girls' Inquiry in Membertou.

Terrance G. Weatherbee, Ph.D., is fully engaged as Professor of Management at Acadia University in the F.C. Manning School of Business. Here, he primarily teaches subjects in management, organizational theory, and advanced research methods. He is an active researcher, generally adopts a critical posture towards his research, and has numerous published articles, edited chapters, and full texts. In the pre-pandemic era, he travelled extensively presenting his work at various international management conferences. He hopes to be able to return to this practice. His research focus lies at the section of management, organization studies, and history. He apportions research activities to three primary areas. Most prominently, he spends significant time attempting to understand the historical processes which have come to define the management discipline and its chosen future. Relatedly, he investigates the oft-times hidden or masked history in the textbook and its impact on management pedagogy. His third area looks at how organizations leverage or employ history. Currently, he is working with a marketing and tourism colleague examining the use of history and historical narrative by firms in the Nova Scotia wine industry. Specifically, the ways in which firms position themselves as legitimate organizations in competition for Old World and New World wineries. When not busy with teaching and researching, he enjoys his responsibilities as the Director of Steamspace. He presently resides with his wife Maria and his two sons, Riley and Corwin, in the Annapolis Valley of Nova Scotia, Canada.

Heidi Weigand, Ph.D
Halifax, Nova Sc
systemic discri
focused on '

change and move towards a state of thriving. She uses a two-eyed seeing collaborative approach in her research collaborations to dismantle systemic discrimination and nurture a strengths-based approach to foster hope and resiliency with Indigenous, Black, and African-Nova Scotian communities. Her current research includes exploring the role of connection and cultural resiliency to address the burnout epidemic during COVID-19, the role of community mental health organizations in reducing wait times for Mental Health support in Nova Scotia, and the role of Indigenous and African Nova Scotian youth in developing community economic prosperity.

Kristin S. Williams, Ph.D. (she/her), is the Director of the FC Manning School of Business and an Associate Professor in Management with Acadia University. She is also Managing Director and Principal Researcher (and Founder) at Prudentia Institute: Youth Knowledge Exchange, with a mission to support the inclusive development and empowerment of youth through research and knowledge mobilization. Prudentia is home to the award-winning Student Research Lab. Kristin has 25 years of executive leadership experience, spanning the non-profit and for-profit sectors. She holds Visiting Researcher appointment at the University of Eastern Finland (Innovation Management). Kristin is co-editor-in-chief at the journal of *Culture and Organization*, and a member of the Editorial Advisory Board of the *Journal of Management History*. Kristin identifies as a polemical feminist engaged in activist writing and narrative methods in critical management studies. Much of her work has focused on uncovering neglected historical female figures, novel theories, and modes of practice in management and organizational history. Her academic awards include the Udayan Rege Best Dissertation Award (Administrative Sciences Association of Canada), the Senior Women ᴀcademic Administrators of Canada Award of Merit, and an Emerald Literati ᴅ for Outstanding Paper (*Journal of Management History*). She is also ɴt of Queen Elizabeth II's Platinum Jubilee Medal for contributions ᴏpy and Social Services.

Acknowledgements

This project was made possible by the support of Dalhousie University's Faculty of Management. We would like to thank Dr. Kim Brooks for her support.

Introduction

Kristin S. Williams, Albert J. Mills, and Heidi Weigand

Introduction

This book was inspired by a growing interest in critical management studies, business history, and management education in Canada, all of which began to make their mark around the year 2000 with the publication of Barbara Austin's edited collection on the history of Business Education in Canada and the establishment of Saint Mary's University PhD in Business Administration, sometimes referred to the "Halifax School" (Bettin, Mills, and Helms Mills 2016).

Austin's book – *Capitalizing Knowledge* – was the first significant offering of perspectives on management education in Canada. Canadian perspectives are generally neglected in management and organizational studies, and this is especially so in management education. Since 2000, there has been relatively little reflection on the development of management education in Canada. Austin's (2000a) book covered a range of perspectives on the major influences in management education, including the United States (US) and industry, the development of what is now called the *Administrative Sciences Association of Canada* (ASAC), the emergence of Canadian business scholarship and sense of legitimacy, and the evolution of business curriculum and factors influencing the expansion of management education and its key drivers. Austin played an important role in the development of the Business History Division of ASAC and was influential in crafting its history (Austin 1994, 1995, 1998, 2000a,b). As editors, we felt much has transpired since Austin's edited collection was published and this new edited collection aims to reengage the conversations that Austin inspired with new contributions. It is due to her role in management education in Canada that we dedicate this book to Barbara Austin.

In the early 2000s, the "Halifax School" was beginning to make its own mark on the field of critical historiography in Canada. Scholars produced from and in association with the Halifax School began writing histories of ASAC (McLaren and Mills 2013); the Atlantic Schools of Business (MacNeil and Mills 2015); Canadian scholarship (Coller, McNally, and Mills 2015); Association to Advance Collegiate Schools of Business (AACSB) (McKee, Mills, and

Weatherbee 2005); the neglect of Canadian management theory (McLaren and Mills 2020); Air Canada (Corrigan and Mills 2017; Myrden, Mills, and Helms Mills 2011; Hartt et al. 2014); the French-English debate (Arsenault, Deal, and Mills 2019); British Airways (Coller, Helms Mills, and Mills 2016; Hendricks et al. 2020); Pan American Airways (Deal et al. 2019; Weigand et al. 2017); gender (Williams and Mills 2017; Williams and Mills 2018; Shaffner, Mills, and Helms Mills 2019), along with several books and edited collections (McLaren, Mills, and Weatherbee 2015).

With these developments in mind, we set out to reflect on the field nearly 25 years on, bringing together leading Canadian management educators from different perspectives, including amodernist, modernist, and postmodernist historical accounts. What has resulted is a deeply insightful, critical set of essays that have a distinct inclination toward historiography vs. history. We also set out to intentionally include voices that are still emerging in the field of management education and ought to receive more consideration. These neglected perspectives include Indigenous and Africentric leadership perspectives as well as some re-engagement with the French-English debates and gender and feminism. Together, this set of essays tells a bigger story about not only the past but also what management education has the potential to be in the future.

The Chapters

Our first chapter critically interrogates university textbooks as a pedagogical object. Textbooks are taken-for-granted objects in management faculty and schools of business. Weatherbee's critique is designed to surface the various ways in which the content of management textbooks does not represent objective or value-free management knowledge, nor a Canadian context. Indeed, Weatherbee argues that there are very few (if any) Canadian textbooks. His chapter seeks to highlight how textbooks quite often perpetuate problematic elements of management and organizational theory, presenting either idealistic caricatures of management and managers or stereotypical views of management and employees. Finally, Weatherbee's chapter draws our attention to the ways in which textbooks assume, unreflexively, that management knowledge is somehow free of political and ideological elements.

Our second chapter delves into where management is taught and by whom. Taking as a starting point the view that business schools have lagged behind developing a record of their past (unlike Schools of Law, Engineering, and Medicine) despite beginning more than 100 years ago. Focusing on the Faculty of Management at Dalhousie University, Williams and Falconer investigate how a federated faculty develops their sense of belonging, defines a common sense of who they are and what they do, and regulates people (negotiating who is in and out) and resources (haves and have-nots). Their study explores how a federated faculty makes sense of their shared history and identity and their explorations consider the temporal, geographic, structural, and conceptual borders and boundaries in which identity construction is transacted. Williams and Falconer employ a socio-linguistic and an intertextual analysis of participant interviews involving staff, faculty, and past deans, along with strategic documents to trace the trajectory of organizational discourse and examine how conflicts and tensions are enunciated, how social identities are cultivated, how borders and boundaries are constructed, and how behaviors and identities are regulated. Their chapter illustrates how dominant discourses prescribe ways of thinking and behaving in shared academic space while also detailing the discursive effects on organizational actors.

Our third chapter sets the stage for future chapters by illustrating how ASAC as a key player and actor in advancing management education in Canada. We felt strongly that a chapter on ASAC was paramount, and it connects with many of the other chapters in this volume, most notably Chapters 4 and 9. Using ANTi-History, this chapter traces how management studies in Canada have come to reflect US models of management. Following members of the ASAC executive members, the annual ASAC conference chair, and division editors, Coller and Weigand surface the tensions that have impacted ASAC, its ability to become a repository of Canadian scholarship and its ability to be seen as a legitimate academic institution within the academic broader field. These accounts are surfaced by examining executive meeting minutes, letters between members of the executive, and journal publications reflecting on the history of ASAC between 1979 and 2009. By tracing the actions of ASAC actors, their analysis reveals how management studies in Canada have been influenced by US values and interests.

In our next chapter (Chapter 4), Deal and Arseneault offer a much-neglected perspective on the role of French business education in Canada. To advance an understanding of why this neglect of Canada's second official language exists in the first place, they problematize the role Anglocentrism has played in business education writ large. Deal and Arseneault forward a new history of French business education by offering three narratives from the recent past including the (mis)representation of the French language across Canadian universities; a disadvantage of French business scholars in mobilizing knowledge in French scholarly outlets; and the prominence and impact of Anglocentrism that presents a conundrum for faculty in French-speaking universities to publish their scholarship in English outlets.

Le développement de l'historique des écoles de commerces est depuis longtemps un élément essentiel de la recherche en études de gestion et d'organisation. Jusqu'à récemment, la plupart des travaux d'historisation de ces institutions ont négligé des contextes nationaux spécifiques comme le Canada. Même dans les histoires de l'éducation commerciale au Canada, il manque une perspective française. Ce que nous faisons dans ce chapitre est de faire avancer la compréhension des raisons pour lesquelles cette négligence de la deuxième langue officielle du Canada existe en premier lieu et, dans le processus, de problématiser le rôle que l'anglocentrisme a joué dans l'éducation commerciale au sens large. Nous présentons une nouvelle histoire de l'enseignement des affaires en français au Canada en offrant trois récits du passé récent, notamment: la (mauvaise) représentation de la langue française dans les universités canadiennes; un désavantage des universitaires français en gestion dans la mobilisation des connaissances dans les débouchés universitaires français; et l'importance et l'impact de l'anglocentrisme qui présente une énigme pour les professeurs des universités francophones de publier leurs bourses dans des médias anglophones.

Chapter 5 explores the potential of Globalization. The chapter begins with an introduction to globalization and discusses its strengths and weaknesses in the context of capitalism. Baba and Chowdhury make the case that the net present value of globalization has been positive for both economic growth and human well-being. Consequently, they argue that globalization may serve as a paradigmatic platform for business education. Emphasis is placed on the MBA program, to advance a new theory of business education that incorporates globalization as a permeating notion in generating a usable body of business knowledge that would serve as the basis for management training. Baba and Chowdhury outline the parameters of management training and theorize a managerial competence model that is globally relevant. In the context of their proposed model, they explain the potential leadership role of Canadian business schools in promoting a globalized curriculum for business education and management training.

Chapter 6 introduces readers to Indigenous perspectives on leadership and the tensions between Western notions of business and management and Indigenous traditional wisdom. Indigenous perspectives remain marginalized due to the legacies of colonialism and ongoing systemic racism. Traditional (Western) management theories continue to dominate management practice. This chapter offers a decolonizing perspective at the intersection of management education and Indigenous ideas. Ward, Williams, and Weigand weave together allegory, autobiography, and Indigenous storytelling. Several lessons are shared, including (1) what constitutes our ideas of wealth, (2) the role of Elders, (3) ceremony, (4) leadership, and (5) the medicine wheel. Underpinning these ideas are the values inherent in the seven sacred teachings. These lessons are shared alongside what contemporary views within management and organizational studies have to say that might relate to these ideas and serve as entry points to broader management education discourse. In a book about the history of management education in Canada, this chapter reflects on the negligence of management education to consider Indigenous ways of knowing, in hopes that it might inspire a more inclusive future practice.

In Chapter 7, our readers are introduced to the Africentric concept of Ubuntu: *I am because we are*. Responding to the call to decolonize the business school, Frempong and Kadam argue that Ubuntu, as a management and leadership philosophy, can be adopted within the praxis of management education to train future managers and leaders to cultivate people-centered mindsets. The Ubuntu philosophy contends that people are inseparably bound to each other's humanity, and a person is a person only through other humans. Ubuntu, which served as a transformative tool for an entire nation – South Africa's transition from apartheid to democracy, is argued herein as a new perspective on organizational and people management that is more compassionate and humanistic. Frempong and Kadam contend that Africentric knowledge systems and values such as Ubuntu are universal and fundamental to our understanding of inclusive learning environments and human development and therefore critical for the field of management learning if it is to remain relevant for all students.

In chapter eight, the authors investigate how to adopt more inclusive practices into management education, by embracing *Sankofa* which translates from Ghanese to mean "it is not taboo to fetch what is at risk of being left behind". In this chapter, Weigand, Sundararajan, and Williams offer insights into Dalhousie University's history of anti-Blackness, anti-Black racism, settler origins, and the recommendations from the Lord Dalhousie Report to help transform the University. According to the report, Dalhousie was the first University in Canada to take part in this self-reflecting examination of its colonial history. The goal was to address Black History and engage in progressive practices to address the considerable neglect of the value of BIPOC's (Black, Indigenous, People of Color) economic activity and influence, business, and consumerism in our society. Authors share stories of advocating and implementing change in administration, research, teaching, and service within the business school context.

Chapter 9 considers the progress of doctoral training in Canada. Hartt, Deal, and Shaffner explore the origins of business and management-related PhD programs and surface a historical narrative of the development of doctoral programs from past to present. They employ non-corporeal actant theory to reveal how tradition, legitimacy, replication, and rigor drive the development of these programs. Through their analysis, Hartt, Deal, and Shaffner contribute to ongoing work tracing the development of a Canadian management discipline and offer an extension of Austin's (2000a) alternative history of the Canadian business school. Ultimately, this chapter helps demonstrate the need to examine how management as a discipline is produced and reproduced in Canada through a largely isomorphic doctoral business education machine and considers the implications of this primarily neoliberal mechanization on the field of business education more generally.

Our final chapter offers a gendered perspective on business education. Williams interviews one of the first women to receive a PhD in Business in Canada, Louise Heslop. Professor Heslop is a Distinguished Research Professor and Professor Emerita in Marketing at the Sprott School of Business, Carleton University. Her research and professional interests focus on marketing and business strategy with an emphasis on consumer behavior and decision-making.

She has authored, co-authored, and edited over 200 publications. She earned her PhD in Business at the University of Western Ontario, graduating in 1977. Professor Heslop shares what it was like as an early female PhD in Business in academia. This chapter features a colloquial methodological approach in which Professor Heslop and Williams co-create a conversation about lived experience.

The chapters presented in this edited collection seek to enlarge our understanding of the history of management education in Canada, whilst also looking forward to what management education in Canada ought to consider. This edited collection of essays brings together diverse perspectives and neglected stories, while also introducing new themes in management education. Additionally, the authors of this edited collection are an esoteric collection of community and business school educators, historians, and critical historiographers, thus evoking consideration not just of what constitutes our notion of the history of management education and how and where it is taught but also how such history is constructed and reproduced and by whom. The authors also introduce new influences in management education, including Indigenous and Africentric perspectives and approaches, while revisiting some of the original topics in Austin's collection, such as the continued development of ASAC.

Conclusion

We see this collection as complementary to other education resources in management education at the undergraduate and graduate levels. In addition to business and management history audiences, readers interested in the broader socio-economic impact of management education, the link between industry and management education, approaches to management pedagogy, and those interested in political economy may be interested in this collection of essays.

References

Arsenault, Rene, Nicholous Deal, and Albert J. Mills. 2019. "Reading "Canadian" Management in Context: Development of English and French Education." *Journal of Management History* 25 (2):180–202.

Austin, Barbara. 1994. "ASAC: The Early Years of the Association.1957-1972." *Proceedings of the 1994 Administrative Sciences Association of Canada, Business History Interest Group, Halifax, 25-28 June* 15 (14):1–11.

Austin, Barbara. 1995. "ASAC And The Crisis In Management Education, 1973-1985." *Proceedings of the 1995 Administrative Sciences Association of Canada, Business History Interest Division, Windsor 3-6 June* 16 (15).

Austin, Barbara. 1998. "The Role of the Administrative Sciences Association in Institutionalizing Management Education in Canada." *Canadian Journal of Administrative Sciences* 15 (3):255–266.

Austin, Barbara. 2000a. "The Administrative Sciences Association of Canada, 1957–1999." In *Capitalizing Knowledge*, edited by Barbara Austin, 266–294. Toronto: University of Toronto Press.

Austin, Barbara, ed. 2000b. *Capitalizing Knowledge, Essays on The History of Business Education in Canada*. Toronto: University of Toronto Press.

Bettin, Caterina, Albert J. Mills, and Jean Helms Mills. 2016. ""The Halifax School": An Actor-Network Analysis of Critical Management Studies and the Sobey PhD in Management Programme." In *CMS: Global Voices, Local Accent*, edited by Christopher Grey, Isabelle Huault, Véronique Perret and Laurent Taskin, 36–53. London: Routledge.

Coller, Kristine, Jean Helms Mills, and Albert J. Mills. 2016. "The British Airways Heritage Collection: An Ethnographic 'History'." *Business History* 58 (4):547–570.

Coller, Kristine, Corrine McNally, and Albert J. Mills. 2015. "The Inner Circle: Towards a 'Canadian' Management History – Key Canadian Contributors to New Institution Theory." In *The Routledge Companion to Management and Organizational History*, edited by Patricia Genoe McLaren, Albert J. Mills and Terrance G. Weatherbee, 342–360. London: Routledge.

Corrigan, Larry, and Albert J. Mills. 2017. "Men on Board: Can Actor-Network Theory Critique the Persistence of Gender Inequity?" In *Insights and Research on the study of Gender and Intersectionality in International Airline Culture* edited by Albert J. Mills. Bradford: Emerald Books.

Deal, Nicholous, Albert J. Mills, Jean Helms Mills, and Gabrielle Durepos. 2019. "History in the Making: Following the Failed Attempt of Wolfgang Langewiesche in Pan American History Project." In *Connecting Values to Action: Non-Corporeal Actants and Choice*, edited by Christopher M. Hartt, 37–51. Bingley: Emerald.

Hartt, Christopher M., Albert J. Mills, Jean Helms Mills, and Lawrence T. Corrigan. 2014. "Sense-Making and Actor Networks: The Non-Corporeal Actant and the Making of an Air Canada History." *Management & Organizational History* 9 (3):288–304.

Hendricks, Kerry, Nick Deal, Albert J. Mills, and Jean Helms Mills. 2020. "Intersectionality as a Matter of Time." *Management Decision* 59 (11): 2567–2582. doi: 10.1108/md-02-2019-0264

MacNeil, Ryan T., and Albert J. Mills. 2015. "Organizing a Precarious Black Box: An Actor-Network Account of the Atlantic Schools of Business, 1980-2006." *Canadian Journal of Administrative Sciences* 32 (3):203–213.

McKee, Margaret, Albert J. Mills, and Terrance G. Weatherbee. 2005. "Institutional Field of Dreams: Exploring the AACSB and the New Legitimacy of Canadian Business Schools." *Canadian Journal of Administrative Sciences* 22 (4):288–301.

McLaren, Patricia Genoe, and Albert J. Mills. 2013. "Internal Cohesion in Response to Institutional Plurality: The Administrative Sciences Association of Canada." *Canadian Journal of Administrative Sciences* 30 (1):40–55.

McLaren, Patricia Genoe, and Albert J. Mills. 2020. "An Analysis of Canadian Management Theory: Where It Is, and Why We Need It?" In *The Routledge Companion to Management and Organizational History*, edited by Patricia McLaren Genoe, Albert J. Mills and Terrance G. Weatherbee. London: Routledge.

McLaren, Patricia Genoe, Albert J. Mills, and Terrance G. Weatherbee. 2015. *The Routledge Companion to Management & Organizational History*. London: Routledge.

Myrden, Susan E., Albert J. Mills, and Jean Helms Mills. 2011. "The Gendering of Air Canada: A Critical Hermeneutic Approach." *Canadian Journal of Administrative Sciences* 28 (4):440–452.

Shaffner, Ellen C., Albert J. Mills, and J. Helms Mills. 2019. "Intersectional History: Exploring the Possibilities of Intersectionality over Time." *Journal of Management History* 25 (4):444–463.

Weigand, Heidi, Shannon Webb, Albert J. Mills, and Jean Helms Mills. 2017. "The Junctures of Intersectionality: Race, Gender, Class and Nationality and the Making of Pan American Airways, 1929-1989." In *Insights and Research on the Study of Gender and Intersectionality in International Airline Cultures Over Time* edited by Albert J. Mills, 417–444. Bingley: Emerald.

Williams, Kristin S., and Albert J. Mills. 2017. "Frances Perkins: Gender, Context and History in the Neglect of a Management Theorist." *Journal of Management History* 23 (1):32–50. doi: 10.1108/jmh-09-2016-0055

Williams, Kristin S., and Albert. J. Mills. 2018. "Hallie Flanagan and the Federal Theater Project: A Critical Undoing of Management History." *Journal of Management History* 24 (3):282–299.

1 Textbooks as Reflections of Who We Are!

Terrance G. Weatherbee

On Textbooks

When I set out to write this chapter, I had assumed that what I had been invited to do for this collection was a relatively straightforward task, craft a historically oriented chapter on management textbooks in the Canadian context. As I was somewhat familiar with both textbooks and with historical studies, I was comfortable in agreeing to contribute along those lines. However, much to my later chagrin, I discovered I had little inkling of what I would eventually learn. Whether it was about textbooks as a class of pedagogical objects in general, or about Canadian management textbooks specifically. What I did learn, the results which I present in some detail in the sections which follow, I found both enlightening and surprising. Perhaps you may as well.

First, and perhaps most contentiously I suspect, I have learned that there are very few, indeed if any, *Canadian* management textbooks. Despite what they declare on the cover! Yes, there are many management textbooks that *appear* to be Canadian. These usually have *Canadian Edition* as a line of text prominently associated with the title. But appearances are often deceiving. I will argue that such is the case more often than not for *Canadianized* management textbooks. By Canadianized, I am referring to the process of taking a textbook usually authored for the U.S. market and amending it in such a way as to incorporate Canadian examples or Canadian cases where appropriate. Otherwise, the management subjects presented in the text remain unchanged. It is typically the case that a Canadian author completes this task.

Second, the taken-for-granted nature of the use of textbooks in our teaching belies the potential significance of their socio-political nature. In using them to support our teaching, we rarely consider how they are produced and the roles they come to play in our classrooms and the impacts they have beyond. The omnipresence of the textbook in our educational systems masks their agential characteristics and the extra-pedagogical influences they have on not only what facts students learn but also how students come to think about these facts. In this

DOI: 10.4324/9781003612612-2

respect, the ubiquity of textbooks at all levels of education veils their ideological or propagandic nature.

Third, even given a broad scholarly acknowledgement of the centrality and critical role that textbooks have at every level in our modern systems of education, our *collective* understanding of textbooks remains limited. Our knowledge of textbooks, whether of their errors and omissions, debatable inclusions and exclusions of fact or theory, or indeed, their extra-pedagogical impacts, is still largely collectively unacknowledged. It is manifest only in isolated snippets, though these may be found across nearly every scholarly field in the natural and social sciences and in the arts and humanities. While there is more-than-sufficient research to form a sub-field with textbooks as the object of study, in the absence of such, some synthesis of what research tells us about textbooks is called for at this point.

A Short Contemporary History of Textbook Research

Textbooks, as didactic tools, were first conceived of as literary devices designed to teach reading and writing (Elson, 1964). Thus, for the hundreds of years of the print era, much of the history of research on textbooks is to be found in literacy and education studies. As intimated in the introduction, however, textbooks also act in other ways than simply as educational devices. Beyond their didactic function, research which began to recognize their socio-political nature commenced over 100 years ago at the beginning of twentieth century. At that time, state-sanctioned school textbooks often portrayed other nationalities or ethnic populations using negative stereotypes or they culturally marginalized these groups in other ways. This practice was so common in European school texts that the League of Nations identified this form of state-sponsored hyper-nationalism as one of the root factors contributing to the outbreak of war in 1914 (Berghahn & Schissler, 1987).

Known as the "textbook problem" (Kawashima, 2014, p. 91), the League's International Committee on Intellectual Cooperation was tasked with promoting and fostering a spirit of international cooperation amongst its member states. Their mandate was to evaluate state-authorized school texts and recommend changes to how national histories were portrayed within them (Osborne, 2016). Both the League of Nations and its effort to address the problematics of state textbooks would unfortunately become failed projects.

However, the textbook would once again come to research prominence just after the Second World War, for two reasons. First, and similarly motivated, the United Nations Educational, Scientific and Cultural Organization (UNESCO), following in the footsteps of the League, instituted a project studying textbooks (Faure, 2011). Again, the goal was to break the perceived contribution of state textbooks to outbreaks of conflict and to reduce the potential reasons for the human cataclysm of war. Unfortunately, despite the worthy intent of these and similar initiatives such as the work of the Georg Eckert Institute, the textbook problematic persists. Hyper-nationalism and "a singular best story" in state-authorized history texts continues well into the twenty-first century (Foster, 2012, p. 49; Schissler & Soysal, 2005).

Second, and contemporaneous with the formation of the renewed UNESCO programme, scholarly interest in the pedagogical function of textbooks after the Second World War also expanded greatly. Most of this research was focused on primary and secondary school history texts rather than on post-secondary texts (Ferguson, Collison, Power, & Stevenson, 2006). Today, while there are quite a few individual studies undertaken across the academy, research on post-secondary textbooks tends to be largely restricted to texts published in the United States (Reed, 2018). So, for objects which are so intimately connected to society's knowledge production at the post-secondary level globally, textbooks remain very much an under-researched object (Manza, Sauder, & Wright, 2010).

This lack is especially true for business/management textbooks (Stambaugh & Quinn Trank, 2010). A surprising situation given the many practitioner and scholarly concerns expressed about the role of business schools in our modern society, the values that business education is perceived to inculcate in our students, and the type of manager and management practices that result from business education (De Vita & Case, 2016; Navarro, 2008). Outcomes and circumstances which largely exist because of the role and impacts of textbooks in business schools.

So, What Are Textbooks Really?

Normatively, textbooks are "books, reusable workbooks, or manuals intended for use as a principal source of study for a given class or group of students" (Mahar, 1966, p. 154). Textbooks accompany students throughout the full range of their educational experiences starting at the beginning of schooling and continuing through secondary and post-secondary levels. Textbooks are globally acknowledged as being foundational to modern pedagogical practices (Granitz, Kohli, & Lancellotti, 2021) and in the Western developed world, student learning is almost exclusively centred around textbooks (Issitt, 2004). Beyond their material ontology as didactic objects (Bölsterli Bardy, 2015), sociologically textbooks are so ubiquitous in teaching and learning that they have become the symbolic icons of education (Altbach, 2017). The very ubiquity and naturalness of textbooks, even the simplest of textbooks – and here I speak of textbooks writ large not just those written for a university or college audience – certainly belies their complexity. As textbooks *live and come into being* at the intersection of the social, the economic, the political, the literary, and the scientific domains of our society (Fuchs, 2014), they are truly complicated epistemological and ontological objects.

Unlike any other form of academic output, textbooks are produced by a unique set of scholarly, organizational, and market forces (Manza et al., 2010; Stambaugh & Quinn Trank, 2010). Textbooks are produced in the Venn overlap of these various spaces and practices. So, textbooks are always composite and compromise creations. Part scholarship, part marketing, part propaganda, and always ideological textbooks are the children of a network of actors; each with different interests, each pursuing different goals (Cameron, Ireland, Lussier, New, & Robbins, 2003a). The resulting content of a textbook, including its layout and format, its price and distribution, is always an amalgam produced by the interactions of these actors. Embodied as textbooks, these very actors are responsible for the creation of what we see as the foundational "building blocks in the architecture of knowledge" and it is these actors who collectively produce "the voices of [our] disciplines" (Issitt, 2004, p. 688).

When textbooks *speak*, they act as the interface between the teacher and student, the scientist and the layperson, and the scholar and the practitioner. Textbooks are the purveyors and carriers of Western societies' knowledge – for all our various scientific and humanistic disciplines and have become the embodied articulation of scientific paradigms (Myers, 1992). And in this regard textbooks perpetuate the arts and the sciences. But textbooks also play a key role in the transmission, maintenance, and perpetuation of particular social ideologies (Apple, 2012; Apple & Christian-Smith, 2017; Luke, 1988) and professional identities (Williams, 1989) as they "are an active agent in its [own] production and reproduction" (Foster & Mills, 2013-2014, p. 444).

Textbooks are both knowledge artefacts and key actors in our systems of education. Individually, they represent the fundamental building blocks of a society's knowledge. Indeed, quite often they are the first exposure that students have to any discipline (Adam, 1986). For the business/management student, even more than scientific journals or monographs, textbooks are *the* mechanism for learning management knowledge and about contemporary business practices (Weatherbee, Dye, & Mills, 2005). In this capacity, textbooks function as both pathways and gatekeepers in the dissemination of what is known.

As pathways they progressively guide students along the course of a society's accumulated knowledge. As gateways, they ensure that students are incrementally inculcated into a society's ways of knowing (van Brummelen, 1990). And as embodied knowledge textbooks have a dual impact, students may learn from them, and students may learn to think in particular ways from them. They represent both *knowledge-as-information*, the factual content of the text itself, and *knowledge-as-a-way-of-thinking*, the ideological nature of where, when, and how the factual content is to be put to use. Thus, in their role as both artefact and actor, textbooks are pedagogically simultaneously both content and process.

In terms of content, textbooks are, by their very nature, conservative expositions of knowledge (Manza et al., 2010). The introduction of the results of contemporary studies of management has been found to take years before being published in introductory management texts (Mills, 2004). They present a discipline's accumulated progress only from the trailing, rather than the leading, edge of disciplinary research. Despite the absence of the latest theoretical or empirical developments in a particular subject area, textbooks are the evolutionary traces of the development of a society's knowledge in a subject area. While textbooks collectively represent the totality of a society's accumulated knowledge – textbooks are not like an archive in any traditional sense.

While textbooks are a collection or storehouse of society's knowledge(s) about a subject, they also stand in an unusual relationship with society and that subject. The various discourses within textbooks serve to constitute, as textbooks themselves are constituted by, the society in which they are produced (Stray, 1994). Textbooks are historically developed and socio-culturally produced with particular ends in mind (Rezat, 2008) and so textbooks are carriers and transmitters of the cultural context within which they are created (Stray, 1994). The impact of textbooks upon student learning is cumulative (van den Ham & Heinze, 2018). Thus, over a lifetime, textbooks, and particularly management textbooks, are just as much ideological and social tools as they are didactic ones (Cameron, Ireland, Lussier, New, & Robbins, 2003a, b). They inculcate *managerial values* and *professional identities* just as much as they *teach* about the management and practices of business.

So, What Do Textbooks Do, Really?

As we have seen, textbooks have agency beyond their didactic function. And in more ways than one! They are both influenced by and influence the politics in and between nations (Foster, 1991). State-authorized texts have been used to promote violence amongst groups (Pina, 2005) yet also as tools to reconcile historic differences amongst them (Lässig, 2009). Textbooks are often central actors in the dissemination and perpetuation of various forms of discourse focused on processes of socialization and normalization (Klerides, 2010) or of fostering particular or desired identities (Koross, 2012). The various discourses contained in textbooks constitute and are constituted by national identities (Anyon, 2011); civics and citizenship (Bromley, 2011; Cramer & Fons, 2020; Hegde, 2021); ethnicity and cultural practices (Provenzo, Shaver, & Bello, 2010); or history and socioeconomic orders (Ferguson et al., 2006; Foster, 1999; Foster & Crawford, 2006). They may speak to heteronormativity and sex roles (De la Torre-Sierra & Guichot-Reina, 2022; Frasher & Walker, 1972), gender (Ferree & Hall, 1996; Kereszty, 2009; Pillay & Maistry, 2018), or portrayals of the marginalized *other* (Alayan & Podeh, 2018; Canale, 2016; Paasi, 1999). In this way, textbooks are often key actors in both collective (Fuchs, 2011) and individual identity development (Ragusa, 2013). And this constitution of the individual within a social context is a process which commences at the time a student enters school and continues for a lifetime of learning until they leave university. For business education the textbook imbricates business knowledge and practice simultaneously with identity development.

Business Schools, Management Texts, and Identity

Throughout their university experience post-secondary education continues the long arc of identity development in young adults. It does so in at least two ways. First, when education is oriented towards, or expected to contribute to, an intended or desired occupation or profession. In this respect, students begin to identify and internalize the norms and practices established for whatever occupation which is being taught or modelled by faculty (Marshall, 2016) or within the text (Wortham, 2006). Second, beyond any one textbook, a curriculum of textbooks plays a role as well. Most significantly, in the manner in which business programmes of study describe social relations in the world.

The subject of management, as taught in business schools, in general terms, is designed to provide tools for students to understand and act as managers (Khurana & Spender, 2012). The management textbook plays a central role in this process as the dominant teaching paradigm in the United States and Canada is to structure course offerings around a particular textbook. In effect, the class pedagogy is to "teach the book" to the students (Thompson, 2005, p. 263). One of the outcomes of this is that the textbooks used, and the curriculum taught, shapes the worldview of students (Vaara & Faÿ, 2012). Beyond teaching students in their classrooms about business and management, business schools become *identity workspaces* where personal and professional identities are developed in students (Ghoshal, Arnzen, & Brownfield, 1992; Grey, 2002; Petriglieri & Petriglieri, 2010).

The portrayal of various social actors, such as managers, employees, and the workers, creates a normative discourse concerning the actions and activities of managers and of management. Management textbooks are cultural products which inculcate business students into what we know *of* and *for* management. This includes the content and form of the textbook and is inclusive of management as a body of knowledge (theory), management as a practice (including representations of managers and management in the world), and as a language (the way in which managers and management is defined and described). Taken together, management textbooks position management as a subject position or type of identity in the world of work and organization (Harding, 2003). Textbooks are a critical part of the structure of management education that serves to "develop a certain kind of person" one that is "deemed to be suitable for managerial work and encultured into some version of managerial values" (Grey, 2002, p. 499). In their pedagogical role in business classrooms, management textbooks socialize business students into the world of management. Thus, textbooks function to literally constitute the business student's identity as that of a future manager.

So, management textbooks "impart ideology as well as information" and consequently, they "have real and tangible effects on what happens at work" (Foster & Mills, 2013-2014, p. 462). In this respect, textbooks have the power to bring "into being that of which they speak" (Harding, 2003, p. 21). Management textbooks act to construct "future organizations and shape future actions by organizational participants" (Bilimoria, 1998, p. 678). Material effects that reach far beyond the classroom into the broader world of work and organizations. Just as primary and secondary education plays a normalization function for society (Corbett, 2001), so too do management textbooks for business schools.

Management as Ideology

The content and form of textbooks serve an educational purpose, whether that purpose is for social, economic, political (both *big* and *small* politics), or scientific reasons. Business schools are an established part of business education in the Western world and their role is to teach and socialize future managers (Grey, 2002). Textbooks comprise a significant part of this educational process. So, whether through text, images, or photographs the particular way in which management textbooks narrate business organizations and management (Czarniawska & Gagliardi, 2003) the text "presents a single – managerialist – worldview" (Mills & Helms Hatfield, 1999, p. 60).

While doing so, textbooks present an overly sanitized version of business and management (Cameron et al., 2003a, b). A version of an idealized world of management and organization. A managerial world that is devoid of the actuality of the messiness (Herath, 2019) and the potential dark sides of the practices of business and the work of managers (Albrecht, Wernz, & Williams, 1995; Crane, LeBaron, Phung, Behbahani, & Allain, 2018; Raufflet & Mills, 2017). There are those who strongly argue that management textbooks carry implicit ideologies (Grey, 2002) embedded in the various assumptions of naturalization, universalization, and rationalization underlaying business and management practice (Boltanski & Chiapello, 1999; Ferguson, Collison, Power, & Stevenson, 2009). Whether the content of business textbooks should be considered as reflective of managerialism as ideology or as management propaganda remains a debatable issue amongst the academy (Cameron et al., 2003a, b; Gilbert, 2003; Mir, 2003).

Research on business and management textbooks demonstrates the way textbooks construct notions of the ideal manager (McLaren & Mills, 2008) and of the employee or worker (Foster & Mills, 2013-2014). For decades, the presentations of idealized managers in textbooks consist predominantly of able-bodied, heterosexual, white males (Weigand & Mills, 2015; Williams & Mills, 2019). The idealization of managers in this way is achieved through the subordination, suppression, or absence of the worker, of women, and of persons of colour. Similarly, business and management textbooks construct images of employees and workers; *optimally* portrayed as "neither too young nor too old"

(Scheuer & Mills, 2017, p. 41). In sum, textbooks perpetuate biases in so far as the presence of individuals who do not fit the dominant societal norms are either marginalized or excluded from the content (Adam, 1986).

Leaving aside the arguments comprising the ongoing critique of management thought, theory, and practice (Fournier & Grey, 2000); it is pretty much universally recognized that the rhetoric employed in business and management texts is intended to persuade the reader that the content is legitimate and scientifically valid knowledge (Cameron et al., 2003a, b; Summers, Boje, Dennehy, & Rosile, 1997). Paradoxically, however, it is equally recognized that much of what is contained in management texts is neither valid from a scientific perspective nor useful from a practical perspective (see, for example, the research of Miner, 1984, 1990, 2003). Management textbooks regularly suffer from "omission, error, inaccuracy, or vague wording" (McQuarrie, 2005). And we find that time and again, theoretical content that has been invalidated is still retained and presented in textbooks (Bridgman, Cummings, & Ballard, 2019; Weatherbee, Dye, & Mills, 2008). A problematic that was clearly identified two decades ago; and one that has yet to be resolved (Miner, 2003).

Unfortunately, one of the outcomes of how textbooks are authored and published is the simplification and reification of management thought and theory over time (Parker & Ritson, 2005). There is an historical inertia to textbook content which is powerfully resistant to change. Management fads and fashions (Abrahamson, 1996) – that is novel practices that are perceived as having the potential to render distinct advantages or improvements over current practices – also make their way into business and management textbooks, despite a lack of scientific evidence of their validity (Brindle & Stearns, 2001). Once a management theory or fad becomes useful in the world of practice – whether it is scientifically valid or not – it persists long after it has been introduced (Benders, Van Grinsven, & Ingvaldsen, 2019).

Business and management textbooks also serve to define for students an overly narrow domain of business and management. One that does not reflect the reality of economic configurations or practices of business. Management textbooks rarely have content that reflects the diversity of modern Western economies or the full range of economic enterprise. The dominant form of enterprise presented in general business and management texts in the United States and Canada is the "investor-owned, for-profit business competing for market share and profit" (Chamard, 2004, p. 34). The corporate form of enterprise has become the pedagogical ideal and alternative forms of business are absent or relegated solely to those textbooks published for what are considered *niche* sub-specialties. Missing forms of enterprise which are quite prominent include cooperatives (Rankin & Piwko, 2022; Schugurensky, 2007), small businesses (Driscoll & Tesfayohannes, 2009; Dunn, Short, & Liang, 2008), family enterprises (Drexler & Frishkoff, 1991), and farms (Hartt, 2018, p. 52).

The process of normalization in management and business teaching becomes a key question when we speak to whether there are really any *Canadian* management texts. Particularly, as there are cultural variations between nations wherein particular aspects of business or management are given priority over others. For example, the role and strategic importance of human resource management varies greatly between the United Kingdom, Canada, and the United States. These differences are a function of the historical trajectory of how industrial relations have developed in each country, the legislative and regulatory frameworks associated with the advance of labour unions, and the associated socio-political perceptions of unionization in each of these countries (Eidlin, 2018; Wright, 1994).

Other manifest socio-cultural differences between business practices in the United States and those in Canada include the fact that Canada has many regional markets with public-sector regulation and oversight; a greater expectation in Canadian society for government intervention for regional economic development; fewer large international corporations (e.g., Fortune 500 firms), more large family-owned enterprises; and a different approach to taxation for the provision of government services such as health care (Boothman, 2000a; Jones, Mills, Weatherbee, & Helms Mills, 2006). Yet, management textbooks used in Canadian business schools rarely speak to differences and so are presented as universal despite national or cultural variations.

Management Knowledge Is Universal and Western

Management has long been considered universalistic in two senses. First, management theorizing as a scientific endeavour is premised upon the notion of the universality of scientific knowledge (Koontz, 1969). The universality thesis is a byproduct of modern thought in the developed West (Giddens, 1990; Toulmin & Toulmin, 1992; Townley, 2002). Management itself is premised upon knowledge conceived within the Western-centric notion of scientific concepts (Banerjee, 2022; Muzio, 2022). Concepts which are considered universal and transferable; in business studies the valorization of rationality and efficiency are prime examples of this (Banerjee & Arjaliès, 2021; Quijano, 2007).

Second, management knowledge is universalized when the implementation of management principles is viewed as applicable across a wide range of organizations regardless of their type or form and whether they are a business enterprise or not (Fayol, 1959; Gulick & Urwick, 1937; Taylor, 1911). It is only in the localized practice of management; management considered as a practiced *art*, where minor changes are needed to account for socio-cultural or technological differences across conditions (Carter, 1969; Koontz, 1969). So, the valorized model of management developed in the twentieth-century textbook effectively ignores "country-specific and time-specific contexts" in such a way as to present management as "rendered generalizable" (Brunsson & Jacobsson, 2000, p. 107) and hence, universal.

In the century plus of modern management theorizing (Crainer, 2003; Voxted, 2017), significant critique of the universality thesis undergirding management theorizing has only been relatively recent. The voices which have begun to question the assumed universality of management knowledge and practice have done so using the lens of place (Nkomo, 2017), colonialism (Fougère & Moulettes, 2009), or national differences (Arseneault, Deal, & Mills, 2019). This begs of us the following question: if management knowledge is not universal and we can articulate national or cultural differences between the United States and Canada, then how can we account for the homogenous nature of the management textbooks that we use (Powell, 1985)?

Textbooks and the Market

After the Second World War, the explosion in attendance at universities (Whitten, 1975) and especially in business schools (Cheit, 1985) in the United States, resulted in a parallel growth in the demand for university and college textbooks. The publishing industry rapidly responded to the demands of this growing market. Where there had been but one dominant publishing house serving the university market before the war, the two decades afterwards saw 50 publishing houses competing to meet the demand for teaching materials in university and college classrooms (Lichtenberg, 1992). And this shift in the publishing market would not stop there. Developments in the next half century saw four factors that would have a significant impact on the post-secondary publishing landscape globally. First, the exporting of U.S.-centric forms of management education. Second, the solidification of the textbook as a feature in post-secondary classrooms. Third, the industry adoption of the *managed textbook* mode of production. Finally, the advent of the Internet and the World Wide Web.

During the three decades after the war, the models of management education developed in the United States would be exported and adopted largely *as is*, throughout Europe and Japan during the rebuilding of these post-war economies (Locke, Toyne, & Nigh, 1999) and the Western hemisphere throughout the ensuing Cold War (Alcadipani & Caldas, 2012; Cooke & Kumar, 2019). The American management textbook followed in the wake of these developments and has become a central element of the management classroom (Apple, 1991).

During this time, the growth of the market – and the growth in business schools especially – saw intensifying competition in the textbook market. This competition led to a new way of producing textbooks, the *managed textbook* (Geersten, 1977). This mode of production saw a shift away from the traditional methods of textbook creation. It became a market-driven rather than a subject-driven approach. The expertise of the publishers would supplant the expertise of authors as the central actors deciding what would get published in a text (O'brien, 1981).

The creative locus saw a shift from the supply side (author) to the demand side (student). Publishers would now conduct market surveys, inspect the offerings of competitor publishers, hold focus groups, and look for ways to maintain core elements of disciplinary or subject knowledge while simultaneously permitting the differentiation of their textbook from competitive offerings. Once this templating process had been completed, publishers would only then contract with authors to complete the textbook in accordance with the publisher's patterning. One of the outcomes of this was that competing textbooks increasingly came to portray similar models of disciplinary and subject knowledges; virtually homogenous at their core, with differentiation to be found only at the edges (Stambaugh & Quinn Trank, 2010). The managed textbook process resulted in significant time and cost savings for publishers (Whitten, 1975) and textbooks became a fully commodified child of the publishing houses. A market logic had come to predominate scholarly production of textbooks.

Similarly, at the close of the twentieth century, the arrival of the Internet and the World Wide Web would again begin to change the structure of the publishing industry and through them the form and content of the post-secondary textbook (Bates, 1996). Over the next two decades, the rise of the Internet facilitated electronic publishing of textbooks while simultaneously allowing pirated textbook copying (Cusker, 2016). While e-texts were growing in presence in the market offerings, the increasing cost of printed textbooks also resulted in the emergence of used and rental textbooks markets.

Each of these factors, e-texts, pirating, costs of production of print texts, and the emergence of secondary markets, would combine to significantly disrupt the way in which textbooks were published and sold. As production processes were disordered and markets reconfigured, intensifying competition would see a further reduction and consolidation of scholarly publishing houses servicing the post-secondary market (Carbaugh, 2020). The twenty-first-century textbook business had become a globalized project dominated by a select oligopoly of publishers.

Textbooks in Canada

Investigating the nature of publishing in Canada is a complex task. First, publishing in Canada takes place in a context where most publishing houses are small enterprises with less than ten employees. Second, education is a Provincial responsibility and post-secondary textbooks are dominated by a few major international conglomerates. In a circumstance where the Federal government is reliant on voluntary reporting by Provincial actors, there is a dearth of publishing data. Third, all of this is compounded by the significant challenges associated with accessing market data. Detailed and consistent data on production and sales of textbooks in the Canadian market is both limited and fragmented (Rollans & de la Chenelière, 2010; Turner & Riggs, 2021). Because Canada's Federalist structure assigns authority and responsibility for education to the provinces, there has never been a national ministry responsible for education. Nor a national set of comprehensive data on publishing. Consequently, there has never been a national-level investment in the authoring or sourcing of textbooks, as there has been in Britain or the United States. And Canada has relied upon these countries as the two primary sources for educational resources in its first century of existence as a nation (Allison, 2004).

The small size of the Canadian book market has meant that the publishing industry in Canada has historically been founded on a *branch plant* configuration. Large international publishing houses would establish subsidiaries in Canada to service the market while allowing profits to be returned to the parent firm. The extra-domestic domination of the Canadian publishing and textbook market happened in two waves. First, British publishing houses set up Canadian operations in the early twentieth century. The dominance of British publishing houses changed with the post-war expansion of the United States economy which saw many of the large American publishing houses open their own Canadian divisions. Both British and American branch plant operations had a distinct economic advantage over the smaller Canadian publishing houses. The capital-intensive nature of the industry combined with the large up-front cost to produce new textbooks meant that British and American publishers could sell their pre-existing texts for much less than Canadian publishers could produce their own originals. Even after the nominal expense involved with the *Canadianizing* of an American text to be sold in the Canadian market, U.S. publishers could still outcompete their Canadian counterparts (Clark & Knights, 2013).

Thus, the large American publishers came to dominate the Canadian textbook market (Young, 1995). So much so that by the middle of the twentieth century less than 30% of all textbooks sold in the country were actually authored in Canada (Clark & Knights, 2011; Eustace, 1972). Over the latter half of the twentieth century, American-based and international conglomerate publishing houses would come to dominate textbook publishing (Buzelin, 2014; McCarron, 2005). As of 2018, trade books (e.g., fiction and non-fiction) comprised 60% of books published in Canada by Canadian publishers. Primary and secondary educational texts were next at 34% while only 6% of Canadian publishing effort was expended on scholarly works intended for the post-secondary market (Nordicity, 2018). Canadian educational textbook production has always been a marginal economic and cultural activity. Hence, the history of economic spill-over and dominance of the vastly larger United States into the Canadian textbook market. A similar pattern is observed in the development of Canadian business schools.

Management Textbooks in Canada

The institutionalization and legitimization of business schools and management education in Canada lagged that of the United States by almost two decades (Austin, 1998). This meant that in the initial stages of their development, business schools in Canada had to draw upon extra-national resources to staff and deliver their programmes. Many of the first management educators were drawn from abroad, primarily the United States, and with them came American textbooks. Canadian graduate students were often sent to get their PhDs from American universities. When they returned to take up positions in business schools in their home country, they often utilized the same pedagogical resources they were exposed to in their own training and education. Thus, Canadian business classrooms become hosts to American management texts.

Three factors have contributed to the circumstance where solely Canadian-authored management texts have remained in the minority. First, the small size of the Canadian market has meant that Canadian publishing houses have always struggled to serve the domestic market. Second, the historical domination of the publishing industry by branch plant operations of large international publishing houses has meant the economics of publishing remain against original Canadian authorship. Third, the assumption of the universality of management knowledge has meant that either American or *Canadianized* versions of American texts have been considered more than sufficient for educating Canadian business students.

So, the post-secondary textbook market for business textbooks remains dominated by primarily American-authored texts (Parker, 2022) which contain a version of management that is U.S.-centric (McLaren & Helms Mills, 2010). There are a few exceptions to this, but those are usually found in subject areas requiring national expertise in authorship, or where institutional and legal differences exist. For example, in the field of human resource management (Fitzgerald & Mills, 2012) or accounting (Gordon, 2011). Canadianized versions of bestselling management textbooks originally authored for the American market still predominate in Canadian management classrooms and are expected to remain so in the future (Fitzgerald & Mills, 2012).

Future of the Textbook

While textbooks have been a foundational and critical element of pedagogy for the last century and a half, educators and scholars are beginning to question the efficacy of the textbook in its current form (Reed, 2018). Some scholars argue that we should abandon the print text since, as a knowledge artefact, it is no longer in accord with the digital world of the twenty-first century and the learning preferences of the net generation (Granitz et al., 2021; Nicholas, 2020). Others suggest that the cost of textbooks combined with the increasing rate of amendment to textbooks editions requiring repurchase (Hammond, Danko, &

Braswell, 2015) is becoming too much of a financial burden upon students. In the United States, for example, textbook costs have increased at double the rate of inflation since the 1980s (Murphy, 2013). Costs of these texts skyrocketed further increasing by 142% between 2001 and 2017. While comparable data is not available for the Canadian market, textbooks in Canada are generally more expensive than prices in the United States due to tariffs and monetary exchange values (Jhangiani, Dastur, Le Grand, & Penner, 2018). Financial burdens on students are also increasing with inflationary pressures on college and university tuitions (Ehrenberg, 2020; Patton, 2015) as these institutions also experience increased expenses in operating costs and in maintaining student resources such as university libraries (Ezeh, 2021; Katz, 2019).

Given the potentials of the digital infrastructure now available to both educators and students (Downes, 2007; Ehlers, 2011), there has been a growing movement calling for less expensive or even free resources for students (Everard & St Pierre, 2014; Farrow, Pitt, & Weller, 2020). Similar to the open software and open access movements, this movement, commonly referred to as Open Educational Resources (Hylén, 2021), follows a similar philosophy with a goal to provide free or inexpensive access to learning resources (D'Antoni, 2009; Otto, Schroeder, Diekmann, & Sander, 2021; Wiley, Bliss, & McEwen, 2014). Indeed, some in the movement call for the privately published textbook to be replaced all together with Open Texts (McIntyre, Wegener, & McGrath, 2018; Pitt et al., 2019). While we are seeing an increasing call for Open Educational Resources, publisher-sold print and e-text formats still predominate in post-secondary classrooms in Canada (Bates, 2018).

Conclusion

Most management courses in American and Canadian business schools are taught using textbooks (Cameron et al., 2003a, b). Unlike Europe, Canada did not have a significant system of business education prior to the introduction of management thought centred in the United States. This meant that there was little, if any resistance, to the adoption of U.S.-centric models of management (McLaren & Helms Mills, 2010).

Even though Canadian management scholars have made significant contributions to management theory (Coller, McNally, & Mills, 2015), there is an absence of study on Canadian contributions to management theorizing over time (McLaren & Mills, 2015). Our understanding of the development of management theory defaults to the dominant published history centred on the United States (Wren, 1972, 1979, 1987, 1994, 2005; Wren & Bedeian, 2009, 2018, 2020). Combined with the assumption that management theory is universal (Alvesson & Willmott, 2012), this has meant that there has been little resistance within the post-secondary environment in Canada to simply adopting American business and management texts. At best, we seek a Canadianized version of such for use in the classrooms of our business schools. In other words, Canadian scholars largely accept a "generically North American" notion of management theory, thought, and practice (Boothman, 2000b, p. 65).

In the realm of business textbooks, it is fair to say that there has never been a time where management education has not been dominated by American-authored texts. Nor a time where Canadian management students were taught using predominantly Canadian textbooks, written by Canadian authors explicitly produced for the Canadian market. That is not to say that there are no Canadian business or management textbooks. In those niche areas of business where institutional or legal mandates demand national differences, such as in accounting or human resource management textbooks, they do exist. But, overall, they remain in the minority. This circumstance is not likely to change anytime soon. Canadian business students will continue to use American, or at best-Canadianized versions of American, texts.

The industrialization and professionalization of textbook production in the twentieth century has meant that publishers and editors increasingly came to influence the form and the content of textbooks (Cameron et al., 2003a, b; DiGiuseppe, 2014; Fuchs, 2014). Consolidation of the publishing industry in the latter half of the twentieth century and the first quarter of the twenty-first has meant that there are only five major publishing houses whose product focus is primarily the post-secondary educational market. These are all large multinationals with little corporate presence remaining in Canada (Lorimer, 2020; Turner & Riggs, 2021). The publication of university textbooks is a "high-risk business" where, in addition to market surveillance, procedures for decision making by editors is premised on "guesswork, intuition, and opinion" (Levitt & Nass, 1989, p. 192). Therefore, there is a great deal of homogeneity, e.g., the copying of content, format, or style of leading (i.e., bestselling) textbooks, amongst publishing houses (Powell, 1985) as this is viewed as a low-risk strategy. But there are implications beyond the economics we must remain cognizant of.

Textbooks themselves become part of the social world apart from their role in education. They are one of the ways in which knowledge is disseminated throughout a society and contribute directly to our collective memory (Halbwachs, 1992). In this way, textbooks influence the social fabric and therefore make us as much as we make them. Textbooks influence how we develop as individuals and members of the societies in which we are enmeshed (Goldberg, Porat, & Schwarz, 2006; Porat, 2004). The presentation of the universality of management knowledge simply exacerbates this problematic.

Longitudinal study of the content of management textbooks reveals that the discourses within them predominantly privilege men and masculinity whilst subordinating both women and femininity (Williams & Mills, 2019). Management textbooks reflect fixed gender binaries associated with heteronormative social practices and with notions of the family, education, or science (Good, Woodzicka, & Wingfield, 2010; Parise, 2021; Snyder & Broadway, 2004).

Textbooks continue to perpetuate a system that discriminates along gender lines and marginalizes our indigenous peoples (Henry et al., 2017; Schaefli, Godlewska, & Rose, 2018).

In Canada, we need to move towards a more culturally responsive pedagogy (Papp, 2019) – which means we must either produce textbooks which are *Canadian* – not *Canadianized* – or in our classrooms we need to speak into our textbooks what is missing from them. Our students need to see themselves in our textbooks. And as future managers, we need them to think about the local and specific as much as about the general and the universal.

Given all of this, I wonder why, even as we have known for over half a century that post-secondary textbooks play several key epistemological and social roles in our society and the enterprise of science (Fleck, 1979; Khun, 1962), we have yet to see a comprehensive sociology of the textbook emerge (Fuchs, 2014). A failing, we cannot attribute to other than ourselves.

References

Abrahamson, E. (1996). Management fashion. *Academy of Management Review, 21*(1), 254–285.

Adam, B. (1986). The construction of a sociological 'homosexual' in Canadian textbooks. *Canadian Review of Sociology/Revue canadienne de sociologie, 23*(3), 399–411.

Alayan, S., & Podeh, E. (2018). Introduction: Views of others in school textbooks—A theoretical analysis. In *Multiple alterities* (pp. 1–17). Springer.

Albrecht, W., Wernz, G., & Williams, T. (1995). *Fraud: Bringing light to the dark side of business*. Irwin Professional Pub.

Alcadipani, R., & Caldas, M. (2012). Americanizing Brazilian management. *Critical Perspectives on International Business, 8*(1), 37–55.

Allison, S. (2004). All quiet on the curriculum front. *Canadian Issues, 21*, 1–21.

Altbach, P. G. (2017). Textbooks: The international dimension. In M. Apple & L. Christian-Smith (Eds.), *The politics of the textbook* (pp. 242–258). London: Routledge.

Alvesson, M., & Willmott, H. (2012). *Making sense of management: A critical introduction*. Sage.

Anyon, J. (2011). Ideology and United States history textbooks. In *The textbook as discourse* (pp. 119–149). New York: Routledge.

Apple, M. (1991). The culture and the commerce of the textbook. In M. W. Apple & L. K. Christian-Smith (Eds.), *The politics of the textbook* (pp. 1–21). New York: Routledge.

Apple, M. (2012). The culture and commerce of the textbook. *Knowledge, Power, and Education*, 152–167.

Apple, M., & Christian-Smith, L. (2017). The politics of the textbook. In *The politics of the textbook* (pp. 1–21): Routledge.

Arseneault, R., Deal, N., & Mills, A. J. (2019). Reading "Canadian" management in context: development of English and French education. *Journal of Management History, 25*(2), 180–202.

Austin, B. (1998). The role of the administrative sciences association in institutionalizing management education in Canada. *Canadian Journal of Administrative Sciences, 15*(3), 255–266.

Banerjee, S. (2022). Decolonizing management theory: A critical perspective. *Journal of Management Studies, 59*(4), 1074–1087.

Banerjee, S., & Arjaliès, D. (2021). Celebrating the end of enlightenment: Organization theory in the age of the Anthropocene and Gaia (and why neither is the solution to our ecological crisis). *Organization Theory, 2*(4).

Bates, T. (1996). The promise and the myths of e-learning in post-secondary education. In M. Castells (Ed.), *The network society: A cross-cultural persepctive* (p. 271). Cheltenham: Edward Elgar Publishing Limited.

Bates, T. (2018). The 2017 national survey of online learning in Canadian post-secondary education: methodology and results. *International Journal of Educational Technology in Higher Education, 15*(1), 1–17.

Benders, J., Van Grinsven, M., & Ingvaldsen, J. (2019). The persistence of management ideas. In A. Sturdy, S. Heusinkveld, T. Reay, & D. Strang (Eds.), *The Oxford handbook of management ideas* (Vol. 270, pp. 271–285). Oxford: Oxford University Press.

Berghahn, V., & Schissler, H. (1987). *Perceptions of history: An analysis of school textbooks*. Oxford: Berg.

Bilimoria, D. (1998). *The editor's corner: The theoretical content of what we teach in the management classroom: needs and issues* (Vol. 22, pp. 677–681). Thousand Oaks, CA: Sage Publications Sage CA.

Bölsterli Bardy, K. (2015). Checklist for competence-oriented textbooks in science. *American Journal of Educational Research, 3*(11), 1450–1454.

Boltanski, L., & Chiapello, E. (1999). *Le nouvel esprit du capitalisme* (Vol. 10). Gallimard Paris.

Boothman, B. (2000a). Canadian management education at the millenium. In B. Austin (Ed.), *Capitalizing Knowledge* (pp. 295–355). Toronto: University of Toronto Press.

Boothman, B. (2000b). Culture of utility: The development of business education in Canada. In B. Austin (Ed.), *Capitalizing knowledge: Essays of business education in Canada* (pp. 1–86). Toronto: University of Toronto Press.

Bridgman, T., Cummings, S., & Ballard, J. (2019). Who built Maslow's pyramid? A history of the creation of management studies' most famous symbol and its implications for management education. *Academy of Management Learning & Education, 18*(1), 81–98.

Brindle, M., & Stearns, P. (2001). *Facing up to management faddism: A new look at an old force*. Greenwood Publishing Group.

Bromley, P. (2011). Multiculturalism and human rights in civic education: The case of British Columbia, Canada. *Educational Research, 53*(2), 151–164.

Brunsson, N., & Jacobsson, B. (2000). *A world of standards*. Cambridge: Oxford University Press.

Buzelin, H. (2014). Translating the American textbook. *Translation Studies, 7*(3), 315–334.

Cameron, K., Ireland, R., Lussier, R., New, J., & Robbins, S. (2003a). Management textbooks as propaganda. *Journal of Management Education, 27*(6), 711–729.

Cameron, K., Ireland, R., Lussier, R., New, J., & Robbins, S. (2003b). Replies to commentaries on "management textsbooks as propaganda". *Journal of Management Education, 27*(6), 739–743.

Canale, G. (2016). (Re)Searching culture in foreign language textbooks, or the politics of hide and seek. *Language, Culture and Curriculum, 29*(2), 225–243.

Carbaugh, B. (2020). The decline of college textbook publishing: Cengage Learning and McGraw-Hill. *The American Economist, 65*(2), 284–299.

Carter, R. (1969). An alternative to comparative management: The functional approach. *Management International Review, 9*(2/3), 139–145.

Chamard, J. (2004). Co-operatives and credit unions in economics and business texts: Changing the paradigm. *International Journal of Co-operative Management, 1*(2), 34–40.

Cheit, E. (1985). Business schools and their critics. *California Management Review, XXVII*(3), 43–62.

Clark, P., & Knights, W. (2011). "Gringo operations": Nationalism and capital in Canadian educational publishing, 1970-81. *Journal of Canadian Studies, 45*(2), 123–161.

Clark, P., & Knights, W. (2013). 'Fratricidal warfare': English-Canadian textbook publishers take on the Americans, 1970–1980. *History of Education, 42*(5), 598–621.

Coller, K., McNally, C., & Mills, A. J. (2015). The inner circle: Towards a 'Canadian' management history–key Canadian contributors to new institution theory. In *The Routledge companion to management and organizational history* (pp. 364–382). Routledge.

Cooke, B., & Kumar, A. (2019). *Academy of Management Learning & Education, 19*(1), 21–39.

Corbett, M. (2001). A protracted struggle: Rural resistance and normalization in Canadian educational history. *Historical Studies in Education/Revue d'histoire de l'éducation, 13*(1), 19–48.

Crainer, S. (2003). One hundred years of management. *Business Strategy Review, 14*(2), 41–49.

Cramer, G., & Fons, C. (2020). Civics for non-citizens. *The High School Journal, 104*(1), 5–27.

Crane, A., LeBaron, G., Phung, K., Behbahani, L., & Allain, J. (2018). *Innovations in the business models of modern slavery: The dark side of business model innovation.* Paper presented at the Academy of Management Proceedings.

Cusker, J. (2016). Online textbook piracy: A literature review. *Issues in Science and Technology Librarianship, 84*.

Czarniawska, B., & Gagliardi, P. (2003). *Narratives we organize by* (Vol. 11): John Benjamins Publishing.

D'Antoni, S. (2009). *Open educational resources: Reviewing initiatives and issues* (Vol. 24, pp. 3–10): Taylor & Francis.

De la Torre-Sierra, A., & Guichot-Reina, V. (2022). The influence of school textbooks on the configuration of gender identity: A study on the unequal representation of women and men in the school discourse during the Spanish democracy. *Teaching and Teacher Education, 117*, 103810.

De Vita, G., & Case, P. (2016). 'The smell of the place': Managerialist culture in contemporary UK business schools. *Culture and Organization, 22*(4), 348–364.

DiGiuseppe, M. (2014). Representing nature of science in a science textbook: Exploring author–editor–publisher interactions. *International Journal of Science Education, 36*(7), 1061–1082.

Downes, S. (2007). Models for sustainable open educational resources. *Interdisciplinary Journal of E-Learning and Learning Objects, 3*(1), 29–44.

Drexler Jr, J., & Frishkoff, P. (1991). Family business management. *Journal of Management Education, 15*(2), 222–231.

Driscoll, C., & Tesfayohannes, M. (2009). "Big" business ethics textbooks: Where do small business and entrepreneurship fit? *Journal of Business Ethics Education, 6*, 25–42.

Dunn, P., Short, L., & Liang, K. (2008). Human resource management importance in small business. *Small Business Institute Journal, 2*(1), 1–22.

Ehlers, U. (2011). Extending the territory: From open educational resources to open educational practices. *Journal of Open, Flexible and Distance Learning, 15*(2), 1–10.

Ehrenberg, R. (2020). The economics of tuition and fees in American higher education. In *The economics of education* (pp. 345–352): Elsevier.

Eidlin, B. (2018). *Labor and the class idea in the United States and Canada*. Cambridge: Cambridge University Press.

Elson, R. (1964). *Guardians of tradition, American schoolbooks of the nineteenth century* (Vol. 553): Lincoln: University of Nebraska Press.

Eustace, C. (1972). *Developments in Canadian book production and design. Royal Commission on Book Publishing: Background Papers* (pp. 38–60). *Canadian Publishers and Canadian Publishing*.

Everard, A., & St Pierre, K. (2014). A case for student adoption of open textbooks. *Journal of the Academy of Business Education, 15*, 66.

Ezeh, R. (2021). Significance of marketing library resources in libraries and information centers: Issues and prospects. *Journal of Library Services and Technologies, 3*(1), 13–24.

Farrow, R., Pitt, R., & Weller, M. (2020). Open textbooks as an innovation route for open science pedagogy. *Education for Information, 36*(3), 227–245.

Faure, R. (2011). Connections in the history of textbook revision, 1947–19521. *Education Inquiry, 2*(1), 21–35.

Fayol, H. (1959). *General and industrial management* (C. Storrs, Trans.). London: Sir Isaac Pitman and Sons, Ltd.

Ferguson, J., Collison, D., Power, D., & Stevenson, L. (2006). Accounting textbooks: Exploring the production of a cultural and political artifact. *Accounting Education: An International Journal, 15*(3), 243–260.

Ferguson, J., Collison, D., Power, D., & Stevenson, L. (2009). Constructing meaning in the service of power: An analysis of the typical modes of ideology in accounting textbooks. *Critical Perspectives on Accounting, 20*(8), 896–909.

Ferree, M., & Hall, E. (1996). Rethinking stratification from a feminist perspective: Gender, race, and class in mainstream textbooks. *American Sociological Review, 61*(6), 929–950.

Fitzgerald, C., & Mills, A. J. (2012). Human resource management a function of the past: A content analysis of the first edition Canadian introductory human resource management textbooks. *Research & Practice in Human Resource Management, 20*(1), 1.

Fleck, L. (1979). *Genesis and development of a scientific fact* (F. Bradely & T. J. Trenn, Trans.). Chicago, IL: The University of Chicago Press.

Foster, J., & Mills, A. (2013–2014). Construction work: Evolving discourse of the 'worker' in management textbooks, 1920's to the first decade of the 21st century. *Journal of Workplace Rights, 17*(3–4), 443–466.

Foster, R. (1991). Making national cultures in the global ecumene. *Annual Review of Anthropology, 20*, 235–260.

Foster, S. (1999). The struggle for American identity: Treatment of ethnic groups in United States history textbooks. *History of Education, 28*(3), 251–278.

Foster, S. (2012). Re-thinking history textbooks in a globalized world. In M. Carretero, M. Asensio, & M. Rodr´ıguez- Moneo (Eds.), *History education and the construction of national identities* (pp. 49–62). Charlotte, NC: Information Age Publishing.

Foster, S., & Crawford, K. (2006). *What shall we tell the children?: International perspectives on school history textbooks*. Charlotte, NC: IAP.

Fougère, M., & Moulettes, A. (2009). On 'cultural' knowledge in international management textbooks: A postcolonial reading. In S. Banerjee, Chio, V., & Mir, R. (Eds.), *Organizations, markets and imperial formations: Towards an anthropology of globalization* (pp. 25–39). Cheltenham: Edward Elgar.

Fournier, V., & Grey, C. (2000). At the critical moment: Conditions and prospects for critical management studies. *Human Relations, 53*(1), 7–32.

Frasher, R., & Walker, A. (1972). Sex roles in early reading textbooks. *The Reading Teacher, 25*(8), 741–749.

Fuchs, E. (2011). Current trends in history and social studies textbook research. *Journal of International Cooperation in Education, 14*(2), 17–34.

Fuchs, E. (2014). The (hi)story of textbooks: Research trends in a field of textbook-related research. *IJHE Bildungsgeschichte–International Journal for the Historiography of Education, 4*(1), 63–80.

Geersten, R. (1977). The textbook: An ACIDS test. *Teaching Sociology, 5*(1), 101–120.

Ghoshal, S., Arnzen, B., & Brownfield, S. (1992). A learning alliance between business and business schools: Executive education as a platform for partnership. *California Management Review, 35*(1), 50–67.

Giddens, A. (1990). *The consequences of modernity*. Cambridge: Polity Press.

Gilbert, D. (2003). Propaganda, trusteeship, and artifact: Locating a new place for the management textbook. *Journal of Management Education, 27*(6), 730–734.

Goldberg, T., Porat, D., & Schwarz, B. (2006). "Here started the rift we see today": Student and textbook narratives between official and counter memory. *Narrative Inquiry, 16*(2), 319–347.

Good, J., Woodzicka, J., & Wingfield, L. (2010). The effects of gender stereotypic and counter-stereotypic textbook images on science performance. *Journal of Social Psychology, 150*(2), 132–147.

Gordon, I. (2011). Lessons to be learned: An examination of Canadian and US financial accounting and auditing textbooks for ethics/governance coverage. *Journal of Business Ethics, 101*(1), 29–47.

Granitz, N., Kohli, C., & Lancellotti, M. (2021). Textbooks for the YouTube generation? A case study on the shift from text to video. *Journal of Education for Business, 96*(5), 299–307.

Grey, C. (2002). What are business schools for? On silence and voice in management education. *Journal of Management Education, 26*(5), 496–511.

Gulick, L., & Urwick, L. (Eds.). (1937). *Papers on the science of administration*. New York: Institute of Public Administration.

Halbwachs, M. (1992). *On collective memory* (Coser, L., Ed.). Chicago: University of Chicago Press.

Hammond, T., Danko, K., & Braswell, M. (2015). US accounting professors' perspectives on textbook revisions. *Journal of Accounting Education, 33*(3), 198–218.

Harding, N. (2003). *The social construction of management: Texts and identities.* New York: Routledge.

Hartt, C. (2018). What are business students taught about farming: Do textbooks paint a negative picture? *International Journal of Management Education, 16*(2), 193–204.

Hegde, R. (2021). Constructing citizenship through textbooks. *Learning Curve* (9), 16–21.

Henry, F., Dua, E., Kobayashi, A., James, C., Li, P., Ramos, H., & Smith, M. (2017). Race, racialization and indigeneity in Canadian universities. *Race Ethnicity and Education, 20*(3), 300–314.

Herath, D. (2019). *Business plasticity through disorganization.* Emerald Group Publishing.

Hylén, J. (2021). *Open educational resources: Opportunities and challenges.* Retrieved from www.oecd.org/education/ceri/37351085.pdf

Issitt, J. (2004). Reflections on the study of textbooks. *History of Education, 33*(6), 683–696.

Jhangiani, R., Dastur, F., Le Grand, R., & Penner, K. (2018). As good or better than commercial textbooks: Students' perceptions and outcomes from using open digital and open print textbooks. *Canadian Journal for the Scholarship of Teaching and Learning, 9*(1), 1–20.

Jones, G., Mills, A. J., Weatherbee, T. G., & Helms Mills, J. (2006). *Organization theory, design, and change* (Canadian Edition ed.). Toronto: Pearson.

Katz, S. (2019). Leveraging library expertise in support of institutional goals: A case study of an open educational resources initiative. *New Review of Academic Librarianship, 25*(2–4), 381–391.

Kawashima, S. (2014). Sino-Japanese controversies over the textbook problem and the League of Nations. In M. Herren (Ed.), *Networking the international system* (pp. 91–106). Cham: Springer.

Kereszty, O. (2009). Gender in textbooks. *Practice and Theory in Systems of Education, 4*(2), 1–7.

Khun, T. S. (1962). *The structure of scientific revolutions.* Chicago, IL: University of Chicago Press.

Khurana, R., & Spender, J. C. (2012). Herbert A. Simon on what ails business schools: More than 'a problem in organizational design'. *Journal of Management Studies, 49*(3), 619–639.

Klerides, E. (2010). Imagining the textbook: Textbooks as discourse and genre. *Journal of Educational Media, Memory, and Society, 2*(1), 31–54.

Koontz, H. (1969). A model for analyzing the universality and transferability of management. *Academy of Management Journal, 12*(4), 415–429.

Koross, R. (2012). National identity and unity in Kiswahili textbooks for secondary school students in Kenya: A content analysis. *Journal of Emerging Trends in Educational Research and Policy Studies, 3*(4), 544–550.

Lässig, S. (2009). History school textbooks as a means of reconciliation? Some remarks on bilateral textbooks and "common histories". *History and Social Science Textbooks, 11*, 11–23.

Levitt, B., & Nass, C. (1989). The lid on the garbage can: Institutional constraints on decision making in the technical core of college-text publishers. *Administrative Science Quarterly, 34*, 190–207.

Lichtenberg, J. (1992). The new paradox of the college textbook. *Change, 24*(5), 10–18.

Locke, R., Toyne, B., & Nigh, D. (1999). International management education in Western Europe, the United States, and Japan: A historian's view. In B. Toyne & D. Nigh (Eds.), *International business: Institutions and the Dissemination of Knowledge* (pp. 25–44). Columbia: University of South Carolina Press.

Lorimer, R. (2020). Canadian scholarly journal publishing: The knowledge economy calls. *Scholarly Research and Communication, 11*(2), 17.

Luke, A. (1988). *Literacy, textbooks and ideology: Postwar literacy instruction and the mythology of Dick and Jane*. Philadelphia: Falmer Publishing.

Mahar, M. (1966). Federal legislation and programs to assist school libraries. *ALA Bulletin, 60*(2), 153–156.

Manza, J., Sauder, M., & Wright, N. (2010). Producing textbook sociology. *European Journal of Sociology/Archives Européennes De Sociologie, 51*(2), 271–304.

Marshall, E. (2016). Cultural identity and school-to-work transitions for post-secondary students. *International Journal of Arts & Sciences, 9*(2), 395.

McCarron, M. (2005). *Marketing in educational publishing: A case study of textbook sales between competing publishers.* Master of Publishing Program-Simon Fraser University, Simon Fraser University.

McIntyre, T., Wegener, M., & McGrath, D. (2018). Dynamic e-learning modules for student lecture preparation. *Teaching & Learning Inquiry, 6*(1), 126–145.

McLaren, P., & Helms Mills, J. (2010). Appropriation, manipulation, and silence: A critical hermeneutic analysis of the management textbook as a tool of the corporate discourse. *Management & Organizational History, 5*(3–4), 408–427.

McLaren, P., & Mills, A. (2008). A product of "his" time? Exploring the construct of the ideal manager in the Cold War era. *Journal of Management History, 14*(4), 386–403.

McLaren, P., & Mills, A. (2015). History and the absence of Canadian management theory. In P. McLaren, A. Mills, & T. Weatherbee (Eds.), *The Routledge companion to management and organizational history* (p. 319). London: Routledge.

McQuarrie, F. A. (2005). How the past is present(ed): A comparison of information on the Hawthorne studies in Canadian management and organizational behaviour textbooks. *Canadian Journal of Administrative Sciences/Revue Canadienne des Sciences de l'Administration, 22*(3), 230–242.

Mills, A. (2004). Feminist organizational analysis and the business textbook. In G. Hodgson & C. Carter (Eds.), *Management knowledge and the new employee* (pp. 30–48). Aldershot: Ashgate Publishing Limited.

Mills, A., & Helms Hatfield, J. (1999). From imperialism to globalization: Internationalization and the management Text. In S. R. Clegg & E. Ibarra-Colado (Eds.), *Global management: Universal theories and local realities* (pp. 37–67). London: Sage.

Miner, J. B. (1984). The validity and usefulness of theories in an emerging organizational science. *Academy of Management Review, 9*(2), 296–306.

Miner, J. B. (1990). The role of values in defining the 'goodness' of theories in. *Organization Studies, 11*(2), 161.

Miner, J. B. (2003). The rated importance, scientific validity, and practical usefulness of organizational behavior theories: A quantitative review. *Academy of Management Learning and Education, 2*(3), 250–268.

Mir, A. (2003). The hegemonic discourse of management texts. *Journal of Management Education, 27*(6), 734–738.

Murphy, M. (2013). Textbooks on reserve: A case study. *Journal of Access Services, 10*(3), 145–152.

Muzio, D. (2022). Re-conceptualizing management theory: How do we Move Away from Western-centred knowledge? *Journal of Management Studies, 59*(4), 1032–1035.

Myers, G. (1992). Textbooks and the sociology of scientific knowledge. *English for Specific Purposes, 11*(1), 3–17.

Navarro, P. (2008). The MBA core curricula of top-ranked US business schools: A study in failure? *Academy of Management Learning & Education, 7*(1), 108–123.

Nicholas, A. (2020). *Preferred learning methods of generation Z. Northeast Business & Economics Association 46th Annual Conference*, 1–12.

Nkomo, S. M. (2017). Time to look in the mirror: Producing management theory and knowledge for Africa. *Africa Journal of Management, 3*(1), 7–16.

Nordicity. (2018). *The Canadian English-language book publishing industry profile: Final report*. Retrieved from https://publishers.ca

O'brien, L. (1981). *Contrasting approaches to curriculum materials development*. Newark: University of Delaware.

Osborne, K. (2016). Creating the "international mind": The league of nations attempts to reform history teaching, 1920–1939. *History of Education Quarterly, 56*(2), 213–240.

Otto, D., Schroeder, N., Diekmann, D., & Sander, P. (2021). Trends and gaps in empirical research on open educational resources (OER): A systematic mapping of the literature from 2015 to 2019. *Contemporary Educational Technology, 13*(4), ep325.

Paasi, A. (1999). The changing pedagogies of space: Representation of the other in Finnish school geography textbooks. In S. Brunn, A. Buttimer, & U. Wardenga (Eds.), *Text and image: Social construction of regional knowledges* (pp. 226–237). Leipzig: Institut fur Landerkunde.

Papp, T. T. A. (2019). Book review: Culturally responsive pedagogy: Working towards decolonization, indigeneity and interculturalism. *: Critical Issues in Education, 3*(2), 10.

Parise, M. (2021). Gender, sex, and heteronormativity in high school statistics textbooks. *Mathematics Education Research Journal, 33*(4), 757–785.

Parker, G. (2022). *The publishing industry in Canada: 1918 to the twenty-first century*. Retrieved from https://digitalcollections.mcmaster.ca/hpcanpub

Parker, L., & Ritson, P. (2005). Fads, stereotypes and management gurus: Fayol and Follett today. *Management Decision, 43*(10), 1335–1357.

Patton, M. (2015). The cost of college: Yesterday, today, and tomorrow. *Forbes Magazine, 19*.

Petriglieri, G., & Petriglieri, J. (2010). Identity workspaces: The case of business schools. *Academy of Management Learning & Education, 9*(1), 44–60.

Pillay, P., & Maistry, S. (2018). The 'firstness' of male as automatic ordering: Gendered discourse in Southern African Business Studies school textbooks. *Journal for Transdisciplinary Research in Southern Africa, 14*(2), 1–9.

Pina, A. (2005). *Palestinian education and the debate over textbooks. Library of Congress, Congressional Research Service.*

Pitt, R., Farrow, R., Jordan, K., de los Arcos, B., Weller, M., Kernohan, D., & Rolfe, V. (2019). *The UK Open Textbook Report 2019. Open Education Research Hub.* The Open University (UK). Available from http://oerhub.net/reports and http://ukopentextbooks.org.

Porat, D. (2004). It's not written here, but this is what happened: Students' cultural comprehension of textbook narratives on the Israeli–Arab conflict. *American Educational Research Journal, 41*(4), 963–996. doi:10.3102/00028312041004963

Powell, W. (1985). *Getting into print: The decision-making process in scholarly publishing.* Chicago: University of Chicago Press.

Provenzo Jr, E., Shaver, A., & Bello, M. (2010). *Textbook as discourse.* London: Routledge.

Quijano, A. (2007). Coloniality and modernity/rationality. *Cultural Studies, 21*(2–3), 168–178.

Ragusa, G. (2013). *STEM literacy and textbook biases in K-12.* Paper presented at the 2013 IEEE Frontiers in Education Conference (FIE).

Rankin, R., & Piwko, P. (2022). An analysis of the coverage of cooperatives in US introductory business textbooks. *Journal of Accounting and Finance, 22*(3), 1.

Raufflet, E., & Mills, A. (2017). *The dark side: Critical cases on the downside of business.* London, UK: Routledge.

Reed, J. (2018). The history of the textbook: The state of the discipline. *Book History, 21*(1), 397–424.

Rezat, S. (2008). Die Struktur von Mathematikschulbüchern. *Journal für Mathematik-Didaktik, 29*(1), 46–67.

Rollans, G., & de la Chenelière, M. (2010). *Study of the Canadian K to 12 educational book publishing sector [report].* Retrieved from https://publications.gc.ca/site/archivee-archived.html?url=https://publications.gc.ca/collections/collection_2010/pc-ch/CH44-139-2010-eng.pdf

Schaefli, L., Godlewska, A., & Rose, J. (2018). Coming to know indigeneity: Epistemologies of ignorance in the 2003–2015 Ontario Canadian and world studies curriculum. *Curriculum Inquiry, 48*(4), 475–498.

Scheuer, C., & Mills, A. J. (2017). Reifying age-related employment problems through the constructions of the "problematic" older and younger worker. In I. Aaltio & A. J. Mills (Eds.), *Ageing, organisations and management: Constructive Discourse and Critical Perspectives* (pp. 41–63). Chamberly: Palgrave Mamillan.

Schissler, H., & Soysal, Y. (2005). *The nation, Europe, and the world: Textbooks and curricula in transition.* New York: Berghahn Books.

Schugurensky, D. (2007). "What knowledge is of least worth?" The coverage of cooperatives and nonprofits in business and economic textbooks. *Academia, Lunchbox Speakers' Series.* Talk at the panel "The Social What? Learning About the Social Economy in Ontario High Schools", Toronto, February 21.

Snyder, V., & Broadway, F. (2004). Queering high school biology textbooks. *Journal of Research in Science Teaching: The Official Journal of the National Association for Research in Science Teaching, 41*(6), 617–636.

Stambaugh, J., & Quinn Trank, C. (2010). Not so simple: Integrating new research into textbooks. *Academy of Management Learning & Education, 9*(4), 663–681.

Stray, C. (1994). Paradigms regained: Towards a historical sociology of the textbook. *Journal of Curriculum Studies, 26*(1), 1–29.
Summers, D., Boje, D., Dennehy, R., & Rosile, G. (1997). Deconstructing the organizational behavior text. *Journal of Management Education, 21*(3), 343–360.
Taylor, F. W. (1911). *The principles of scientific management*. New York: Harper.
Thompson, J. (2005). *Books in the digital age: The transformation of academic and higher education publishing in Britain and the United States*. Cambridge: Polity.
Toulmin, S., & Toulmin, S. E. (1992). *Cosmopolis: The hidden agenda of modernity*. Chicago: University of Chicago Press.
Townley, B. (2002). Managing with modernity. *Organization, 9*(4), 549–573.
Turner, K., & Riggs, C. (2021). *Economic profile of the Canadian book publishing industry: Technological, legislative and market changes in Canada's English-language book industry, 2008–2020 [report]*. Retrieved from www.canada.ca/en/canadian-heritage/corporate/transparency/open-government/economic-profile-book-publishing-industry.html#a3
Vaara, E., & Faÿ, E. (2012). Reproduction and change on the global scale: A Bourdieusian perspective on management education. *Journal of Management Studies, 49*(6), 1023–1051.
van Brummelen, H. (1990). The role of textbooks in inducting children into society. *Journal of Educational Thought (JET)/Revue de la Pensée Educative, 24*(3A), 135–137.
van den Ham, A., & Heinze, A. (2018). Does the textbook matter? Longitudinal effects of textbook choice on primary school students' achievement in mathematics. *Studies in Educational Evaluation, 59*, 133–140.
Voxted, S. (2017). 100 years of Henri Fayol. *Management Revue, 28*(2), 256–274.
Weatherbee, T., Dye, K., & Mills, A. J. (2005). *The paradox of management theory*. Paper presented at the Administrative Science Association of Canada, Toronto, Canada.
Weatherbee, T., Dye, K., & Mills, A. J. (2008). There's nothing as good as a practical theory: The paradox of management theory. *Management & Organizational History, 3*(2), 147–160.
Weigand, H., & Mills, A. J. (2015). Analysis of the role of sport in the management textbook: A study of sports images in organizational behaviour textbooks from 1992 to 2011. *Journal of Sports Science, 3*(1), 246–256.
Whitten, P. (1975). College textbook publishing in the 1970s. *Annals of the American Academy of Political and Social Science, 421*(1), 56–66.
Wiley, D., Bliss, T., & McEwen, M. (2014). Open educational resources: A review of the literature. In *Handbook of research on educational communications and technology* (pp. 781–789). New York: Routledge
Williams, B. (1989). A class act: Anthropology and the race to nation across ethnic terrain. *Annual Review of Anthropology, 18*, 401–444.
Williams, K., & Mills, A. J. (2019). The problem with women: A feminist interrogation of management textbooks. *Management & Organizational History, 14*(2), 148–166.
Wortham, S. (2006). *Learning identity. The joint emergence of social identification and Academic Learning*. Cambridge: Cambridge University Press.
Wren, D. (1972). *The evolution of management thought*. New York: The Ronald Press Co.
Wren, D. (1979). *The evolution of management thought* (2nd ed.). New York: John Wiley & Sons, Inc.

Wren, D. (1987). *The evolution of management thought* (3rd ed.). New York: John Wiley & Sons, Inc.

Wren, D. (1994). *The evolution of management thought* (4th ed.). New York: John Wiley & Sons, Inc.

Wren, D. (2005). *The history of management thought* (5th ed.). Hoboken, NJ: John Wiley & Sons, Inc.

Wren, D., & Bedeian, A. (2009). *The evolution of management thought* (6th ed.). Hoboken, NJ: John Wiley & Sons, Inc.

Wren, D., & Bedeian, A. (2018). *The evolution of management thought* (7th ed.). Hoboken, NJ: John Wiley & Sons, Inc.

Wren, D., & Bedeian, A. (2020). *The evolution of management thought* (8th ed.). New York: John Wiley & Sons, Inc.

Wright, M. (1994). A comparative study of the contents of personnel and human resource management textbsooks. *International Journal of Human Resource Management, 5*(1), 225–247.

Young, D. (1995). The Macmillan Company of Canada in the 1930s. *Journal of Canadian Studies, 30*(3), 117–133.

2 Making History

Identity Work within a Business School

Kristin S. Williams and Chantelle Falconer

Introduction

A neglected area of inquiry in management education history is how business schools and management faculties construct their sense of history and contributions to the field. Unlike Schools of Law, Engineering, and Medicine, business schools have largely lagged behind in developing a record of their past. This is partly due to the fragmented nature of such histories, beginning more than 100 years ago and stretching across various disciplines such as political economy, social work, home economics, and commerce. The roots of management education first took shape in skills-based or commerce courses, with an eye to vocational training, then shifting over time to the advancement of theoretical insights and broader contributions to management research and practice. Focusing on the Faculty of Management at Dalhousie University in Halifax, Canada, we investigate how a federated faculty with an interdisciplinary mandate makes sense of their history and identity, including their sense of belonging (or lack thereof).

To guide our investigation, we ask, "how does this federated faculty make sense of their shared history and identity?" We consider the temporal, geographic, structural, and conceptual borders and boundaries in which identity construction is transacted. We undertake a socio-linguistic and an intertextual analysis to trace the trajectory of organizational discourse. Specifically, we examine how conflicts and tensions are enunciated, how social identities are cultivated, how borders and boundaries are constructed, and how behaviors and identities are regulated. Our study illustrates how dominant discourses prescribe ways of thinking and behaving in shared academic space while also detailing the discursive effects on organizational actors. As a result, our study contributes to the larger conversation about how we *do* management education and how we forge academic identities within management faculties.

A Necessary Primer

Until quite recently, Dalhousie University's Faculty of Management, the subject of our case study, had a unique structure in which four schools, including its business school, were united under a federated faculty model with an interdisciplinary mandate. Therefore, it is important to offer a two-fold primer: (1) what is management (in the context of management education) and (2) what does it mean to be interdisciplinary?

Initially, we took for granted that a *faculty of management* understood *management* in the same ways, and it was only upon deeper reflection that we realized that some feel management is a general umbrella term that unites various schools conceptually under one roof, whereas others feel it is what unites various disciplines by describing the action of managing, be it people, resources, or data. Many management faculty members do not think of management as a central part of their identity but rather make sense of their association to management in terms of how their field of study informs management and organizational practices (e.g., financial practice, regulation/policy, the movement of goods through the supply chain, the sustainable use of environmental resources, leadership and human resources, governance, and data and information management). The concept of management as practice instead of (or as well as) management as an academic field is perhaps partly to blame for this confusion. In this way, management is understood as a practice and something that you *do*. Dalhousie's Faculty of Management orientation toward management is probably better understood as an administrative strategy to unify what some might consider disparate fields of knowledge in the *management of management*. As a result, the associated organizational actors experience different senses of belonging and fit.

An *interdisciplinary* identity is also not well understood within the faculty and a definition lacked consensus. For some it is perceived as activity belonging within discrete disciplines and involving a combination of novel methods in the study of social phenomenon, but still ontologically and epistemologically bounded. Whereas for others it speaks to a spectrum of collaborative research behaviors across disciplines that may or may not transgress epistemological boundaries. One participant described these activities as moving from "singular tracks" to "crosscuts" (P20). Whereas another spoke of it in terms of achieving a common direction and agreement on resource allocation: "[a]common, a strategic decision, common administrative decision and orderly instead of competition for resources" (P19). Conceptually, the federated model boasts in strategic documents the idea of the four schools blurring disciplinary borders to provide a more holistic education.

There have been many deliberate attempts to make business and management education consider curriculum related to a more holistic education. Indeed, we can trace a pattern in which over the course of management education at

Dalhousie, there have been various attempts to both integrate insights from social sciences and humanities and then reject such adoptions in favor of more business-focused courses, such as finance and marketing. Of late, such integrations have favored the adoption of perspectives on sustainable resource development and other ethical business practices. Management scholars cite the need for "enthusiastic support" and support at "several levels" to achieve sustained interest in such integration (Rusinko, 2010, p. 516). Though this is not restricted to business schools, higher education is increasingly being asked to take a significant role in promoting well-rounded perspectives, and viewing sustainable development and other ethical considerations in global management plans and integrating impact measures and drivers in organizations, and in management strategies and decision making (Lozano & von Haartman, 2018; Yáñez et al., 2019).

Additionally, research into higher education has sought to signal unmet needs in management education, such as work-based pedagogical approaches, developing global perspectives and integration skills in executive learning, and reflective practices within leadership (Waddock & Lozano, 2013). As a result, the design of management schools has been much debated by universities, largely due to the need for management education to address the management of business in complex times and the perceived merit for greater engagement with arts and humanities to create more empathic and creative leaders (Starkey & Tempest, 2009). It has been argued that in order to create a venue for new and innovative thinking, including improvisational skills, an attitude of inquiry and curiosity, management schools need new design principles (Starkey & Tempest, 2009). Business schools have also had to address a vastly competitive landscape and the worldwide expansion of higher education (Schofer & Meyer, 2005). It is on this backdrop that we lay the foundation for why Dalhousie chose to structure its management education as a federated model with an interdisciplinary mandate.

Background: Dalhousie University's Faculty of Management

In 1975, the Faculty of Administrative Studies was created with four schools: the School of Business Administration, the School of Public Administration (SPA), the School of Library Studies, and the School of Social Work. It was in 1984 that it became the Faculty of Management Studies, and in 1987, the Faculty of Management. The schools organizing under the banner of management have shifted over time, as has the curriculum, and degrees offered. Until recently, the Faculty of Management consists of the Rowe School of Business (RSB), the School of Information Management (SIM), the SPA, and the School for Resource and Environmental Studies (SRES). Structural changes initiated in 2022 have resulted in the departure of one school (SRES) and the amalgamation of the three remaining to be acknowledged collectively as the "Faculty of

Management" (business, information management, and public administration). Between 1975 and 2022, the Faculty of Management was a dynamic faculty, with schools moving in and out over time. One constant has been its federated composition and interdisciplinary orientation. This composition and orientation has also been much debated. Our review of strategic documents did not yield a succinct rationale for the combination of schools as representing the faculty, and faculty members have called the federation everything from a "faculty of convenience" to a "faculty of mismatched schools" to a faculty which is "nervously federated". We do not believe that these are fair descriptions, but they give you, as our reader, a sense of the confusion our participants feel about the model.

Under the most recent configuration, the RSB was the largest school, representing approximately 70% of faculty members (including part-time faculty) and enrollments in the order of 80% of students for the faculty (Balser, 2019). The RSB has four programs: a Bachelor of Commerce, the Corporate Residence Master of Business Administration (MBA), the distance/online MBA (Financial Services/Leadership) (Faculty of Management, 2019), and MSc in management. Approximately 50% of the courses offered in the Bachelor of Management program[1] are offered by the RSB and 50% are offered by the other three schools in the Faculty of Management (as reported in 2020).

Dalhousie University is a U15[2] research university. Management has held an awkward place at Dalhousie University, given the university's emphasis on research and the faculty's dual role as both a professional school with the goal of training leaders and managers, and as a faculty that produces knowledge and research with real-world application. When the first commerce courses were introduced in the 1920s, a prerequisite of funding was that the university retain strong ties with the business community and be in service to the business community (P21). This combined directive of both producing "ready-to-work" professional graduates and meeting the U15 research-intensive culture in a competitive landscape presents many challenges. Management scholars have reflected on this double academic identity with grave concern for reconciling the instrumentalism of careerism (for themselves and students) with the images of being a "proper academic" and exploring new knowledge for knowledge-sake (Learmonth & Humphreys, 2012). However, Dalhousie's history is even more complicated.

Each of the four schools has been targeted for redundancy over the history of the faculty. Two of our participants (P8 and P13) shared that during Howard Clark's presidency (1986–1995), he attempted to restructure parts of Dalhousie, using the argument of financial constraints that the university was facing (at the beginning of the 1990s). The SPA was designated for closure, and the School of Library and Information Studies was expected to become more closely aligned with the School of Business Administration. This plan was vigorously resisted by members of the faculty and administration including the dean of the faculty at the time. The Dalhousie Faculty Association launched a grievance (on the grounds that it did not follow the requirements of the Collective Agreement regarding financial exigency) and won. None of the closures were implemented and the units designated for closure or restructuring may have been strengthened in the process, due to the shared threat. Under the next president, Tom Travis (serving until 2013), Dalhousie expanded. The Faculty of Management benefited from a new administrative view, which led eventually to a new building for the faculty where all four schools were finally co-located in 2005.

For context, it is also important to note that the Nova Scotian government has periodically considered "rationalizing" the number of universities in the province, including floating the ideas of a University of Nova Scotia and a University of Halifax (O'Neill et al., 2010). One of these initiatives (late 1990s) was of particular concern to the business school as the business programs offered by the universities in Halifax (Dalhousie University and Saint Mary's University) were targeted for potential merger, with the possibility of the programs being consolidated at Saint Mary's University. Such a consolidation did not happen, in part because of considerable push back from Dalhousie advocates, including members of the Advisory Board.[3] Dalhousie has been in the position of having to defend its worth and place within the Nova Scotian post-secondary landscape several times.

The managerial turn in academia may have also been a factor in these profound shifts in approaches to management education in Nova Scotia. The managerial turn in academia has promoted characteristics of professional organizing which have led to a profound restructuring, the increase in higher-level administrative positions and management units to address quality control (increased surveillance), technology, career service, and increased managerial demands on academics (Clarke & Knights, 2015; Krücken et al., 2013).

Theory Building

Identity work is a central, constitutive feature of organizing (Mumby, 2016). Contemporary management schools are under scrutiny for how neoliberal capitalism is seeping into identity and exploits, extracts, and transacts value (processes of discursive production) (Pohle, 2016). The branding of management and business schools has become the epicenter for organizing processes and leveraging equity and translating potential or actual economic value (Mumby, 2016). Additionally, universities are sites of dynamic social ordering, shared meaning-making and governed in a multistakeholder setting where input may not be a good indicator of output (Latour, 2005; Pohle, 2016).

On a microlevel, business and management scholars are also contending with different identity pressures which create various anxieties about what it means to be an academic. The business and management scholar must be an excellent teacher who produces ready-to-work graduates, sometimes with or without the assistance of service learning and cooperative placements. The business and management scholar must attend to what is required for promotion in terms of grants, publications, and service. A business and management scholar must find the right orientation to scholarship in an environment where ontological and epistemological camps are not only clearly demarcated but fervently defended as "the right way" to do research. These frictions call into question the stability of academic identities within business schools (Clarke & Knights, 2015; Learmonth & Humphreys, 2012). In many cases, the legitimacy of business school scholars is viewed in terms of their experience as researchers *and* practitioners. Instructors may acquire more intellectual capital if they are convincing performers occupying various tropes from the *aloof and distant researcher*, to the *aggressive corporatist* (Bell & Clarke, 2014). Younger academics must quickly slay their imposter syndrome and achieve confidence and credibility to go head-to-head with business-savvy MBA students who are already established organizational actors and leaders (Crozier & Woolnough, 2020). Ultimately, business and management scholars must negotiate the appropriate scholastic attitude, the most persuasive instructor performance, while pursuing careerist instrumentalism in a highly competitive, self-interested environment of increasing scarcity (Bell & Clarke, 2014). The strain on business scholars caused by these environmental stressors is now more well understood, but solutions are illusive (Clarke & Knights, 2015; Quijada, 2021).

Conceptually, there are three components of identity that are advanced by Alvesson and Willmott (2002): (1) identity regulation (expectations and regulation), (2) identity work (becoming and belonging), and (3) self-identity (outcomes and repercussions) (as cited in Crozier & Woolnough, 2020). We add to these ideas about identity both macro (collective) and micro (individual) level sites of enactment. On the macro level, our analysis will consider the temporal, geographic, structural, and conceptual identity boundaries, whereas on the microlevel, we will look more closely at social identities.

Methodological Approach

Our work is framed in a postmodern tradition, wherein we attempt to decode embedded social significances and uncover shifting meaning-making, while charting how narratives perform (performativity and language games) (Prasad, 2005). In writing an organizational story, we apply two forms of analysis in the reading of both the texts we collected and reviewed and in analyzing our narrative accounts (participant interviews).

First, we apply Social Linguistic Analysis (Phillips & Hardy, 2002) to interrogate the prominent domains in which our identity discourses are framed, namely temporal, geographic, structural, and conceptual. We compare the "official" records with that of personal narratives and sense making. We illustrate how narratives are replicated and rejected. In so doing, we also reveal the discursive effects of organizational narratives.

Second, to chart the trajectory of organizational discourse, we apply an interpretation of Boje's (2001) Intertextual Analysis. Intertextual Analysis sees text as a dynamic production. We take a critical reading of history as "intertextual scenes" (p. 76). Specifically, we draw on Boje's social questions for intertextual analysis, which he presents on an axis of immediate and distance contexts and the historicity of preceding and anticipated texts (Boje, 2001).

Our data consists of interviews with faculty, administrators, and alumni. We interviewed 21 individuals with longstanding connections to the faculty. As tenured individuals with their confidentiality protected, they felt free to share their opinions and thoughts. We asked them to share their memories and perspectives on the history of the faculty. This chapter is part of a larger project of history-making for the faculty, which has been initiated to help the faculty develop an understanding of who they are and where they have been. As part of this study, we also examined various internal reports. In organizations, reports, such as the ones we reviewed, contain conventions, interpretation, and interweave multiple voices, and they represent social and cultural identity work (Boje, 2001). By examining the text of our interviews alongside these reports, we can also see how actors legitimize and construct their own identity against or in agreement with this institutional one. It is through this exercise that we uncovered dissonance between historical records and the narrative accounts of our participants, and it is this dissonance that we wish to explore. Discourses attempt to represent a common sense of certain actors (Burrell & Morgan, 1979), but this is not what we saw. Concepts that you might expect to be common sense were far from taken for granted, including a shared sense of history and important events, and the core umbrella term that unites the faculty (management) might in fact not.

We bring to consideration our emic perspectives as we examine accounts of past and present faculty members (see participant list, Appendix 2.1)[4] and documents such as Senate and internal faculty reviews (see Appendix 2.2). One of our first steps was to create a comprehensive timeline for the faculty, which had not been undertaken before. We charted the history of schools, centers, programs, key achievements (see Appendix 2.3), as well as a history of the deans (see Appendix 2.4). The timeline project allowed us to create an organizational record by which to help us navigate and interpret our data.

Data and Analysis

In Table 2.1 (Social Linguistic Analysis), we arrange our data across two dimensions (macro/collective through formal documents and micro/individual

Table 2.1 Social linguistic analysis

	Formal Documents	Narrative Participant Accounts
Temporal	• The study of business at Dalhousie University goes back to the early 1920s with the development of the Bachelor of Commerce degree in the Department of Commerce. The Department of Commerce was a part of the Faculty of Arts and Science (FAS). The Master of Business Administration (MBA) program was launched in 1967 (Advisory Committee to the Rowe School of Business, 2020, p. 26). • The federated faculty model was established in 1975. • The faculty was co-located in the same building in 2005.	• "In my recollection is that it started out with the Business School… over the years, different schools, I guess, joined together" (P6). • "In 1975, when Faculty of Business Administration at that time it was the name, was faculty of Business Admin. It was established to include business education and public administration education and I think library at that time, library education" (P20). • "The justification of bringing the four schools in like what was the selling feature that got the president to say 'yeah, sure, I'll give you a new building and we will bring these three or these four schools together'" (P5).
Geographic	• Until 2005, the various schools were located across campus in different buildings and houses. In 2005, they were co-located in a new dedicated and named building. Formerly, SIM was located in the library and SPA and RSB were collocated within a church with the Gallery of Nova Scotia. Prior to that the business school was located in the basement of the library. • The building was named the Kenneth C. Rowe Management Building when opened in 2005.	• "Yeah, the building was, I mean the main purpose of the building was to, uh, teardown, I guess some of those silos…it put everybody under one roof with hopes that there would be more collaboration…I think it's more collaborative now than it was when we first moved in but…it took time" (P6). • "Moving into this new building definitely was a significant event" (P2). • "I always thought that that was the one thing that the building in 2005 and gave us that we did not have as a faculty before the building because we were all over campus and we were all housed poorly" (P21).
Structural	• "The Faculty of Management (originally the Faculty of Administrative Studies) was created in 1975. Since then, there have been structural changes with Schools added and removed" (Senate Review Committee, 2012, p. 5).	• "Well, I definitely think that just given our own unique set of circumstances where we have a faculty that is comprised of one very large school and a satellite set of smaller schools" (P2).

Table 2.1 (Continued)

	Formal Documents	Narrative Participant Accounts
	• The faculty has included the Maritime School of Social Work and the unit of Marine Management. Marine Management was part of the faculty (though not a school) and co-located with the faculty until 2013. • "Unique among Canadian Universities, the Faculty of Management is home to four Schools: the Rowe School of Business (Rowe), the School of Information Management (SIM), the School of Public Administration (SPA), and the School for Resource and Environmental Studies (SRES)" (Review Committee, 2014, p. 3). • "RSB is structured comparably with other U15 universities in Canada, however, the majority of other business schools in Canada have independent faculties" (Advisory Committee to the Rowe School of Business, 2020).	• "In the current discussion about the configuration of the school, it needs to be understood that this is something that has plagued us for well, as long as I've been here and probably longer so" (P2). • "I think that the intention was pure about why they wanted to bring diverse perspectives on management under one faculty... and people just aren't willing to let it die because we know it's the right thing" (P3). • "a kind of fraught collaboration" (P20). • [SRES] "never thought they belong[ed] to the faculty of management" (P19). • [being] "interdisciplinary...never happened. Whatever the reason was, and every Dean has tried very hard" (P19).
Conceptual	• "Particularly hopeful and positive about the Faculty position in that there is a strong and well respected Dean in place, the constituent units are co-located in a purpose-build, modern and beautiful building and there is a healthy mix of new and experienced faculty members productively engaged in their work" (Senate Review Committee, 2012, p. 1).	• "And right now, there's conversations where one of the schools do not feel like they are part of the strategic objective" (P6). • "But there has always been this kind of rivalry between the faculty and the School of Business. Or now, the Rowe School in some form or other" (P2).

(*Continued*)

44 *Management Education in Canada*

Table 2.1 (Continued)

Formal Documents	Narrative Participant Accounts
• "The thread that appeared to glue the disparate schools in FAS was management (in a broad sense of the term). In some sense, the idea that the MBA was an all-purpose management degree implied that it had features common to the management of libraries and public sector organizations" (Advisory Committee to the Rowe School of Business, 2020, p. 26).	• "They don't do research in the School of Business…in many places the faculty of management is or certainly was not viewed as a hotbed of research" (P2). • "I don't think it's ever really, if I'm being frank, unfolded the way the vision was originally [planned]…I think everyone busy into that diverse multi lens perspective on solving problems, but historically, I think the academic set up and historical tenure system … like academia gets in its own way" (P3). • "Stitched together, parts of our faculty in a way that would really enrich and student experience, and some of those have been kind of fulfilled and some of them have not. Some of them are kind of midway through right" (P20). • [the perspective] "from the outside is better than it has worked" [within]…so perception from the outside is much, much better than it actually [is] working together" (P19). • "It was a shotgun wedding" (P5).

through participant narratives) and across different identity boundaries (temporal, geographic, structural, and conceptual) to determine where there is dissonance and agreement. Our formal documents originate from several different dates, whereas our participant data was collected in fall 2021/winter 2022.

Participants used several anchors to communicate their history. On the macro level, participants generally commented on the aforementioned temporal, geographic, structural, and conceptual identity boundaries. Temporally, many actors have only a vague sense of when the federated faculty was formed. Many believe it was not until they were co-located in the same building. Our records indicate it was always a federated faculty, though (as we have stated) courses in commerce began very early in the university's history. As previously mentioned, one participant characterized the faculty as a *faculty of convenience*, in that many programs and schools had come and gone over the years often arriving as a program and leaving as a more fully fledged school, and that this has left the faculty feeling porous. This also supports some of the narrative from reports which appear to need to reassert, over and over, who belongs to the faculty. In contrast, narratives from participants continue to reflect on existing tensions between schools.

Geographically, most actors speak fondly of being independently located in their own buildings. This was seen as a more friendly and intimate arrangement, despite functional deficits. The building is set up to support the distinctiveness of each school and the administration (with its own doored hallways and sets of suites and rooms) with few common spaces outside of each school. A critique was levied by some participants that co-location did not inspire more formal or informal engagements across schools. For example, P12 spoke of the need for more "collision opportunities". Indeed, several participants remarked that the only engagement with other school faculty members tended to happen by happenstance in the stairwell: "As you run into somebody on the stairs, and you stopped to talk with them and then 20 minutes later you've both had a brain wave for some future research" (P21). The two significant program collaborations (the Bachelor of Management and the Management Without Borders graduate course) were both created irrespective of location.

Structurally, the faculty has always been federated though membership has varied. Both the School of Social Work and the Marine Management program have come and gone. It was interesting to note that many members did not recall Marine Management as joining the rest of the schools when moving to the new building in 2005, despite their presence there until 2013. "When I joined the faculty, they were part of the faculty even when we sort of moved over to the new building. They just didn't come with us" (P6). Currently discussions have led to the departure of another school: the School Resource and Environmental Studies[5] who will be joining the Faculty of Science. This departure is happening along the folding of the school structure entirely in favor of a more united Faculty of Management.

Conceptually, there are two threads that are replicated across most formal documents, and this includes the following: (1) the benefits of being a federated faculty and (2) an interdisciplinary identity of the faculty and a holistic approach to management education. However, neither of these two conceptual (linguistic) imperatives are shared in our faculty narratives. Instead, our participants acknowledge these strategic priorities but suggest that they have never fully been realized. The cohesiveness noted in official reports in some places is not replicated by faculty that we interviewed, who instead see the faculty as disconnected at best, competitive at worst. Additionally, the formal documents do not delineate between an interdisciplinary mandate and a federated faculty and therefore the meaning and outcomes of such priorities are unclear. It is our observation that the notion of being interdisciplinary and offering a holistic form of management education is a *strawman* and the notion of a federated faculty as

Table 2.2 Reference – Intertextual analysis framework

Social Identities	Conventions
What social identities get constituted?	What conventions get incorporated?
What text gets quoted?	Who are the audiences designed to be?
What institutions commission the text?	Who is the text consumed by?

Organizational Artifacts	Metaphorization
How are parts of the text incorporated?	What are the insider terms?
How are various stories incorporated?	What are the examples of metaphor?
What are the organizational artifacts?	What text is selected for the audience?

Note: Based on Boje (2001, p. 77).

a decision that serves the faculty is an *organizational artifact* that was discursively constructed (Phillips & Hardy, 2002).

Table 2.2 outlines our interpretation of Boje's (2001) Intertextual Analysis Framework and applicable social questions for cultural activity. Social identities consider who is talked about and who does the speaking. They are in a constant state of becoming, dynamic, unfinished, and interrelated (Boje, 2001). Conventions consider the rules of the organization and the immutable structures, as perceived by the organizational actors. Organizational artifacts consider how stories are replicated and reproduced and what may not come to pass but is held on to as having value (or not). Finally, metamorphization refers to the examples of organizational experience that are translated into something that is perceived as real by the organizational actors.

As illustrated in Table 2.3 (Intertextual Analysis of Formal Documents), those commissioning the text consist of faculty members participating in committees, external reviewers, and others associated with the university, whereas the focus of identity work is on the faculty writ large, leadership, and governance (upper left quadrant). It was clear that school dispositions toward one another and leadership are working against the strategic imperative to be both federated and interdisciplinary.

Conventions apparent in formal reports include research outputs, which were difficult to evaluate (upper right quadrant). Even in the business school, there is confusion about what constitutes management or business education and what the conventional approach is. If one of the schools is having trouble in understanding their core purpose, it is easy to appreciate that a federated identity is even more challenging to conceive. This is evident in legacy of comments related to the standing of the business school, the uneven structure, and lack of collaboration between all four schools (organizational artifacts, lower left quadrant).

However, on balance, the formal reviews and reports speak to the value of integration and the merit of a merged identity (metamorphization). However, these merits do not appear to be enough to carry the strategy forward. According

Table 2.3 Intertextual analysis of formal documents

Social Identities	Conventions
• "The Faculty and School have been experiencing changes in leadership since 2015, with one interim Dean (2015–16), another Dean (2016–18), a new interim Dean (2018–19), two interim RSB Directors (2015–16; 2016–17), and a churn of faculty members" (Faculty of Management, 2019, p. 17) • "It quickly became apparent to the Committee that many of the challenges facing the school are unrelated to structure, and they will not be resolved partially or totally by a change to the structure… Some of these problems and challenges can be attributed to RSB's membership within the Faculty with the same autonomy and status of other three much smaller schools" (Advisory Committee to the Rowe School of Business, 2020, P. 11)	• "The Committee does not have a finely tuned sense of the internal research and publication norms for the various sub-disciplines in the Faculty… research intensity varies between the four schools" (Review Committee, 2014, p. 4) • "The view of the MBA as the flagship program of RSB has generated some vision problems. The MBA focuses on 'management', which is hardly the core of business. In fact, the core disciplines are finance, marketing, management, strategy, and operations. Understanding that 'business' is at the heart of Western society and culture, the academic study of the core disciplines would seem to be central to the business school mission. There is a strong argument that marketing, and operations have been largely ignored in the RSB. It is not that the base of the RSB is a one-legged stool, but strength in core disciplines is required" (Advisory Committee to the Rowe School of Business, 2020, p. 27)

Organizing Artifacts	Metaphorization
• "Not only is the RSB less visible within the University or among its competitors, it has a structure that is hard for important external organizations to understand, evaluate and serve" (Advisory Committee to the Rowe School of Business, 2020, p. 11) • "Lack of goal congruence, cultural differences between schools. We do have a group of faculties who just are not very collaborative or open to working with others" (Advisory Committee to the Rowe School of Business, 2020)	• "Surviving external and internal threats set the FAS on a more united path forward. A succession of Deans … promoted integration. In 2005, a new management building, named after Kenneth C. Rowe, facilitated the housing of all schools under one roof. A faculty-wide 'Management Without Borders' course, required of all graduate students, was created. However, the identities of the individual Schools were also enhanced by the physical facilities in the Rowe Building" (Advisory Committee to the Rowe School of Business, 2020, p. 27).

to a recent review on the structure of the business school, a recommendation was made to further investigate the viability of the business school becoming a stand-alone faculty (Advisory Committee to the Rowe School of Business, 2020, p. 21). Ultimately though a trajectory of discourse across the formal reports appeared to call for a separation of the business school, this has not come to pass.

As illustrated in Table 2.4 (Intertextual Analysis of Participant Narratives), the social identities (upper left quadrant) of concern in our participant narratives were that of the formal leadership and the deans. Many remarked that turn over had caused confusion in strategic direction and delays in key decisions. When narrating the past, our participants often associated the deans symbolically with the strategy of the faculty and used these social figures to make sense of doing research and teaching in an interdisciplinary space. One participant remarked that it was both difficult to attract and maintain top leadership historically (P3). Deans are often depicted as "multi-talented, high-status achievers", but they are also often the high-profile targets of criticism (Brown et al., 2021, p. 823). One former dean commented that he felt it was a "common academic assumption that deans are expected to have dollars available for a variety of 'significant' faculty projects" (P16). Another said, "I was put in a real box as a dean" (P7). Appreciably, when probed for additional clarity, many participants reveal the relatively little structural power a dean possesses, instead relying tremendously on their persuasiveness and social influence. For example, "We cannot really give all the credit or all the blame to the deans." (P19) was a common refrain. However, it was routinely noted that stability was lacking and is simultaneously very important. This speaks to the uncertainty about accountability within an academic environment and begs the question: if a strategy is jointly approached, who then is accountable when it fails to be realized?

We noted constraints (sometimes rules) presented as conventions of the organization (upper right quadrant) and were thus incorporated into the text and narratives. An example we have provided here speaks to the sense that things move slowly within universities and change is difficult. Such conventions are taken for granted and often unchallenged. Another example is the notion of "busy work" or work that is irrelevant and timewasting. A third observation is that the system produces skepticism. And finally, our most concerning convention was the understanding that the structure advantages some over others. We share an example in our analysis of this underlying idea that the business school is propping up the other schools, and though this chapter cannot trace that narrative in its entirety, we do think it is relevant to the identity work within the federated faculty as promoting competition over collaboration and working counter to a collective sense of belonging within the faculty. In turn, this serves as a stumbling block for articulating a unique space for Dalhousie's approach to management education in the provincial, national, and global post-secondary sphere.

In the lower left quadrant, we note key stories onboarded and espoused by faculty. These include the approach to management education as being more holistic and *ahead of its time*. We feel that this is recognition that the federated

Making History 49

Table 2.4 Intertextual analysis of participant narratives

Social Identities	Conventions
• "That's seemed [in] my opinion anyway, over the last 10 years or so that the leadership has been, I guess, scattered…the deanships have been uh, quite plentiful" (P6). • "['name' became dean and] was not a manager. Zero management ability … You know, the role of a leader is to lead. And I'm not sure universities are set up very well, to allow for that" (P1). • "Every dean is busy setting up their own strategy and completely ignoring anything that has happened before…and it has always struck me as incredibly wasteful and demoralizing" (P2). • "The president at the time decided to cut [the] school of public admin and the school of library [sciences]… at the time the Dean said no…so eventually we decided to carry them from the budget of the business school" (P19). • "But in none of those, uh, you know, all the credit or blame goes to the Dean, because [even though] these are the decisions that we collectively make" (P19). • "It's tough because we've gone through so many freaking deans …and that's nobody's like, that's no one's fault…I think there was a dean in there too, who might have overemphasized how one school might be better than others because they were smaller, but they had lots of researchers. So then that kind of fanned, fans fanned the flames" (P17). • "It was a struggle when I was the dean to try and think about how we could make these units work together…My predecessors had the same struggle to try and get the different schools to you, have meaningful collaboration and do that instead of just being a patchwork quilt" (P7).	• "In the sense that it is forcing the issue to work as fast as you can within a university setting. Which is very slow. Yes. Very slow. And I think we'll get as good an outcome as we can from it" (P1). • "Uh, so I run into a colleague of mine in the hallway as I'm rushing out to the meeting, which was not in the building and I'm… he's asking me well where you going? And I've said the faculty of management meeting and he basically said oh don't bother, that's just more busy work" (P2). • "I hate to say it over the years one does get cynical" (P2). • "I am sure you have heard the stories [of] struggle and tension…I wish I could like pull up every email on strategy for the faculty that I've ever gotten in my 12 years and like it. Just you feel like you never are actually working the plan. You're just continuing to talk about the plan like that, and I think it's in part because we've never found the way to actually integrate these schools and get buy in from everybody" (P3). • "Actually, I believe that these smaller schools have a right to grow, but the growth has to be justified and bring budget from outside, not from the Management budget envelope of the of the faculty, because this would be a sort of cannibalism. One part that grows. The other part you know goes down, and so forth. So, we have to be able to bring resources in for the growth of every part of this faculty" (P19). • "I always thought that the Rowe School of Business thought that they were better than everybody" (P17).

(*Continued*)

Table 2.4 (Continued)

Organizational Artifacts	Metamorphization
• "I think management education I mean used to be just business and now it's more holistic ... managing for the greater good I guess, and not just for profit, and I think that's a change that's reflected in in education... I think there is a lot of opportunity out there for management in and across sectors [and] fields" (P6). • "The Bachelor of Management... it looked like it had really lots of potential, but it's like so many other entities around the globe, uh, it's the program of the future and always has been, always will be" (P2). • "Management should include not only just business for profit, but also management of public admin and management of environment... It needs some profit for corporations, but it need to save the environment for our grandchildren" (P19).	• "I think that Management Without Boarders was... A good thing to bring the faculty together... And the Bachelor of Management [was] another program that had brought all the all the schools under one roof" (P6). • "I think I think our focus around experiential learning has always been a strength at Dal and that has manifested through the co-ops [and] through the MBA" (P3). • "I think the Bachelor of Management was one example of how the four schools can work together" (P19). • "When the Bachelor of Management program came on one, where it was an interdisciplinary (mandate), and it was to include pieces from each of those schools, it was a great idea, but no one thought it through as to like they ended up being, you know, the unwanted orphan" (P17).

faculty and its commitment to interdisciplinarity (even if not entirely realized) are seen as positive and instrumental to management education in Canada. We also see this as an organizational artifact or *strawman* in that it is notion that is clung to, though not entirely representative.

In the lower right quadrant, we examine how key ideas have been expressed. A significant example of interdisciplinary activity across the schools is the Management Without Borders graduate course, which is mandatory for all graduate students in all schools. This was broadly considered an exemplar of how the federated faculty demonstrated interdisciplinarity and it serves as a key metaphor in the intertextual framework. Many feel that it was something that the faculty could have been *known for* if it was more embraced by all schools. It was novel when introduced in 2006, and students were being challenged in positive ways to see beyond their disciplines:

> And it was tough for them. The business students could see no reason in the world why they would ever meet with an environmentalist. Why they would ever meet with a government official, or why they'd ever want to know anything about information management. And I'm not kidding, to a person, why would we ever do that? The environmentalist felt exactly the same thing.
>
> (P1)

Similarly, the Bachelor of Management degree, which is also open to all schools, was similarly seen as a tangible example of how the schools came together. The cooperative programs (part of the Corporate Residence MBA and the Bachelor of Commerce) were also praised for being something the faculty is known for (even though it resides in the business school). One participant remarked that these initiatives made the faculty better: "I mean, this is going to make this business[6], this Management faculty better" (P1).

An intertextual analysis considers the hegemonic and heterogeneous weave of utterances from and within texts, as well as the way that text is a part of an ongoing dynamic production, distribution, and consumption of narratives (Boje, 2001). Crucially, it charts the direction of discourse. It would appear from our analysis that the trajectory is away from a holistic and interdisciplinary approach to management with some exceptions. The narratives seem to describe the issues of coming together and belonging but speak to the structure of federation as getting in the way. However, feelings of belonging and fit have not become deeply anchored beyond the confines of the schools. It will be interesting to see as the amalgamated faculty moves forward if the challenges mentioned herein can be resolved.

Discussion – Doing Management

Here we wish to highlight a few key learnings. First, we wish to capture the specific factors we feel that point to ongoing dissonance within the federated model. Second, we also wish to return to provide a few remarks on the components of identity and how this also contributes to the dissonance within the federated model. This dissonance is what we feel is responsible for the trajectory of the discourse of the faculty to move away from a federated model, which strategically seemed to hold significant promise for the delivery of management education.

On balance, our participants view the federated model and its interdisciplinary mandate as unrealized potential. The two examples of the four schools collaborating and attempting to embrace its interdisciplinary mandate are the Bachelor of Management degree and the Management Without Borders graduate course. These initiatives have and continue to hold much promise and have done considerable good for the faculty and its students. However, they are generally viewed as being, at best, underdeveloped and, at worst, neglected. One participant offered this summary: "I still think that the benefits are the untapped potential of, uh, a degree in management that has straddled different subject areas and different industry areas" (P18). The functional and ethical benefits to students and businesses are seen as tremendous and the interconnectedness that the federated model promotes makes those benefits more obvious. Regrettably, these conceptual ideas are not sufficient to promote within the faculty of these disparate disciplinary areas enough will and energy to fully exploit said potential.

Dalhousie's federated model of management education is a cautionary tale. There are several threads within our narratives that seem to reveal forces that are working against the idea of being united as a federated model and suggest concern for those educational environments that may wish to embrace such an approach. Two are prominent. Firstly, participants pointed to uneven resources as one such barrier. The business school is perceived to have more revenue generating capacity than the other schools. Secondly, the large size of the business school in comparison to the other schools and the uniform level of bureaucratic support for all schools appear to be a factor inhibiting more close association between the schools. Some remarked that it is an unnecessary level of resources. For example, one participant pointed to these pressures as reducing the business school's ability to hire anyone to meet the course load requirements, and to an associated concern that the smaller schools were permitted to grow under this arrangement at the cost of others (P19). This was difficult to reconcile with narratives from the other schools, who feel self-sufficient, successful, and independent financially (P5).

Our analysis was able to draw out not only the primary impediments to the federation, but also the trajectory of the discourse. The shared identity of being federated, though lured by a very seductive conceptualization of "doing management better", was not enough for individual identities to map onto it. However, it is interesting to note that in conducting interviews with our participants, there was considerable investment in these conversations about structure, while simultaneously eschewing the subject altogether. We believe that this speaks to the level of attachment faculty members have with the university, the faculty, its programs, and its students. In other words, the faculty wants on the one hand to protect the faculty and the collection of schools, but on the other hand, to separate its schools into different faculties or have a simpler model altogether where benefits could be ultimately realized. The newly adopted amalgamated faculty hopes to finally embrace the benefits of different disciplinary areas working together, without structural or resource politics getting in the way.

Our participants were quite emotional and passionate in their interviews. We read this to represent an investment into the collective identity. We also see this as representing individual fears and feelings of insecurity and uncertainty. These feelings of uncertainty are linked to implications for individual academic identities either as management scholars or as members of a faculty to which they can show pride in association. The faculty's most recent structure-based conversations, though challenging, have been an opportunity to reflect on where we have been so we can better understand where to go from here. For some it represents a juncture "where we should recognize and celebrate all that has happened within" (P18). Both sentiments seem to point to an ending and a new beginning.

We now return briefly to the three components of identity that are advanced by Alvesson and Willmott (2002): (1) identity regulation (expectations and regulation), (2) identity work (becoming and belonging), and (3) self-identity (outcomes and repercussions) (as cited in Crozier & Woolnough, 2020). We saw that identities are being *regulated* and limited by the conventions of academia, funding, the structures of the schools within the faculty, and the faculty structure itself. Individual *identity work* tended to be transacted within the schools, with organizational actors finding it easier to relate to school colleagues than the larger faculty. We feel that with the pressures on individual academics, a school is a sufficiently complex place to forge an individual academic identity, especially if one considers the challenges we discussed earlier in this chapter. In some instances, our participants reflected that school identities were passed on to students who they felt were far more likely to associate with their program than their faculty (P4, P5, P3). Finally, the repercussions of *self-identity* work were clear with respect to the tension between the business school and the other schools. Ultimately this tension within the faculty model is leading to an *outcome* by which the federated model has again been transformed in terms of its membership and strategy.

Conclusion – Making a History

In undertaking this study, which simultaneously contemplates the practice of making a history, while creating a history for the faculty, we naturally asked our participants what such a history should include. Answers varied so vastly that we feel we could present many histories. Conceptually, our participants thought a history of the faculty ought to include everything from formal reports to biographies of noteworthy faculty and students through to various prestigious milestones. Participants shared stories of navigating legislative and political turmoil, funding gaps, the vagaries of donor expectations and investments, and the influence of industry, as all playing a critical role in developing management education. We started with the data that examined identity construction. We have come to appreciate through our study of Dalhousie that business schools and faculties of management, in their various forms and how they organize, can serve as a rich site of inquiry. However, the complexity of such environments might also be a clue as to why charting a history has been an elusive task (for Dalhousie and we suspect perhaps for others too). Undertaking history work takes time, people, and resources and making the case for funding such work can be challenging.

Many of our participants felt that having a history of the faculty was critical, whether it was to develop "a collective narrative" (P20), a "sense of purpose" (P19), to "look back and reflect and make sure that we have our facts in order" (P6), or the pragmatics of having "a history of the programs" (P6), understanding origins (P12, P21), or research outputs (P2). Some spoke to the merits of understanding key influencers, "seminal events" and "seminal strategies" (P1) and recognizing being at the forefront of innovations (P2, P14, P21).

Some believe that capturing a historical perspective "would even generate more buy in as we evolve moving forward" (P3). Others focused on history as needing to recognize the student experience and their accomplishments, including the acquisition of relevant job ready experience, case competitions, scholarships, cooperative placements, and successful graduates (P2, P3, P7, P9). Having a history even appears to have the potential to generate pride in association through recognizing and capturing various ideas of what a faculty is known for: "we provide our students with true experience that they can lean on and leverage" (P3). Many remarked that it was important to know both the good and the "instructive" parts of our experience:

> It's very instructive to know these things not only the good otherwise you might as well forget about it. If it doesn't have the bad if there aren't learning moments in there, where we could look back and say we could have done better.
>
> (P1)

One participant aptly remarked that the history of an organization is like the *history of a life*, and it becomes a way to get to know something (P1). All this is to say that it is very difficult to pick just one focus and one story to tell. Writing about the past can take you in unexpected directions. In the case of Dalhousie's Faculty of Management, its history is an eclectic collection of memories, some written, and some recalled, and perhaps in either case, not terribly reliable ... but no less important. Perhaps documenting a history has the potential to bring a faculty together under a shared identity, bridging the critiques and dissonance inherent in conversations about structure.

In developing a history, we encountered many challenges. There was no collection strategy for archived materials, which for the most part was collected and stored based on the proclivities of individuals in various leadership or administrative roles. Some administrators were very methodical in keeping key reports, strategic documents, and individual files from their terms. However, in general, materials were stored in a variety of places, including the library archives, digital archives, and various faculty offices or homes. Indeed, we are still in the midst of tracking down various records as part of ongoing history project. Downsizing of space also saw some interesting material lost including an origin paper on the Centre for International Business, penned at the 25th anniversary (in 2000, P21). Somewhat frustrating was the discovery that when the faculty became digital, much was lost when individuals moved on because there was initially no shared common computer drive. Materials that might once have been kept in hard files were lost because they were instead stored only on individual computers: "I've heard of people leaving and taking their laptops with them [or] their laptops are completely wiped" (P6). Even analyzing research output is challenging as the central repository is an opt-in system and used unevenly across the faculty.

As with most history-making, efforts are hindered and aided by circumstances, context, and a bit of luck. We were aided by a strategic mandate of the current dean who put it simply: "we need to understand where we have been in order to understand where we are going". Additionally, those that we interviewed helped us to make sense of what we did find, and piece together key events and dates and they offered candid insights. Materially, their memories are what constitute their ideas of the past and helped us to form at least this one story of this faculty's history. This process helped us understand why such undertakings are challenging, but also critical to understanding what underpins the organization of management education in Canada and how it has developed over time.

Appendix 2.1 Participants

P1	Joined in the 1970s, Former Faculty, Advisor
P2	Joined in the 1980s Faculty
P3	Joined in the 1990s, Senior Administrator, Alumni Relations
P4	Joined in the 1980s, Administration, Senior Administrator
P5	Faculty
P6	Faculty, Senior Administrator
P7	Senior Administrator and Faculty
P8	Joined in the 1970s, Senior Administrator and Faculty
P9	Management, Career Services
P10	Faculty
P11	Joined in the 1970s, Former Faculty, Advisor, Investor
P12	Senior Administrator and Faculty
P13	Joined in the 1980s, Former Dean
P14	Former Senior Administrator and Faculty
P15	Senior Administrator and Faculty
P16	Former Senior Administrator and Faculty
P17	Joined in the 2000s, Administration
P18	Joined in the 2000s, Administration, Career Services
P19	Joined in the 1980s, Faculty
P20	Faculty
P21	Joined in the 1990s, Alumni, Senior Administrator and Faculty

Specific centers have not been named to protect the anonymity of participants. Specific dates have been approximated (rounded to decades) to also protect anonymity. Senior Administrators may comprise deans, heads of centers, chairs, or other similar senior administrative roles within the faculty.

Appendix 2.2 List of Documents

Senate Review Committee. (2012). *Faculty of Management Senate Review.*

Faculty of Management. (2019). *Dalhousie University – AACSB Report – 2013–18 Rowe School of Business – Faculty of Management.*

Rowe School of Business. (2020). *The School of Business Report on BSB Structure Advisory Committee, Appendix II – The History of the Faculty of Management and the Rowe School of Business.*

Balser, T. (2019). *AACSB PRT Site Visit and Report – March 2019 – Response from Provost*

Dalhousie Faculty of Management. (2020). *Faculty of Management: Action Plan in Response to the Report by the Senate Review Committee.*

School of Information. (2019). *Self Study: Prepared for The Committee on Accreditation American Library Association* (Issue August).

Advisory Committee to the Rowe School of Business. (2020). *Advisory Committee on RSB Structure – Report to School.*

Dalhousie University. (2021). *Personal and Professional Effectiveness – Corporate Residency MBA – Dalhousie University.* www.dal.ca/academics/programs/graduate/corporate_residency_mba/program-details/personal-and-professional-effectiveness.html

The Commerce Co-op Program. (2021). *CELEBRATING 100 YEARS OF COMMERCE.* https://blogs.dal.ca/mgmtalum/2021/10/06/feature-the-commerce-co-op-program/

Review Committee. (2014). *Faculty of Management Senate Special Review of the Faculty.*

Office of the Dean. (2020). *Continuous Improvement Review Committee – Response Letter.*

Appendix 2.3 Faculty of Management Timeline

1818	Dalhousie was established with custom funds collected in the War of 1812
1863	Dalhousie University was established under Chapter 24 of the Acts of 1863
1891–1902	Dalhousie course calendars sporadically listed in two-year course in "Subjects Bearing On Commerce" and training was supplemented by practical training
1920	First courses offered in commerce (three-year program)
1921	The School of Commerce was started with funding from William A. Black (donation of $60,000 c1919). Bishop Carleton Hunt was appointed the first William Black Professor of Commerce in 1921. Courses taught led to the formation of a Bachelor of Commerce degree.

	Link: https://findingaids.library.dal.ca/dalhousie-university-faculty-of-management-rowe-school-of-business
1923	First Bachelor of Commerce degrees awarded (Faculty of Arts and Sciences)
1930	James MacDonald replaced Hunt and was appointed the first head of the Department of Commerce
1936	First-degree programs in public administration were established
1941	The Maritime School of Social Work was incorporated in 1941 as an independent school. Courses were taught by volunteers under the direction of the school's first director Samuel Henry Prince, Professor of Sociology at Dalhousie, and the University of King's College. In 1944, Phyllis Burns became the school's first full-time employee and was appointed Assistant Director and Registrar. In 1949, Lawrence Hancock was appointed the first regular Director of the School (until 1973). In 1969 the school officially amalgamated with Dalhousie University. The school initially operated under the auspices of the Faculty of Administration but is now currently one of eight schools (and a college) grouped within the university's Faculty of Health Promotion. In the early 1980s, the school added a Bachelor of Social Work. Link: https://findingaids.library.dal.ca/maritime-school-of-social-work-fonds
1949	The Faculty of Graduate Studies was established in response to pressures from science faculty. Between 1930 and 1950, the university granted over 300 master's degrees. With an infusion of federal funding, graduate programs were expanded to include a PhD program in biological sciences (1956) and a PhD program in chemistry (1960). The Master of Business Administration was created in 1967. Link: https://findingaids.library.dal.ca/dalhousie-university-faculty-of-graduate-studies
1967	Master of Business Administration program was initiated in the Faculty of Graduate Studies
1969	First MBA Degrees awarded (first graduate: Hugh Brown)
1969	School of Social Work amalgamated with Dalhousie University
1969	The School for Information Management was established in 1969 as the School of Library Service, housed in the Faculty of Graduate Studies. The first Master of Library Service degrees were awarded in 1971. In 1975, the School of Library Services joined the Faculty of Administrative Studies and remained connected to the faculty through its iterations.

The School of Library Service became the School of Library and Information Studies in 1987. In 2005, the name was changed to the School of Information Management. Between 1979 and 1985, the library services curriculum was subject to ongoing revisions. It continued to offer a Master of Library and Information Studies degree which in 2019 became a Master of Information. In 2008, the school launched a graduate program for mid-career professionals leading to a Master of Information Management. The school has been continuously accredited by the American Library Association since 1971.

Link: https://findingaids.library.dal.ca/dalhousie-university-faculty-of-management-school-of-library-and-information-studies

1973   Institute of Environmental Studies: The School for Resource and Environmental Studies grew out of the Institute for Environmental Studies which was established by biologist Ronald Hayes in 1973. The institute expanded to the Institute for Resource and Environmental Studies in 1978 and began offering a Master of Environmental Studies degree in collaboration with TUNS in 1979/1980. In 1987/1988, the institute was established as a school. In 1991, the school joined the Faculty of Management.

Link: https://findingaids.library.dal.ca/dalhousie-university-faculty-of-management-school-for-resource-and-environmental-studies

1974   Creation of the Faculty of Administrative Studies comprised programs in business administration, public administration, education, health, and welfare services. The Schools of Library Services and Social Work were brought forward from the Faculty of Graduate Studies and added to the Schools of Business and Public Administration

1975   The School of Public Administration was established in 1975 as the new Faculty of Administrative Studies opened. The tradition of public administration dated to 1936 when Dalhousie became the first university in Canada to offer classes in public policy and public management. Between 1938 and 1949 the Faculty of Graduate Studies awarded the Master of Public Administration degrees through the Institute of Public Affairs. The graduate program was dormant from 1951 to 1969 when three programs were launched to meet the needs of practicing and prospective civil servants

through the MPA program. These were administered by the Department of Political Science with decisions and structures shared with the Department of Commerce. The School of Public Administration was attached to the Faculty of Administrative Studies (1975–1985), then the Faculty of Management Studies (1985–1989), and today remains part of the Faculty of Management (1985 to present).
Link: https://findingaids.library.dal.ca/dalhousie-university-faculty-of-management-school-of-public-administration

1975	Center for International Business established as one of four in Canada with federal funding. The mandate of the center was to build global business
1975	Faculty established as the Faculty of Administrative Studies, a federated faculty of the School of Business Administration, the School of Public Administration, the School of Library Services, and the Maritime School of Social Work. For a short time, it also administered a Program in Educational Administration and a Program in Health Services Administration. Link: https://findingaids.library.dal.ca/dalhousie-university-faculty-of-management
1976	A year after the establishment of the Faculty of Administrative Studies, the School of Business Administration replaced the Department of Commerce. The Bachelor of Commerce became a four-year program, and the Centre for International Business Studies was created
1978	First students admitted to the Master of Environment Studies program (approved in 1976)
1979–1986	School of Library and Information Studies curriculum substantially revised
1980	School of Public Administration established internship program
The 1980s	The then School of Library and Information Studies launched a combined MLIS LLB program, which was the first in Canada of that combination. The MLIS/LLB mimicked the MBA/LLB. The school later launched a combined MLIS/MBA, and then MLIS/MPA, and MLIS/MREM
1984	Name changed to Faculty of Management Studies
1985/1986	Name changed from School of Library Service to School of Library and Information Studies
1986	The Institute of Resource and Environmental Studies became the School of Resource and Environment Studies

60   *Management Education in Canada*

1986	The Master of Library Service was changed to Master of Library and Information Studies
1987	Name changed to Faculty of Management
1988	The Marine Affairs Program was first offered
1989	The School of Resource and Environmental Studies joined the Faculty of Management
1991	Commerce Degree became a mandatory cooperative program (placing 100% of students in first year)
1991	School of Resource and Environmental Studies joined the Faculty of Management
1992	Significant changes were introduced to modernize the MBA program
1996	MBA Financial Services/Leadership program established
1999	Bachelor of Management program established (programming across all schools)
2000	Federal funding for the Centre for International Business ended
2004	Construction began on the new Kenneth C. Rowe Management Building
2004–2013	The Faculty of Management housed Marine Affairs Studies starting in 2004. The Marine Affairs Program was initiated in 1988 and originally housed in the Faculty of Law (until 1992) and then the Faculty of Graduate Studies (until 2004). The program was developed from teaching and research programs dating back to 1945. In 1970, the program incorporated marine-related law and social sciences. The program was initiated as a one-year interdisciplinary graduate diploma through the Law School. In the period of 1992–1993, the program offered a Master of Marine Management degree. The current home was the Faculty of Sciences. *There was a discrepancy in the record which dates the relationship back to 2001 not 2004.* Link: https://findingaids.library.dal.ca/dalhousie-university-faculty-of-science-marine-affair-program
2005	The School of Library and Information Studies was changed to the School of Information Management
2005	September – Opening of the Kenneth C. Rowe Management Building, bringing together the Faculty of Management's four schools: Rowe School of Business, School of Information Management, School of Public Administration, School for Resource and Environmental Studies
2005	Two Canadian Research Chairs were assigned to the faculty: CRC in Risk Management and CRC in Management Informatics

2006	Management Without Borders: A Foundation Course for masters' students in Management established (across all Schools)
2007	The School of Public Administration also launched an MPA (Management), following the model of the MBA (Financial Services) of offering a degree for mid-career professionals via a blended online mode
2008	The School of Information Management launched a Master of Information Management, which followed the model of the MBA (Financial Services) of offering a degree for mid-career professionals via a blended online mode
2009	First cohort of the Corporate Residence MBA
2011	Ken Rowe announced $15-million commitment to the School of Business, and the business school became a named school
2012	The School of Business Administration was renamed the Rowe School of Business after Kenneth C. Rowe
2013	Marine Affairs Program (aka Marine Management) joined Faculty of Science
2015	The tenth anniversary of the Rowe Building
2018	Rowe gift paused after receipt of just under $5 million
2018	200th anniversary of Dalhousie University

Appendix 2.4 List of Deans

2023–present – Mike Smit
2020–2023– Kim Brooks
2016–2020: Sylvain Charlebois
2015–2016: Bertrum MacDonald (acting)
2009–2015: Peggy Cunningham
2006–2009: David Wheeler
2005–2006: Philip Rosson (acting)
1999–2005: Abol Jalilvand (responsible for new building)
1994–1999: Philip Rosson
1992: Introduction of Associate Dean and Assistant Dean
1988–1994: Jim McNiven
1987: Roy E. George
1983–1986: Norman Horrocks
1980–1983: Tom Kent
1975–1980: Peter A Ruderman (first Dean of Administrative Studies)

Notes

1 The Bachelor of Commerce program is unique to the Rowe School of Business and includes a mandatory cooperative placement that produces approximately 3,000 graduates per year. The Bachelor of Management program spans all four schools and does not have a mandatory cooperative placement.
2 U15 refers to the group of Canadian research universities that are the most research intensive. It is a directorate that fosters various research interests across different research environments: https://u15.ca/.
3 Part of Nova Scotia's provincial identity is one of "doing more with less". This was apparent in some of our interviews as underlying assumption. An example we can give here is that according to one review conducted by fellow faculty at another prominent business school they had in the order of six times the resources per student as Dalhousie (P19).
4 It is critical to note that our participants felt that they could freely participate without reprisal, and this is largely due to either their tenured position or their leadership roles. Longstanding members of the faculty were identified because of their longer affiliation with the faculty and that affiliation providing useful clues to the faculty's history. It was quite useful that these individuals were also not encumbered by concerns for their participation. Most of our participants have been associated with the faculty for at least two decades and some for as many as four (P1, P8, P11, and P13).
5 Members of SRES wish to stay in the building for another five years.
6 Though we could not elaborate in this chapter, we do find this theme of bringing business principles into a management faculty as interesting and perhaps unique to management education, whereas other faculties of science or social science are not expected to adopt business principles to be considered successful. It is in this increasing neoliberal position that business schools must perform like businesses and it would appear that funding is increasingly tied to business-like deliverables.

References

Advisory Committee to the Rowe School of Business. (2020). *Advisory Committee on RSB Structure – Report to School*.

Balser, T. (2019). *AACSB PRT Site Visit and Report – March 2019 – Response from Provost*.

Bell, E., & Clarke, D. W. (2014). 'Beasts, burrowers and birds': The enactment of researcher identities in UK business schools. *Management Learning*, 45(3), 249–266. https://doi.org/10.1177/1350507613478890

Boje, D. M. (2001). *Narrative Methods for Organizational & Communication Research*. Sage Publications.

Brown, A. D., Lewis, M. A., & Oliver, N. (2021). Identity work, loss and preferred identities: A study of UK business school deans. *Organization Studies*, 42(6), 823–844. https://doi.org/10.1177/0170840619857464

Burrell, G., & Morgan, B. (1979). *Sociological Paradignms and Organizational Analysis*. Heinemann Educational Books.

Clarke, C. A., & Knights, D. (2015). Careering through academia: Securing identities or engaging ethical subjectivities? *Human Relations*, *68*(12), 1865–1888. https://doi.org/10.1177/0018726715570978

Crozier, S. E., & Woolnough, H. (2020). Is age just a number? Credibility and identity of younger academics in UK business schools. *Management Learning*, *51*(2), 149–167. https://doi.org/10.1177/1350507619878807

Faculty of Management. (2019). Dalhousie University – AACSB Report – 2013-18 Rowe School of Business – Faculty of Management.

Krücken, G., Blümel, A., & Kloke, K. (2013). The managerial turn in higher education? On the interplay of organizational and occupational change in German academia. *Minerva*, *51*(4), 417–442. https://doi.org/10.1007/s11024-013-9240-z

Latour, B. (2005). *Reassembling the Social: An Introduction to Actor-Network-Theory*. Oxford University Press.

Learmonth, M., & Humphreys, M. (2012). Autoethnography and academic identity: Glimpsing business school doppelgängers. *Organization*, *19*(1), 99–117. https://doi.org/10.1177/1350508411398056

Lozano, R., & von Haartman, R. (2018). Reinforcing the holistic perspective of sustainability: Analysis of the importance of sustainability drivers in organizations. *Corporate Social Responsibility and Environmental Management*, *25*(4), 508–522. https://doi.org/10.1002/csr.1475

Mumby, D. K. (2016). Organizing beyond organization: Branding, discourse, and communicative capitalism. *Organization*, *23*(6), 884–907. https://doi.org/10.1177/1350508416631164

O'Neill, T. J., Nova Scotia. Office of the Premier, & Canadian Electronic Library. (2010). Report on the University System in Nova Scotia (Issue September). https://novascotia.ca/lae/HigherEducation/documents/Report_on_the_Higher_Education_System_in_Nova_Scotia.pdf

Phillips, N., & Hardy, C. (2002). *Discourse Analysis: Investigating Processes of Social Construction*. Sage Publications.

Pohle, J. (2016). Multistakeholder governance processes as production sites: Enhanced cooperation "in the making". *Internet Policy Review*, *5*(3), 1–19. https://doi.org/10.14763/2016.3.432

Prasad, P. (2005). *Crafting Qualitative Research: Working in the Postpositivist Traditions*. M.E. Sharpe.

Quijada, M. A. (2021). My mental health struggle in academia: What I wish all business school faculty, students, and administration knew. *Journal of Management Education*, *45*(1), 19–42. https://doi.org/10.1177/1052562920958433

Review Committee. (2014). Faculty of Management Senate Special Review of the Faculty.

Rusinko, C. A. (2010). Integrating sustainability in management and business education: A matrix approach. *Academy of Management Learning and Education*, *9*(3), 507–519. https://doi.org/10.5465/AMLE.2010.53791831

Schofer, E., & Meyer, J. W. (2005). The worldwide expansion of higher education in the twentieth century. *American Sociological Review*, *70*(6), 898–920. https://doi.org/10.1177/000312240507000602

Senate Review Committee. (2012). Faculty of Management Senate Review.

Starkey, K., & Tempest, S. (2009). The winter of our discontent: The design challenge for business schools. *Academy of Management Learning and Education*, *8*(4), 576–586. https://doi.org/10.5465/AMLE.2009.47785476

Waddock, S., & Lozano, J. M. (2013). Developing more holistic management education: Lessons learned from two programs. *Academy of Management Learning and Education*, *12*(2), 265–284. https://doi.org/10.5465/amle.2012.0002

Yáñez, S., Uruburu, Á., Moreno, A., & Lumbreras, J. (2019). The sustainability report as an essential tool for the holistic and strategic vision of higher education institutions. *Journal of Cleaner Production*, *207*, 57–66. https://doi.org/10.1016/j.jclepro.2018.09.171

3 The Administrative Sciences Association of Canada and the Development of Management Studies
1979–2009

Kristene E. Coller and Heidi Weigand

Introduction

Increasingly there have been management scholars concerned about the "Americanization" of management theory (Gantman, Yousfi, & Alcadipani, 2015; Usdiken, 2004). The idea has been that US-based studies are equivalent to being seen as universal knowledge (Booth & Rowlinson, 2006; Elteren, 2006; Kieser, 2004; Symons, 1978), across various national contexts, including Canada (Coller, McNally, & Mills, 2015; Foster, Helms Mills, & Mills, 2014; McLaren, Mills, & Weatherbee, 2015; McLaren & Mills, 2013, 2015; McQuarrie, 2005; Russell, 2015, 2019, 2021; Symons, 1978;). While there has been considerable discussion illustrating examples of "Americanization," there has been little in-depth study of how the Americanization of management studies takes hold across national boundaries. This chapter sets out to understand some of the processes through which the "Americanization" of management studies (Booth & Rowlinson, 2006; Elteren, 2006; Kieser, 2004; Symons, 1978) has occurred, specifically in Canada.

Understanding the process of Americanization is important as "knowledge" is seen as being an objective representation of scientific knowledge. That is, "knowledge" that is viewed as being universal, incrementally builds upon theoretical foundations. In the process of making scientific knowledge objective, the framework within which knowledge is realized is influenced by "taken-for-granted assumptions" and deeply held values and beliefs (Johnson & Duberley, 2000, p. 7) that shift our understanding of what "knowledge" is. Thus, "scientific knowledge" has come to be viewed as "universal" or generalized models void of context (Booth & Rowlinson, 2006) rather than representing the values and beliefs of the scholars creating knowledge. When knowledge is viewed as a science, and therefore universal, there is no relationship between one's nationality and the type of knowledge produced (Cormier, 2004, p. 29). Kieser (2004)

DOI: 10.4324/9781003612612-4

has argued that generalized models of knowledge have shifted from being universal to representing values and traditions that are predominantly American (Kieser, 2004). These predominantly American accounts of management knowledge have arguably resulted in the marginalization of other accounts of knowledge and have implications for scholarship and identity within the academy. Hiller and Luzio (2001), for example, argue that the universalist view renders the idea of Canadian content as "inconsequential." Similarly, Papadopoulos and Rosson (1999) argue that universal thinking has encouraged Canadian researchers to "follow closed system models, guided by American thinking..." (p. 78). In Canada, concerns over following American models resulted in a movement to protect issues of Canadian identity and sovereignty (Cormier, 2005; Nosal, 2000) and has influenced Canadian (and other non-American) accounts of history in the arts (Edwardson, 2008), media (Collins, 2000; MacDonald, 2009) and the socialization of Canadians (Cormier, 2004) and has extended into management theory and the absence of any notable Canadian studies (Coller et al., 2015; Cooke, 1999; Kieser, 2004; McLaren & Mills, 2015; Wanderley & Faria, 2012). This chapter will trace Canadian actors in Administrative Sciences Association of Canada (ASAC) to understand how management knowledge has come to represent an Americanized model. ASAC was chosen as it is the only national-level association for management scholars in Canada. The ASAC has been a constant presence in Canadian business schools since its inception in 1957 and has provided a space for Canadian scholars and practitioners to debate the role, policies, and nature of research and management education in Canada.

Methodology

This chapter adopts ANTi-History to understand how prevailing models of management have been collectively known as management studies by following what has been left behind in the process and reassembling them in a new way (Durepos & Mills, 2012). These traces can include a variety of sources such as biographies, letters, meeting minutes, and photographs that indicate how knowledge is organized and performed. Thus, ANTi-History recognizes that knowledge is an outcome of the relationships, politics, and underlying assumptions involved in the development of management studies and how it has come to represent Americanized traditions.

This chapter uses biographies, letters, meeting minutes, and ASAC conference proceedings between 1979 and 2009 to surface the institutionalized practices within academia. The year 1979 is the first available conference proceeding and 2009 was chosen as the end point to be able to evaluate the impact that articles may have had on the field. ASAC was chosen because it is the only national scholarly business conference in Canada and there is a database of conference proceedings, meeting minutes, and other available archival material established by the "Halifax School" (at the Sobey School of Business at Saint Mary's University—Bettin, Mills & Helms Mills, 2016) that could be used to understand how and why decisions were made over the span of decades.

The Organizational Behavior (OB), International Business (IB), and Policy/Strategy divisions of ASAC were selected for study given the stability of these divisions over time and given that they provided the ability to compare conference themes with articles in CJAS (*Canadian Journal of Administrative Sciences*). These comparisons are important to help identify similarities and differences that occur at different stages of the publishing process. 1027 papers were accepted to these three divisions between 1979 and 2009 and included 1147 authors from more than 30 Canadian institutions and businesses.[1] Selecting these three stable divisions facilitated the process of analysis by providing a manageable number of human and non-human actors (i.e., authors and articles) to follow but also means that notable contributions by individual scholars, or the role of specific institutions, may not have been fully realized. Incorporating additional divisions or choosing different divisions would have resulted in surfacing different human or non-human actors and could have changed the findings of the management knowledge traced.

In total, 49 authors had three articles accepted across the three divisions and 16 authors had articles accepted more than five times when listed as the primary author during the timeframe. The 16 authors and multiple acceptances represented a more manageable number of actors to trace to understand the processes involved in producing management knowledge. Table 3.1 lists the 16 actors in alphabetical order with more than five articles, their institutional affiliations, authorship information, language of accepted articles, and additional information related to the articles that were accepted for presentation at an ASAC conference. Listing the authors in alphabetical order was simply a way of being able to easily work through the list of actors across multiple sources and does not reflect a level of importance or prominence in the actor network.

Of the 16 ASAC contributors identified in Table 3.1, 4 became ASAC presidents (Etemad, Irving, McShane, & Miller), and 6 served at the divisional level. At the divisional level, Rugman, Etemad, McShane, Beamish, Miller, and Lévy all participated as divisional editors and chairs acting as gatekeepers to articles that would ultimately be accepted to the annual conference.

Growing a National Conference

To address concerns regarding Canadian scholarship and identity, ASAC decided to grow its annual meeting, where scholars gathered to discuss Canadian-related research, into an annual conference that would actively seek out submissions from the broader academic community. The development of an annual conference was seen as a way of providing scholars a venue to present papers on issues of importance to Canadian businesses and strengthening overall scholarship in Canada (Austin, 2000). Two considerations that were important to the ASAC executive were choosing desirable locations as a venue for the conference and the selection of conference themes (see Table 3.2 for the list of conference locations and themes). A decision was made early on to switch between Eastern and Western Canada on an annual basis to address membership concerns regarding the cost of travel (Austin, 2000) and had implications for the number of people attending the annual conference. Although the ASAC executive chose locations to facilitate travel, there are implications for the development of management knowledge. Because of limited funding, scholars choose which conferences to attend each year based on a number of factors (conference prestige, location, cost, language, subject, and appropriateness; Gur, Hamureu, & Eren, 2016). As a result, ASAC is competing with other, more prominent (e.g., *Academy of Management*) conferences.

Conference themes are seen as one way to encourage research with a Canadian focus and to be in line with funding opportunities from organizations like the Social Sciences and Humanities Research Council (SSHRC; Austin, 2000). Alan Blair, the president of ASAC in 1979, stated that the "theme, the choice of speakers, and the contacts planned with officials of funding and granting agencies, are all meant to make us more visible in the larger community when it counts" (ASAC, 1979, p. 2). Themes that lined up with institutions like SSHRC were viewed as a way of enhancing the legitimacy of the annual conference (Austin, 2000). Conference themes may also reflect an effort by the ASAC executive to appeal to a broader management membership base and to appear more legitimate within the broader field of management or to coincide with global issues and research trends. In addition to reflecting the broader research trends and priorities of funding agencies, conference themes can also reflect the values of conference organizers and the goals of executive members to meet institutional objectives. For example, Bill Wedley, conference chair for the 1985 conference, provided the rationale for the selection of the theme "*Business in its international dimension: Implications for management education, and research*":

> This is the first time that international business has been featured as a theme for an ASAC Conference. It is a topic which fits in well with the concepts of Expo '86, and it provides relevance for all of ASAC's divisions. Moreover, issues of trade, investment, and cultural relations with other nations are becoming major public policy issues for Canada.
> (ASAC Bulletin, Fall 1985)

Wedley's explanation suggests that the choice of theme was to adhere to ASAC's mandate of focusing on Canadian issues but also fits in with the broader socioeconomic conditions and notable events of the time (e.g., Expo '86). Conference themes can impact the direction of conference papers for that year but can also signal shifts and trends in management topics for future years. In this case, the emphasis on how the topic addresses general trends associated with IB and how Canada fits into the broader academic field reinforces ideas consistent with how management studies come to represent American dominant models. As a result, the themes of a conference are discursive and impact how subsequent models of management are developed and reinforced.

Conference Growing Pains

Despite efforts of the ASAC executive to increase membership and interest in the annual conference through themes and location choices, many established scholars viewed ASAC as a developmental conference for graduate students before beginning their academic careers in the larger (and more legitimate) academy. Based on the experience of the authors, some Canadian business school faculty, who supervise graduate students, deter graduate students (particularly PhD students) from submitting papers to ASAC because of the questions this could raise about the quality of their students or their abilities as a graduate supervisor and continues to present challenges to the ASAC executive. There is also a growing number of master's degree students attending ASAC which, although it serves to strengthen the academic base of quality scholarship over the long term, has further called the legitimacy and quality of the ASAC conference into question by some business schools that privilege top-tier conferences with an international focus. The *Academy of Management* is generally considered to be a top-tier conference for management scholars and generates submissions from around the world (Johnson, 2008). One way that ASAC sought to develop and grow the annual conference and develop a strong Canadian identity was to focus on the development of Canadian scholars.

One issue with which ASAC was confronted was the hiring of faculty in Canadian business schools. This concern was echoed by the Symons Report (1978)[2] which highlighted that "[t]he shortage of qualified Canadian graduates… . forced business schools in this country to go outside Canada to recruit faculty in large numbers" (p. 192). Some faculty obtained their PhD education outside of Canada (Burke, University of Michigan; Etemad, University of California, Berkeley; McShane, Michigan State University) and were later recruited to work in Canada. Hiring foreign faculty was justified by Canada's business schools stating,

> [w]e continue to hire top-flight Americans only because we feel their help is essential in developing our PhD programmes and thereby acquiring the ability to graduate first-class Canadian-born and educated students who will begin to fill the gaps in Canadian business education.
>
> (Symons, 1978, p. 192)

Boothman (2000a) highlighted that when American-trained scholars were recruited to work at Canadian institutions, they "usually maintained their professional credentials through American academic societies" (p. 65) continuing to develop work that would appear "in American conferences or journals, concentrated upon American practices, and applied models or theories based upon American experiences" (Boothman, 2000a, p. 65). University leaders and ASAC executives were concerned that importing American and American-trained academics might lead to an over-reliance on American models. The maintenance of their professional credentials and participation in American conferences demonstrates how actors were performing the activities required to be successful in the academic field.

To address concerns related to the lack of available Canadian faculty, the development of PhD programs in Canadian universities was paramount to ensuring that Canadian knowledge and identity could be developed within Canada. As a result, there was a push to increasingly develop PhDs who could later be recruited to work in Canadian institutions. Both Beamish and Irving for example received their PhDs at the University of Western Ontario, Miller received hers at the University of Victoria and Saks received his from the University of Toronto. Developing Master and PhD programs in Canada was a challenge. Students often privileged European and US programs (i.e., Etemad, University of California, Berkeley), which were seen as being more prestigious and legitimate than their Canadian counterparts who were still struggling to institutionalize basic undergraduate programming. Students privileging international institutions over Canadian ones provides another example of how management studies are performed and influenced by funding, supervising faculty, and other reputational factors. With funding support from SSHRC, ASAC actively worked to encourage students to remain in Canada when completing graduate school throughout the 1990s (e.g., Irving, Beamish, and Miller). With an emphasis on management, the ASAC executive discussed a number of initiatives including the possibility of placement services; a PhD best paper award; a pre-convention consortium; and a best dissertation award (ASAC, 1979). The proposal of these ideas mirrored national-level initiatives with which ASAC was involved, including membership on the steering committee for the National PhD program (ASAC, 1979) which occurred during Etemad's tenure as ASAC president. The National PhD program was founded by the Canadian Federation of Deans Management and Administrative Sciences (CFDMAS). The CFDMAS has a mandate to promote management education by bringing Deans from different business schools together. Arising from concerns regarding the lack of PhDs in Canada, the CFDMAS founded the National PhD program; however, despite initial efforts, it does not appear that the National PhD program was successful (ASAC, 1990) and even with the addition of government scholarships, many students still traveled outside of Canada to pursue their education (Austin, 2000a).

Despite the suggested lack of success of the National PhD program, the development of graduate students at the Master's and PhD levels have continued to grow across Canada. Many of the actors traced in this chapter have actively participated in the development of graduate students. Beamish, for example, actively worked with students and had articles accepted to ASAC. Beamish's staff profile at the University of Western Ontario indicates that he has supervised 35 doctoral students and has taught for the Executive MBA at Ivey's Hong Kong campus (University of Western Ontario, staff profile accessed June 30, 2020). Elangovan co-authored papers with three PhD students at ASAC and Tallman co-authored one paper with a health sciences PhD student. Working with graduate students provides supervisors with the opportunity to mentor like-minded students who share similar values and research interests. In doing so, supervisors impact subsequent generations of scholars in the type of research seen as acceptable within the broader academic field by imparting their values to the next generation of students. The mentorship activities also reinforce how academic activities should be performed and influence the content, context, and language of articles pursued by graduate students.

Content, Context, and Language at ASAC

ASAC conference articles written by the 16 faculty identified were analyzed for their content, their context (i.e., framing as Canadian), and their language (i.e., English or French). Reviewing conference articles across these three dimensions can reveal how articles build upon their respective fields over time and reflect the values predominant in management studies. As a result, reviewing the titles, content, and references of accepted ASAC articles can be instrumental in understanding how academic literature is constructed and developed.

One way to evaluate the development of management studies is to examine the content of accepted articles. For example, 2 of Beamish's 20 accepted ASAC articles specifically mention Canada in the title. One article titled *A Corporate View of International Business Education in Canada: National and Provincial Assessments* (Beamish & Calof, 1989) looked at how curriculum at business schools in Canada should internationalize content to maintain global competitiveness. Although the article focuses on a survey sent to Canadian corporations, public sector organizations, and universities, the reference list relies heavily on articles from the *Academy of Management, Journal of International Business Studies*, and books published by American publishers. This article specifically addresses the need to legitimize Canadian business schools by identifying the ideas and training that experts expressed as being important. By relying on American sources in the development of a paper on the internationalization of management education, the inference is that American models of education are privileged as being "reality par excellence" (Berger & Luckman, 1967, p. 21). Privileging high-tier (i.e., predominantly American) sources could suggest to readers that Canadian business schools are unable to be competitive unless American ideals are adopted or that there is an absence of available Canadian literature from which to draw. We are not suggesting that Beamish and Calof (1989) were deliberately restricting themselves to Americanized examples to define quality management education; rather, that this example reflects broader institutional pressures governing academia that motivate actors to perform accepted activities in the management studies network. Beamish's articles were not an anomaly.

The use of American sources to develop conference papers was evident among many of the 16 authors' work. Ashforth and Saks (1996) for example did not reference any Canadian publications and relied exclusively on American publications like the *Academy of Management, Journal of Management*, and *Journal of Applied Psychology* in their honorable-mention-winning paper on socialization practices of new employees. Withey's (1988) award-winning paper only referenced two Canadian publications—a previous submission of his from the 1985 ASAC conference proceedings and his doctoral dissertation. The only reference to the Canadian context in Withey's 1988 paper was the involvement of Ontario commerce graduates in understanding organizational commitment using models from the OB literature. The privileging of American journals has a cascading effect that influences Canadian scholars to select American journals over Canadian ones to increase their chances of getting published. While the availability of Canadian sources is limited the lack of sources combined with context-free content is a slippery slope that leads to discrediting Canadian-relevant content and channels.

When looking at other articles written by our 16 authors it became apparent that regardless of the context of the article, the reference lists appear to privilege predominantly American journal publications (e.g., *Organization Studies, Administrative Sciences Quarterly, Academy of Management*, and *Harvard Business Review*). Dastmalchian, Javidan, and Pasis (1985), for example, reference *Administrative Sciences Quarterly* and *Organization Studies* regularly in their article titled *Centralization of Decision Making, Organizational Context and Dependence: Evidence from Canadian Provincially Controlled Organizations.* Although the article focuses on the Canadian context, references to Canada are limited to the structure of provincial and crown corporations and play a limited role in the discussion of the findings. Unlike Beamish and Calof's (1989) article, which suggested the need for internationalization, Dastmalchian et al. (1985) emphasized the need for more research in a Canadian context. For example, Dastmalchian et al. (1985) highlight how their research supports some variables of decision-making models that are American; however, they also highlight how there are different cultural and political explanations for other aspects of their findings and identify the need for more research in this area.

Although many of the ASAC authors relied heavily on American sources to inform their articles, some incorporated Canadian and European journals more frequently. Etemad, for example, frequently referenced European journals in addition to an Australian and a Brazilian journal to inform his papers (Etemad, 1981, 1982, 1986a, 1986b). Rugman (1986) referenced a number of sources: the *Canadian Journal of Economics*, a book about Canada, the Ontario Economic Council, and the Canadian Tax Foundation in his paper titled, *The Determinants of Canadian Outward Direct Investment* which focuses on Canada's investment in the United States. The article emphasizes reasons why Canadian firms seek to expand into the United States, references the different contexts of the Canadian market (i.e., smaller population), and discusses the political environment of Canada to explain how organizations make investment decisions. Despite the inclusion of Canadian references in his 1986 article, Rugman's articles are submitted to the IB division, and the content and context generally worked to internationalize management studies. The internationalization of articles sought to remove context from the articles to improve their generalizability. Although some of the authors incorporated Canadian content and sources in their articles, this was not common and only comprised a small number of the total references. Who the authors were citing in conference papers signaled to other scholars what were appropriate sources of information and the lack of availability of Canadian sources and abundance of American when constructing and submitting papers. Although references are an important aspect of building on what was taken as scientific knowledge, the prominence of American sources in the reference lists, even when papers were discussing Canadian issues (i.e., political, economic, and cultural dimensions) served to reinforce broader institutional values that privilege American journals as top-tier and marginalize other accounts of management studies that could add to our understanding of OB, Strategy/Policy, and IB. The prominence of American journals and values espousing universal knowledge further eroded efforts to grow and develop Canadian publications.

In addition to analyzing the reference lists of the authors for the type of references used in their conference papers, the references were also examined to see if any of the other ASAC scholars or other identifiable Canadian scholars (e.g., Mintzberg, Barling) were referenced in their conference papers. Identifiable Canadians in the reference lists were, however, minimal. Beamish and Calof (1989) referenced an article by Rugman and Verbeke (who served as an editor for CJAS) but aside from referencing Beamish's dissertation and another University of Western Ontario dissertation, no other identifiable Canadians were referenced. In Beamish and Jung's (2005) award-winning paper, Etemad was referenced as was Delios (who served as an Associate editor for CJAS). Delios and Beamish have co-authored other papers together and were referenced in addition to another article that Delios had co-authored with other individuals. The Saks and Ashforth (1996) article referenced Ashforth's and Mudrack's work, two individuals who have made contributions to ASAC both as authors and as divisional editors at ASAC and CJAS. Although some of the authors referenced others on our list, many did not. Elangovan (1994) and Irving (1995) did not reference any of the 16 scholars identified on our list and only referenced one identifiable Canadian, Henry Mintzberg, in their articles.

The extensive use of American sources when constructing conference articles, even when the article is designed to address Canadian issues, reveals the dominance of American journals throughout management studies. Canadian scholars wanting to incorporate Canadian sources are further constrained by having only a single general management journal (CJAS) and a relatively small number of Canadian discipline-specific journals (i.e., *International Business Research*). Relying on American journals and scholars when writing an article about the Canadian context shifts management studies to reflect and generalize the findings in the broader academic field and reduce potential connections to the Canadian context. Through the permanence of accepted articles, the articles become instrumental in signaling what steps scholars need to take to be successful in performing management studies. The reliance on American journals when developing management studies in Canada has been a concern highlighted by scholars over the past forty years (Boothman, 2000b; Symons, 1978). The number of American journals cited, however, only provides part of the picture in understanding the context and content of accepted ASAC articles.

The Devaluation of Canadian Sources

In addition to looking at the types of sources used in conference articles, it appears that ASAC authors draw on a broad body of literature when developing their papers and go beyond journal articles. Beamish and Calof's (1989) article about IB education, for example, referenced two doctoral dissertations (one was Beamish's PhD dissertation) both from the University of Western Ontario, as well as the Academy of International Business Conference in London, England. Dastmalchian et al. (1985) reference the Institute for Research on Public Policy and a book called *Crown Corporations in Canada* to inform their article on the centralization of decision-making policy in Canada. Referencing a variety of sources at the conference level appears to be common and demonstrates that when writing papers at the conference level, scholars draw on a greater variety of sources to help develop their ideas with different subject areas (Coller, 2021). Elangovan (1998, for example, referenced a working paper series from the University of Wisconsin as well as an *American Psychological Association* conference paper presented in 1986 and an *Academy of Management* paper presented in 1991. Etemad referenced the Government of Canada, the Economic Council of Canada, working papers, books, texts, and magazines (1981, 1982).

Although a broad number of sources were used in accepted ASAC articles, there were very few references by the 16 authors to the ASAC annual conference and CJAS. There was one reference to the Atlantic School of Business conference (Irving, 1995), a Canadian regional conference. Irving also referenced research bulletins and an unpublished manuscript. Irving, Kovacheff, Coleman, and Wood (1995) referenced a paper presented at the 1993 ASAC conference. Withey did reference ASAC once in his paper (1988); however, it was his own paper presented at a previous conference.

Canadian sources are only used when providing context (i.e., bilingualism, geography, politics) in ASAC articles rather than in the development of theory. These sources are used to highlight the economic, political, and cultural dimensions that journal articles published in American publications generally do not address. Although there are Canadian sources to inform the context of the articles, the annual ASAC conference is not generally seen as a source for individuals writing about Canadian-specific content.

Context-Free Content

In addition to using a variety of sources to construct the conference paper, there were differences in how the articles addressed the content and context. Although many of the article titles were general, some article titles did reference Canada and other geographic regions. Etemad, for example, authored and co-authored 15 articles for ASAC. Etemad referenced Canada four times in the title of the articles and referenced China, South Korea, Taiwan, the Netherlands, and Finland in various articles and appears to have deliberately incorporated research with varied geographic regions. Elangovan, Finegan, Irving, McShane, Miller, Saha, Stone, Tallman, Withey, and Withane, on the other hand, did not have any articles listed with Canada in the title and in some of those articles, the context for the topic studied was unclear. One way to try to identify the context of the paper was to review the methods sections of the papers. The methods sections identified differences in how the authors described respondents.

Finegan, for example, did not include references to Canada in any of the article titles and the methods section of her 1995 article simply read "Questionnaires were distributed to 10, 300 employees at a subsidiary plant of large petrochemical company" (p. 60).[3] As a result, it is unclear whether the research was conducted in Canada, the United States, Europe, or elsewhere. When the geographic context is removed from the article, the implication is that the knowledge applied is universal and value-free and could be motivated by "academics feeling that they need to conduct 'context-free' research to be successful in their careers in Canadian universities" (McLaren and Mills, 2015a, p. 321). "Context-free" has increasingly come to represent American models of knowledge. Finegan, working for a Canadian institution, may have removed references to Canada to make it easier for the paper to be accepted by a non-Canadian journal. The conference paper was developed and accepted for publication in the *Journal of Occupational and Organizational Psychology*, a British publication, in 2002. The article's publication at the journal level further demonstrates that actors perform activities consistent with the development of management studies which privileges the idea that knowledge is value-free and therefore does not need to reflect specific contexts.

Saks and Ashforth (1996) took a similar approach when describing their research participants as "members of the 1991 and 1992 graduating classes of an undergraduate business program" (p. 13) omitting all geographic references in their longitudinal study. Given that they were looking at the lived experiences of business school graduates in their first post-graduate jobs, one would expect that the graduates' experiences could be impacted by broader societal conditions such as the economy, politics, and cultural context. Examination of articles written by Saks and Ashforth reveals a similar article, using longitudinal data from recent business school graduates, published in the *Academy of Management Journal* (Ashforth & Saks, 1996). That article, although with a different title than the conference paper, does examine similar constructs and matches the timeframe of the ASAC conference piece. Authors may eliminate geographical references to increase the likelihood of publication in an American top-tier journal, but it also supports the idea that context need not be a consideration when developing papers in management studies (McLaren & Mills, 2015a) reflecting the taken-for-granted assumption that the results are value-free and could be applied universally. In essence, Canadian content does not have value in an American journal, so by stripping away the Canadian context, it is perceived to raise the quality of the paper.

Another consideration involves analyzing the models used to conduct studies with Canadian data. Irving (1995), for example, indicated that the subjects in his study were students from a University of Western Ontario introductory psychology class, but did not include any additional discussion regarding the Canadian context of the study. In the section discussing the model used in the study, the limitation of using university students to evaluate the conflict resolution interventions made by managers using vignettes was discussed, but no consideration was given to understanding how geographic context could impact the generalizability of the findings (Irving, 1995). Discussing the geographic context would be important in this research as it relied on models and vignettes that were developed and tested using American data. The model adopted by Irving (1995) was Vroom-Yetton's decision model. Vroom was born in Canada, obtained his PhD from the University of Michigan, and developed the model while a professor at the University of Yale. In addition to the ties of Vroom to the United States, Vroom, and Yetton used managers from a management development program (presumably in the United States) in their landmark model. Adopting a model based on United States data does not mean that the model cannot be of use to understand decision-making in a Canadian context. Rather, the purpose is to understand how we came to view management studies as being value-free and universal rather than acknowledging the conditions around which knowledge has been produced.

Although not including identifying information is seen as protecting the identity of respondents, the removal of pertinent geographic information from the methods section is problematic. The lack of discussion regarding the generalizability of the findings based on economic, political, and sociocultural dimensions in Canada further influences the Americanization of management studies. Some of the decisions by authors could reflect institutionalized standards by conferences, journals, and universities to improve the chances of acceptance and eventual publication by journals. It could also reflect the idea that "[r]esearch on Canadian issues was little understood in American associations and not readily accepted by U.S. journals" (Austin, 2000, p. 275). As a result, it may have been easier to omit geographical references rather than explain their relevance or applicability to a broader audience. Although the removal of geographic information could make it more appealing to prospective journals, the exclusion of important contextual information does not inform the reader about the political system, culture, or other distinguishing features that could impact the application of the information.

The Privileging of English Contributions

Another dimension of ASAC that differentiates it from American conferences is that it is bilingual. Despite recognition of its bilingual status, dominant accounts of ASAC's history have glossed over the impact of language on ASAC's development. Austin (1998) for example reduces the impact to "ASAC is bilingual and tries to balance regional representation on its executive" (p. 255). The bilingual nature of the conference is an important dimension to consider in the development of management studies in Canada. Of the 16 ASAC scholars who had papers accepted to the annual conference, 15 write solely in one language, English, likely in order to increase the chances of publication. As a result, the individuals they collaborate with tend to also be English-speaking. Brigitte Lévy is the only exception from our list. Six of her seven accepted articles were written in French, and she has gone on to write in both of Canada's official languages. Five of her seven articles reference Canada in the title. Unlike our English-speaking actors who exclusively draw on English articles, Lévy draws on both English and French articles to inform her conference papers, referencing journals such as *Interventions economique* (in 1986) and *Analyse de politique* (in 1989). Lévy also drew on the French version of government publications, a French working paper from the University of Ottawa, and included a variety of sources to inform each of her accepted ASAC articles.

Language also appeared to be influential with those who served at the divisional and editorial levels of ASAC. There have historically been French-speaking members of ASAC, the representation at the executive level and at the divisional levels has been fewer than their English-speaking counterparts. Based on a review of Google Scholar and published articles, it appears that between 1979 and 2009 there have been four bilingual presidents of ASAC, but the majority of divisional chairs and editors have been English-speaking. Recognizing that there are fewer French-speaking members at ASAC as contributors and in leadership positions is important to acknowledge as English is the standard language accepted for premier journal articles (i.e., American). The privileging of English could signal to authors that for their work to be published and accepted in the broader institutional field they must adhere to specific language requirements.

Management Studies in Canada

Unlike other accounts suggesting Americanization was contested in Europe (Tiratsoo, 2004), management studies in Canada have a different starting point. Tiratsoo (2004) highlights how Americanization in Britain occurred in part because of market pressures. Management studies in Canada, on the other hand, intentionally modeled conferences and journals after their more prestigious American counterparts. Modeling conferences and journals after American equivalents appeared to be influenced by geographic and cultural similarities between Canada and the United States (Russell, 2019) and the growing acceptance worldwide of an American model of management. The modeling of the conference and journals was further facilitated through the hiring of American-trained scholars to Canadian universities. These individuals brought their training and experience to their Canadian institutions and to the roles that they took on in ASAC. As a result, it appears as though management studies in Canada were founded with American values and traditions from its inception.

Although modeling ASAC after American counterparts was designed to enhance the perceived legitimacy of the institutions, it also provides guidance regarding how the annual conference and associated journal should be structured. Adopting similar divisional and editorial structures, conference themes, and special issues were commonplace among conferences and journal publications. The generally accepted format impacted decisions on the review process and development of strategic directives. Basing decisions on American models was designed to improve the likelihood that Canadian scholars would view ASAC as a legitimate venue for their research, and also resulted in human actors inadvertently adopting traditional American conventions that would increase the likelihood that their work would be accepted by the broader institutional field.

The conventions adopted by actors in the management studies network are further reinforced by editors and division chairs at ASAC. Authors who use certain more acceptable references as a cue of what is acceptable can also reinforce the decisions made by editors at each level to accept or reject articles that do not adhere to these informal rules. The rules governing the responses of editors influence the apparent Americanization of management studies. As McCarten (2010) highlights, each stage of the peer review process provides "different levels of feedback as a piece of a research develops into a formal journal article" and is a hierarchical process (p. 244).

This process is further impacted by decisions made by editors. Editors consciously and unconsciously make decisions designed to reinforce the mandate of ASAC (i.e., to increase membership) which reflects the values of the prevailing model of management studies (i.e., American). In doing so, editors make decisions that not only impact the annual conference, but rather, make decisions that continue to influence management studies long after the conference has concluded. The decisions made by editors also impact readers and potential contributors regarding the standards, content, and applicability of their work to ASAC.

These human actors also influence others in the management studies network through mentorship roles. It is an important aspect of academia and is broadly incorporated through institutionalized processes (i.e., graduate student supervisor, divisional progression). Rugman, for example, is recognized for his support of incoming Division editors and chairs at ASAC. In taking on these mentorship roles, Rugman would presumably instill his values in incoming members and upcoming students. Ideas, like the acceptability of conferences (i.e., ASAC and AOM), journal articles (CJAS, *Harvard Business Review*, etc.), methodology (i.e., quantitative and qualitative), and sources (time frame for sources, type of sources, etc.) are all implicitly and explicitly communicated through mentorship of graduate students. Graduate students then progress through their careers adopting similar approaches when developing, submitting, and publishing their work. Instilling acceptable ways of navigating through academia ensures the perpetuation of values and traditions that support the dominant American model, having an enduring impact that extends beyond the supervisor-student relationship.

Revealing Tensions in the Network

Not all scholars accepted the Americanization of management studies in Canada. Some of the scholars traced throughout this chapter sought to infuse Canadian content in management studies and decenter the apparent dominance of American models. The original intent behind the founding of ASAC was to provide a venue for scholars to present and publish research addressing Canadian-specific issues in response to concerns raised by the Symons Report (1978). The ASAC executive worked to increase the prominence of the annual conference among Canadian business schools by selecting desirable Canadian locations, choosing themes that would be of interest, and working to develop a National PhD program to promote homegrown academics who could then obtain faculty positions in Canadian institutions. The ASAC executive further promoted a vision to support Canadian scholarship through the founding of CJAS. The efforts by ASAC leadership were taken up by committed scholars who were, and continue to be, motivated to develop scholarship and content within Canada. The support of funding agencies like SSHRC further reinforces established national priorities designed to protect Canadian studies and influence policies at an institutional level. These policies and actions reflect the values of the scholars who work with others to promote a Canadian account of management studies. As a result, ASAC, the programs, themes, and contributions reflect the value of trying to preserve Canadian identity through the development of venues and publishing opportunities.

In trying to preserve Canadian identity, some scholars appear to try to influence the development of Canadian-trained PhDs. McShane, for example, during his tenure as ASAC president, was involved in securing funding for the establishment of the doctoral consortium at the annual conference. Etemad, also an ASAC president, saw the National PhD program proposed during his term. Both initiatives were developed with the intention of strengthening the ability to attract home-grown PhD scholars. This influenced the actions of potential graduate students to select a Canadian institution when selecting potential programs. In addition to supporting the development of PhD students in Canada, the two programs aligned with the goals of SSHRC. The development and funding by Canadian Government agencies explicitly and implicitly communicate the values that are important to the development of management studies in Canada. Despite the provision of funding and alignment with the mandate of ASAC, the National PhD program was viewed as being unsuccessful. Creating intentional space for knowledge production to grow in situ, in Canada, arguably opens the doors for Canadian scholars.

In addition to the development of Canadian-trained scholars and an annual conference, ASAC founded CJAS with the intent of providing an outlet for Canadian-specific research. Despite the clear mandate of ASAC, our analysis supports other accounts that document how the journal struggled to be seen as legitimate (McLaren & Mills, 2015). The further analysis we conducted also surfaced how scholars responded to pre-existing, embedded values and traditions consistent with American-dominated models of management studies. These values are reflected in the work of the scholars traced in this chapter and provide a novel account of how management studies developed in Canada.

Etemad, for example, had 17 conference papers accepted to ASAC and was an ASAC president. His ASAC articles appear to reflect the values of ASAC's mandate of providing an outlet for Canadian-specific research. Dastmalchian is another scholar who appears to reflect the mandate of ASAC. Dastmalchian et al. (1985) acknowledge how the differences between the Canadian and American contexts could impact the generalizability of their findings; however, they were among the only actors that we traced actors traced whom we can make this statement regarding. Recognition that their research could be influenced by taken- for-granted assumptions underlying the foundations of the model is powerful and accepts that their research may not reflect the accepted dominant model.

Etemad and Dastmalchian are not the only scholars that we traced who wrote extensively on the Canadian context. Lévy, for example, had a number of accepted articles to ASAC based on Canadian-specific topics and these are almost exclusively written in French. Although ASAC is a bilingual conference, Lévy was the only actor identified who had articles accepted in French and almost exclusively wrote about Canadian issues (e.g., NAFTA and free trade). It appears, however, that Lévy recognized and responded to broader institutional pressures when publishing her work outside of ASAC. One article, published in the *International Business Review*, was titled "The interface between globalization, trade and development: Theoretical issues for international business studies" (Lévy, 2007). The article has been cited 80 times (Google Scholar, accessed January 2, 2021) and is broader in its context than the articles accepted to ASAC. Many of Lévy's articles listed on Google Scholar appear to adopt a more generalized context than her ASAC articles. This difference could reflect how Lévy responded to institutional pressures when developing and submitting articles to journals outside of Canada. In addition to a more generalized context for articles published outside of ASAC and CJAS, Lévy—despite writing extensively in French for ASAC—tends to write in English. Given that many journals adopt English in their publication and appeal to broad issues of interest to their readership, Lévy may have recognized and adapted to these institutional pressures to obtain widespread acceptance of her ideas. Despite the attempts to provide a venue for Canadian scholarship through her contributions to ASAC, her collective efforts appear to be overshadowed by institutional pressures to stabilize the dominance of the American model of management. In the process, some scholars, whose work focuses on Canadian-specific research topics or who wrote in a language other than English, found that their work needed to change to reflect the values of more prominent (American) journals.

Implications for Canadian Identity

This chapter surfaced how the movement to provide a venue for Canadian scholarship involved ASAC. We demonstrate how some individual actors take on personal risks when sharing their research, whilst others conform more to a so-called American ideal. ASAC represents the protection of Canadian identity during a time when this was viewed by some as unscholarly and unscientific. We surfaced various tensions by tracing the scholars; the work they publish and how they respond to broad institutional pressures that privilege American values and traditions.

With the apparent acceptance of American models of management studies in Canada and with scholars following conventions designed to support prevailing such models, we argue that this has implications for Canadian identity. As content and context are removed to appeal to a broader and more American and International market, scholars are not able to identify relevant research to address specific issues confronting nations. Over time, this has made it increasingly difficult to identify what "Canadian" issues are in relation to the dominant American models. The increasingly generalized research also broadens the gap between practitioners and corporations who rely on scientific expertise to address business issues and provide guidance about proposed directions, policies, and strategies based on the unique political, cultural, and social dimensions of a particular region. As a result, systems and policies reflect the values of scholars who are motivated to maintain prevailing models to secure coveted funding and international recognition. This works to increase the gap between what businesses have identified as needed from the workforce, with what is being taught at universities, and how theoretical contributions can help resolve Canadian business issues. When scholars unintentionally focus on research that will appeal to American conferences and journals to secure grants and funding, it leaves the Canadian story of management studies unexamined. The inference is that the Canadian context can be easily substituted by American concepts and theories and that Canadian businesses share the same concerns and challenges as their American counterparts. The idea that Canadian businesses have similar issues as American ones supports the idea that some actors view management studies as universal and "…therefore existing research applies to both Canadians and Americans equally" (McLaren and Mills, 2015a, p. 323). Although there are many similarities between the two countries, there are many differences (Russell, 2015). As the Symons Report (1978) highlights; "[i]n the case of Americans, for example, while we have much in common, our differences are many and diverse" (p. 25) and should be recognized. There are differences in the political systems of the two countries, socioeconomic conditions, and culture (McLaren and Mills, 2015; Symons, 1978). As a result, Canadian corporations have different laws that need to be followed, different barriers and opportunities, and are governed by the values of a nation that has approached business differently. This issue is not unique to Canada alone. European and Middle East nations, and many others are all confronted with similar issues resulting from prevailing models of management studies. The United States, as the current prevailing model of management, does not need to have these same discussions since the standards established reflect what is defined as being American (i.e., American scholars; American context and American publishers = American knowledge).[4]

Conclusion

As this chapter highlights, management studies in Canada remain based on American models. This process was facilitated by modeling ASAC after its American equivalents and was reinforced through the actions of individual scholars who adhered to conventions that were inherently American and served to further reinforce values and traditions privileging the dominant American model. Some scholars sought to protect Canadian identity; however, their efforts were largely unsuccessful. Finally, this chapter examined the implications that this has had on the development of Canadian management studies.

Table 3.1 List of notable contributors to the annual ASAC conference 1979–2009

Name	Affiliation(s)	Range of years articles were accepted to ASAC	Primary author acceptances	Sole author	Total number of articles accepted[5]	Language of accepted articles	Paper awards and recognition
Beamish, Paul W.	University of Western Ontario Wilfrid Laurier University	1982–2005	7 times	1 time	20 times	English	Best IB paper (2005)
Dastmalchian, Ali	Athabasca University University of Lethbridge	1982–200	6 times	3 times	7 times	English	
Elangovan, A. R.	University of Toronto University of Victoria	1991–2006	5 times	4 times	5 times	English	
Etemad, Hamid	McGill University	1981–2009	15 times	7 times	17 times	English	IB Honorable Mention (2003)
Finegan, Joan	University of Western Ontario	1992–2005	7 times	2 times	9 times	English	
Irving, Gregory P.	University of New Brunswick Wilfrid Laurier University	1995–2004	8 times	2 times	12 times	English	OB Honorable Mention (1995) OB Honorable Mention (2002)

(*Continued*)

Table 3.1 (Continued)

Name	Affiliation(s)	Range of years articles were accepted to ASAC	Primary author acceptances	Sole author	Total number of articles accepted[5]	Language of accepted articles	Paper awards and recognition
Lévy, Brigitte	University of Ottawa	1986–2006	7 times			English and French	
McShane, Steven L.	Queen's University Simon Fraser University	1983–1986	5 times	4 times	5 times	English	Best OB paper (1983) Honorable mention in OB (1986)
Miller, Diane L.	University of Toronto University of Lethbridge	1992–2004	5 times	3 times	8 times	English	Best OB paper (2003)[6]
Rugman, Alan M.	University of Toronto Dalhousie University Indiana State University	1981–2003	11 times	5 times	12 times	English	
Saha, Sudhir K.	Memorial University	1981–2004	5 times	3 times	6 times	English	
Saks, Alan M.	Concordia University University of Toronto	1991–2005	6 times	2 times	7 times	English	OB Honorable mention (1996)
Stone, Thomas H.	York University McMaster University University of Iowa Oklahoma State University	1981–2005	5 times	1 time	7 times	English	

Name	Affiliation(s)	Range of years articles were accepted to ASAC	Primary author acceptances	Sole author	Total number of articles accepted	Language of accepted articles	Paper awards and recognition
Tallman, Rick	University of Manitoba University of Northern British Columbia	1996–2004	5 times	2 times	5 times	English	
Withey, Michael	Memorial University	1985–2005	8 times	4 times	9 times	English	Best OB Paper (1988)
Withane, Sirinimal	University of New Brunswick University of Windsor	1984–1992	7 times	5 times	7 times	English	

86 Management Education in Canada

Table 3.2 List of ASAC conference themes and locations by year

Year	Conference location/sponsor	Conference theme	Year	Conference location/sponsor	Conference theme
1979	University of Saskatchewan	"Managing in the 1980s: Themes for management research"	1994	Halifax (Dalhousie)	"Looking South: The Canadian perspective on North American trade"
1980	Montreal	"Towards excellence in the 80's"	1995	Windsor (Windsor University)	
1981	Dalhousie University		1996	Montreal (HEC)	
1982	University of Ottawa	"The Future: Today's Challenge"	1997	St. John's (Memorial)	"Discovering new worlds"
1983	University of British Columbia	"Linking Knowledge to Action"	1998	Saskatoon (University of Saskatchewan)	
1984	University of Guelph	"Management Education: Its Place in the Community"	1999	Saint John (UNB Saint John)	"Managing on the digital frontier"
1985	University of Montreal	"The information society: Its implications for teaching and research"	2000	Montreal (UQAM)	"Taking Stock: a look at competing paradigms"
1986	Whistler (Simon Fraser)	"Business in its International Dimension"	2001	London (University of Western Ontario)	
1987	University of Toronto		2002	Winnipeg (University of Manitoba)	"Where East meets West"
1988	Halifax (Saint Mary's University)	"Management education in the 90's: Challenges and Changes"	2003	Halifax (Saint Mary's University)	"New paradigms for a new millennium"
1989	Montreal (McGill)	"Changes and challenges of the 1990's and beyond: Le future commence aujourd'hui"	2004	Quebec City (Laval University)	"Research Agenda for the next decade"

Year	Location	Theme
1990	Quebec City (Laval)	"Adapting to Turbulent Environment"
1991	Niagara Falls (Brock University)	
1992	Quebec, Quebec	
1993	Lake Louise (Calgary)	
2005	Toronto (Ryerson University)	"Managing in Turbulent Times"
2006	Banff (University of Lethbridge)	"Reaching new heights"
2007	Ottawa (University of Ottawa)	"The essentials of leadership"
2008	Halifax (Dalhousie University)	"Managing the responsible enterprise"
2009	Niagara Falls (Wilfrid Laurier University)	"Creating Knowledge in the New Economy"

Notes

1 There were also authors who had articles submitted from international affiliations. In all, 31 authors were associated with institutions outside of Canada. These authors were not included in the study as they did not meet the selection criteria for making a sustained contribution to ASAC over multiple conferences.
2 The Symons Report was commissioned by the Canadian Government to provide guidelines about how to incorporate Canadian content into university curriculum (Coller, 2021).
3 Finegan later published the same article in the *Journal of Occupational and Organizational Psychology* (2002), a British journal and has been cited 247 times (ProQuest, Retrieved October 3, 2020).
4 On my Twitter account on April 30, 2019, for example, Minna Salami @MsAfropolitan, who describes herself as being Scandinavian laments; "I find the Americanisation of culture suffocating. Its not just pop culture, but also academia, social media and even our innermost thoughts, all Americanised in ways that way too few people even question anymore."
5 As an author or co-author of an accepted article.
6 Miller was the second author. Leonard Karakowsky was the lead author and Kenneth McBey was the third author.

References

Administrative Sciences Association of Canada (ASAC). (1979, April 6–9). Minutes of the Executive Meeting. Archives of Canadian Management.

Administrative Sciences Association of Canada (ASAC). (1985, Fall). Bulletin. Archives of Canadian Management.

Ashforth, B. K., & Saks, A. M. (1996). Socialization tactics: Longitudinal effects on newcomer adjustment. *Academy of management Journal*, *39*(1), 149–178.

Austin, B. (1998). The role of the administrative sciences association of Canada in institutionalizing management education in Canada. *Canadian Journal of Administrative Sciences*, *15*(3), 255–266. Retrieved from http://libproxy.mtroyal.ca /login?url= www-proquest-com.libproxy.mtroyal.ca/scholarly-journals/role-administrative-sciences-association-canada/docview/204872592/se-2?accountid=1343

Austin, B. (2000). Introduction. In B. Austin (Ed.), *Capitalizing knowledge: Essays on the history of business education in Canada* (pp. 3–10). Toronto, ON: University of Toronto Press.

Austin, B. (2000a). The administrative sciences association of Canada, 1957-1999. In B. Austin (Ed.), Capitalizing knowledge: essays on the history of business education in Canada

Beamish, P. W., Jung, J. C. (2005). *The performance and survival of joint ventures with asymmetric parents*. Proceedings of the annual general conference of ASAC IB division, 1–16.

Beamish, P. W., & Calof, J. L. (1989). International business education: A corporate view. *Journal of International Business Studies*, *20*, 553–564.

Berger, P. L., & Luckmann, T. (1967). *The social construction of reality: A treatise in the sociology of knowledge.* New York, NY: First Anchor Books.

Bettin, C., Mills, A. J., & Helms Mills, J. (2016). "The Halifax School": An actor-network analysis of critical management studies and the Sobey PhD in management programme. In C. Grey, I. Huault, V. Perret, & L. Taskin (Eds.), *CMS: Global voices, local accent* (pp. 36–53). London: Routledge.

Booth, C., & Rowlinson, M. (2006). Management and organizational history: prospects. *Management and Organizational History, 1*(1), 5–30. https://doi.org/10.2307/2093510

Boothman, B. (2000a). Culture of utility: The development of business education in Canada. In B. Austin (Ed.), *Capitalizing knowledge: Essays on the history of business education in Canada* (pp. 11–86). Toronto, ON: University of Toronto Press.

Boothman, B. (2000b). Canadian management education at the millennium. In B. Austin (Ed.), *Capitalizing knowledge: Essays on the history of business education in Canada* (pp. 295–356). Toronto, ON: University of Toronto Press.

Coller, K., McNally, C., & Mills, A. J. (2015). The inner circle: Towards a 'Canadian' management history – Key Canadian contributors to new institution theory. In P. Genoe McLaren, A. J. Mills, & T. G. Weatherbee (Eds.), *The Routledge companion to management and organizational history* (pp. 342–360). London: Routledge.

Collins, R. (2000). *Culture, communication and national identity: The case of Canadian television.* Toronto, ON, University of Toronto Press.

Cooke, B. (1999). Writing the left out of management theory: the historiography of the management of change. *Organization, 6,* 81–105. https://doi.org/10.1177/135050849961004

Cormier, J. (2004). *The Canadianization movement: Emergence, survival, and success.* Toronto, ON: University of Toronto Press.

Cormier, J. (2005). The Canadianization movement in context. *The Canadian Journal of Sociology, 30*(3), 351–370. https://doi.org/10.1353/cjs.2005.0047

Dastmalchian, A., Javiden, M., & Pasis, H. (1985). Centralization of Decision Making, Organizational Context and Dependence: Evidence from Canadian Provincially Controlled Organizations. *Proceedings of the Annual Conference of Administrative Sciences Association of Canada,* 23–32.

Durepos, G., & Mills, A. J. (2012). *ANTi-History: Theorizing the past, history, and historiography in management and organizational studies.* Charlotte, NC: Information Age Publishing.

Edwardson, R. (2008). *Canadian content: Culture and the quest for nationhood.* Toronto, ON: University of Toronto Press.

Elangovan, A. R. (1994). *Managerial intervention in disputes: A comparative study of factors affecting strategy selection.* Proceedings of the annual general conference of the Administrative Sciences Association of Canada, 52–61.

Elteren, M. (2006). *Americanism and Americanization: A critical history of domestic and global influence.* Jefferson, NC: McFarland & Co.

Etemad, H. (1981). *Are domestic and international marketing dissimilar? A re-examination and extension.* Proceedings of the annual conference of the Administrative Sciences Association of Canada, 24–38.

Etemad, H. (1982). *World product mandating in perspective.* Proceedings of the Annual Conference of the Administrative Sciences Association of Canada, 107–119.

Etemad, H., Zhou, L. (1986a). *Foreign trade arbitration in China*. Proceedings of the annual conference of the Administrative Sciences Association of Canada, 1–7.

Etemad, H. (1986b). *International marketing at the crossroads: the new technologies and strategies of the past*. Proceedings of the annual conference of the Administrative Sciences Association of Canada, 69–82.

Finegan, J. E. (2000). The impact of person and organizational values on organizational commitment. *Journal of occupational and Organizational Psychology, 73*(2), 149–169.

Foster, J., Helms Mills, J., & Mills, A. J. (2014). Shades of red: Cold War influences on Canadian and U.S. business textbooks. *Journal of Management Education, 38*(5), 642–671.

Gantman, E. R., Yousfi, H., & Alcadipani, R. (2015). Challenging Anglo-Saxon dominance in management and organizational knowledge. *Revista de Administração de Empresas, 55*(2), 126–129. http://dx.doi.org/10.1590/S0034-759020150202

Gür, S., Hamurcu, M., & Eren, T. (2016). Selection of academic conferences based on analytical network processes. *Multiple Criteria Decision Making, 11*, 51–62. http://dx.doi.org.library.smu.ca:2048/10.22367/mcdm.2016.11.04

Hall, R. I. (1984, January 3). [Letter to Wallace Crowsten]. Canadian Management archive.

Hiller, H. H., & Di Luzio, L. (2001). Text and context: Another" Chapter" in the evolution of sociology in Canada. *Canadian Journal of Sociology/Cahiers canadiens de sociologie*, 487–512.

Irving, P. G. (1995). *Dimensions of managerial third-party conflict intervention strategies*. Proceedings of the annual general conference of the Administrative Sciences Association of Canada, 11–21.

Johnson, C. D. (2008). "Doing well by doing good" garners broad appeal for academy of management conference. *Equal Opportunities International, 27*(7), 646–653. http://dx.doi.org.library.smu.ca:2048/10.1108/02610150810904337

Johnson, P., Duberley, J. (2000). *Understanding Management Research*. Thousand Oaks, CA: Sage Publications.

Kieser, A. (2004). The Americanization of Academy of Management education in Germany. *Journal of Management Inquiry, 13*(2), 90–97. https://doi.org/10.1177/1056492604265301

Lévy, B. (2007). The interface between globalization, trade and development: Theoretical issues for international business studies. *International Business Review, 16*(5), 594–612.

MacDonald, P. K. (2009). Those who forget historiography are doomed to republish it: empire, imperialism and contemporary debates about American power. *Review of International Studies, 35*, 45–67. https://doi.org/10.10171so260210509008328

McCartan, P. (2010). Journals and the production of knowledge: a publishing perspective. *British Journal of Political Science, 40*(2), 237–248. http://dx.doi.org.library.smu.ca:2048/10.1017/S0007123410000062

McLaren, P. G., & Mills, A. J. (2015). History and the absence of Canadian management theory. In McLaren, P. G., Mills, & Weatherbee T. G. (Eds.), *The Routledge Companion to Management and Organizational History* (pp. 319–331). New York, NW: Routledge.

McLaren, P. G., & Mills, A. J. (2013). Internal cohesion in response to institutional plurality: the Administrative Sciences Association of Canada. *Canadian Journal of Administrative Sciences, 30*(1), 40–55. Retrieved from http://libproxy.mtroyal.ca/login?url=www-proquest-com.libproxy.mtroyal.ca/scholarly-journals/internal-cohesion-response-institutional/docview/1326901615/se-2?accountid=1343

McLaren, P. G., & Mills, A. J. (2014). History and the obfuscation of Canadian management theory. Atlantic School of Business Proceedings.

McLaren, P. G., & Mills, A. J. (2015). History and the absence of Canadian management theory. In P. G. McLaren, A. J. Mills, & T. G. Weatherbee (Eds.), *The Routledge companion to management and organizational history* (pp. 319–331). New York: Routledge.

McQuarrie, F. A. E. (2005). How the past is present(ed): a comparison of information on the Hawthorne studies in Canadian Management and Organizational Behaviour textbooks. *Canadian Journal of Administrative Sciences, 22*(3), 230–242.

Nossal, K. R. (2000). Home-grown IR: The Canadianization of international relations. *Journal of Canadian Studies, 35*(1), 95–114.

Papadopoulos, N., & Rosson, P. (1999). Inventory and analysis of Canadian research and scholarship in exporting and international marketing. *Canadian Journal of Administrative Sciences, 16*(2), 77–94.

Russell, J. (2015). Organization men and women: making managers at Bell Canada from the 1940s to the 1960s. *Management & Organizational History, 10*(3–4), 213–229. https://doi.org/10.1080/17449359.2015.1098546

Russell, J. (2019). Finding a turn in Canadian management through archival sources. *Journal of Management History, 25*(4), 550–564. http://dx.doi.org.libproxy.mtroyal.ca/10.1108/JMH-02-2018-0020

Russell, J. (2021). *Canada, a working history*. Toronto: Dundum.

Rugman, A. (1986). The determinants of Canadian outward direct investment. *Proceedings of the annual conference of ASAC IB division*, pp 96–108.

Symons, T. H. B. (1978). *To know ourselves: The report of the Commission on Canadian Studies*. Ottawa: Association of Universities and Colleges of Canada.

Tiratsoo, N. (2004). The "Americanization" of management education in Britain. *Journal of Management Inquiry, 13*(2), 118–126. https://doi.org/10.1177/1056492604265329

Usdiken, B. (2004). Americanization of European management education in historical and comparative perspective: A symposium. *Journal of Management Inquiry, 13*(2), 87–89. doi: 10.1177/1056492604265224

Wanderley, S., & Faria, A. (2012). The Chandler-Furtado case: A decolonial (re)framing of a North/South (dis)encounter. *Management & Organizational History, 7*(3), 219–236.

Whithey, M. (1988). Antecedents of value based and economic organizational commitment. *Proceedings of the Annual Conference of the Administrative Sciences Association of Canada*, 124–133.

4 French Language as a Missing Context in Histories of 'Doing' Business Education in Canada

Nicholous M. Deal and René Arseneault

Introduction

Few topics are as controversial in Canada as the state and placement of the French language. This is not a recent phenomenon. Histories of Canada commonly offer narratives of a progressive nation-state that has always been welcoming to all (cf. Brown, Doucette, & Tulk, 2016) including French cultures. Indeed, in a country as diverse as it hopes to be inclusive, it is generally accepted that the coexistence of numerous national, racial, and ethnic groups – each comprising its own unique cultural and social backgrounds – contribute to a milieu best typified in the cultural mosaic metaphor[1] (Schwind, Uggerslev, Wagar, & Fassina, 2022). The Canadian ideal thus encourages a vibrant combination of different cultures on a grand scale. Admirable as this may be, these sentiments of pluralism are sadly not practiced in many aspects of Canadian society (see Bannerji, 2000; Doucette, Gladstone, & Carter, 2021). Certainly, this is a political challenge but also one we feel history may play a role in remedying. If we can understand how the narrative of French business education is excluded from histories of Canadian management education and business schools, we may be better suited to help bridge the divide.

We take the history of 'Canadian' business education (Austin, 2000) as an exemplar of 'difference' in this chapter, specifically the absence of any substantive consideration for French business knowledge in Canada. Herein, we attempt a problematization of how Canadian management education has been historicized by offering redress to the neglect of the French socio-cultural context. The absence of French management education in the literature follows a similar posture of federal biculturalism over the past 50 years, beginning with the legacy of *The Royal Commission on Bilingualism and Biculturalism* and the mixed results it has produced for the French cause (Fraser, 2007). What we set out to do is build on the work of Arseneault, Deal, and Mills (2019) by further pluralizing the historical foundations of Canadian business studies to include the enfranchisement of the French and, in the process, offering a 'new history' of Canadian business education.

DOI: 10.4324/9781003612612-5

To do all this, we need to build context (McLaren & Durepos, 2021) around the neglect of French in Canadian management education's past by revisiting the evolution of Canadian business schools. As a way to set the stage for how our arguments about the neglect of French business education in Canada, we offer a short primer on new and anti-histories of management in historical organization studies. The first part of our chapter begins with an account of the early business school: first at English universities like the University of Toronto, and later, in French institutions. Except for small commercial colleges in Quebec, École des Hautes Études Commerciales de Montréal (HEC Montréal) is recognized as the first school of management in French Canada (McKeagan, 2014). We take these early, problematized accounts along with the development of Canadian business education and the Anglocentric character of management knowledge (Barros & Alcadipani, 2022), to form a theoretical background. Since the historical contours of Canadian business education are rather limited in their breadth, namely Barbara Austin's (2000) *Capitalizing Knowledge: Essays on the History of Business Education in Canada*, we scrutinize this interregnum of the recent past to understand the status of French business education. We take the time since Austin's work to generate and focus on three narratives: (1) the situation of French representation across Canadian universities; (2) a disadvantage of French business scholars in mobilizing knowledge in French scholarly outlets; and (3) the prominence and impact of Anglocentrism that presents the conundrum of faculty in French-speaking universities to publish their scholarship in English outlets. The chapter concludes by offering our own reflections about French business education and its place in history.

(Anti)Histories in Business: A Primer

There is no shortage of histories that attempt to tell the origin story of where and how business education received its start (see Arseneault, Deal, & Helms Mills, 2021; Usdiken & Kipping, 2014). As is the case in most histories, getting the 'facts' straight and the narrative just right has been a source of debate among scholars. Take, for example, the efforts to historicize the origin of the world's 'first' business school. A great deal of time and space has been taken up in management and organization studies (MOS) by scholars who offer their version of events. Andreas Kaplan's (2014) work posits that business schools first began from within a European management context that defined management as an interdisciplinary practice rather than a function of 'doing business.' Accordingly, École Supérieure de Commerce de Paris is said to be *the* pioneer of formal business education having been founded in 1819. Of course, this story conflicts with others like Steven Conn (2019) – an American historian – who raised the Wharton School of Finance and Economy at the University of Pennsylvania in 1881 as *the* beginning of business education. Regardless of whose history is more palatable, it is obvious that from the way most of these histories read, the one narrative that stands out is management education was founded in the United States (US). Period. It would seem quite trivial then to even consider an alternative history. Well, not so fast.

More recently, scholars in historical organization studies, and especially those with an interest in writing critical histories (Durepos, Shaffner, & Taylor, 2021), have set their sights on historicizing the business school (McLaren et al., 2021). For them, the idea is that conventional histories have played an important part in providing insights into these institutions of higher learning and how they have evolved over time. If it were not for the work of traditional scholars like, for example, Wren and Bedeian (2020), who devoted an entire career to tracing the 'evolution' of management thought, important insights about management's past – like the role of the Conservation and Progressive movements played in the development of Scientific Management[2] – could otherwise go unnoticed. There is no shortage of histories of this ilk in MOS. However, what often gets neglected in the mainstream – be it intentional or otherwise – are 'new or anti-histories of management' (Durepos & Mills, 2012; Deal, Hartt & Mills, 2024) that help us consider what is missed (and should be included) in management's history.

Take the conventional history of the Harvard case method as an example. It is widely believed that the history of the case method in management pedagogy follows a narrow path through to Harvard Law School (Gill, 2011; Khurana, 2007; Mesny, 2013). A counter-history of the case method at Harvard, as argued by Cummings, Bridgman, Hassard, and Rowlinson (2017), found that it was in fact the groundswell support for organized labor within the US that presented the need to have students consider business from perspectives other than management (i.e., labor). So, for those doing critical history about management and/or business schools, the whole point of this work is to inspire new thinking within the context of management learning and education. While we count ourselves as part of this growing collective in MOS, we also cannot help but notice that in the process of unearthing anti-histories of management, the American narrative retains its power. It appears to be the research context by which most histories of management education are used.

With each new knowledge published that historicizes overlooked figures, social movements, and even key junctures in management history (e.g., Hawthorne Studies), opportunities to offer a history from anything other than an American ethos are scant. A corpus of work that explores the historical character of management learning and education in other national contexts exists yet specific interest in Canada lacks attention (McLaren & Mills, 2015). This begs us the question: Is there even a Canadian business school? If so, how has it been characterized? Which narratives are privileged and marginalized? To answer these questions, we look back at the narrative of how management education developed in Canada.

Where It All Started? Early Business Education in Canada

It is difficult to pinpoint exactly the origins of management education in Canada. Such is/has been a tall order even by those whose work predates this chapter. The primary reason behind this seemingly futile task is the fact that most business schools in Canada have borrowed inspiration from American institutions modeled at Wharton, Harvard, and Dartmouth, for example (Contardo & Wensley, 2004). What this means is that histories of management education have been difficult to trace because the point at which Canadian business schools have cut free from entanglements of American influence is fuzzy at best. In essence, assembling the history of early Canadian management, stories of American schools are mingled throughout. Nevertheless, we do our part in this chapter by starting with Boothman's (2000) account and going from there.

Something from Nothing: Upper Canada

If it were possible to place the development of business education in Canada, the public school system in Upper Canada (a colloquial term used to describe modern-day Southern Ontario during the 19th century) would be a fitting start. We come to understand that the earliest forms of business education in Canada traced back to the British colonial era in the late 18th century. At the time, formal education was of little value. The Industrial Revolution had barely begun to take root in the Western world. The economy in Canada was small and mainly revolved around local agriculture from the family homestead (Bullock, Richard, & Deal, 2023). Few occupations required more from a person than their physical labor. However, as time went on, subtle shifts in economic and personal structures (e.g., traditional artisan-craftworkers becoming proletarianized) meant that for the first time, work was being reimagined beyond domestic labor. New shops processing raw goods like iron and steel were becoming popular (Kristofferson, 2005). By the early 1800s, enough time had lapsed to see the need (and value) of training; thus began the move of shop masters to offer instruction in practical work skills like bookkeeping and writing (Dunning, 1997). All at once, as these 'students' became proficient, so did market opportunities flourish in filling the gap for practical, workplace learning.

Useful knowledge demanded by those in the early settling of Canada – mainly the Upper Canada region – coupled with the prestige of occupations being normalized in Western Europe and growing industrialization, contributed to a sense that prosperity would entail a greater role for formal education. The transition toward machine-based production meant that the old model of apprenticeship training had broadened to include other skill-based occupations like commercial banking. What would need to happen instead was an alternative: commercial colleges, owned by independent operators, as a short-term solution.

Harbinger of Canadian Business Schools: Commercial Colleges

Business schools were not the first to act as an organizing force formalizing teaching and learning 'business.' Learning-by-doing had already been underway for some time in shops and on factory floors. Boothman (2000) notes in his narrative of Canadian business education that because of three factors – population growth, immigration, and the construction of railway systems that expanded the size of markets – foremen [sic] were no longer able to teach laborers themselves. Even if they could, with new innovations (e.g., assembly lines) placing a greater demand on increasing output, their organizations had become ever more complex and thus difficult to manage. This change created an opening for the commercial college business that had already been successfully prototyped in the US.

The concept of commercial colleges (Russell, 2018) originated in American industrial cities like Detroit whose local economy relied almost exclusively on the success of manufacturing. There, starting in the 1830s, were these small private institutes with a loosely compiled curriculum that supported learning stenography, typewriting, and data entry methods (Brubacher & Ruddy, 2017). They had no affiliation with universities, seeking only to help train functionaries in industry. The first commercial college, British Canadian Commercial College, opened its doors in Toronto[3] in 1860 (Axelrod, 1997). In just a few short years, colleges began popping up across Ontario in Ottawa, Belleville, Hamilton, and London – all early Canadian industrial cities.

Following the decline of clerical apprenticeship in the wake of industrialization, the curriculum in commercial colleges responded to gaps in skills like bookkeeping and typewriting. Their purpose was to impart practical knowledge and skill development that no other institution of learning (i.e., the university) would dare sully their reputation of prestige. Ironically, the applied nature of the curriculum in these colleges was, at least in part, the reason why universities eventually moved to include business courses in extant programs and later, establish schools of business. More on that topic is in the next section. For now, the business of commercial colleges served as a success model that could not be ignored.

... and Then There Was Queen's University

Any historical account that traces how early management education in Canada evolved should include a point about the significance of key junctures within the narrative. For this chapter, we draw attention to the context formed around the evolving beliefs about the purpose of Canadian universities in the late 1880s. Canada had only been a nation-state for just over two decades when universities in developed nations were reorienting themselves to industrial society. The

Wharton School of Finance and Economy had formed in the US and, at roughly the same time, HEC Paris in France. It would seem as though the philosophical idealism of the natural sciences and humanities was slowly giving way to a professionalization of vocationalism. Eventually, this context produced the Queen's undergraduate business program.

In Canada, it was a slow slog at first. As the American and French models of business education became a proven concept, Canadian business learning and education were still being conceived in other departments. Boothman (2000) traces the political economy and psychology departments at Queen's University as giving business a start as a 'learned profession.' There, at Queen's, economics was treated as an applied field with an emphasis on studying institutional practices in public and private sectors. The question of the production of wealth led to the curriculum in new courses, such as bookkeeping (i.e., accounting), decision-making (i.e., organizational behavior), and forecasting (i.e., operations management). It became clear as time went on that the nebulous business curriculum was taking shape and would need a more fitting home than in an arts or science program.

A smattering of diploma programs across the country represented the tepid interest of institutions to experiment with business education: Mount Allison University introduced a one-year course in commercial and secretarial topics (Reid, 1984); the University of Toronto developed a two-year commerce program featuring extensive coursework in descriptive economics (Friedland, 2013); and McGill University's two-year commerce diploma beginning 1907 (Frost, 1984), to name few examples. Regardless of the apparent progress, these diploma programs were kept separate from an academic degree. That all changed at Queen's. In 1919, Queen's University became the first institution in the country to offer a fully credentialed undergraduate degree program in commerce (Daub & Buchan, 2000). What had distinguished Queen's from the rest, aside from the obvious fact that it was a degree at the baccalaureate level, was their program was housed in their faculty of science; engineering to be exact.

Queen's success at being the first to establish a truly university-level program in business may have been a coincidence of timing. In the same year that Queen's launched its degree, McGill University in Montreal had also approved its Bachelor of Commerce degree as a three-year program. Shortly thereafter, in the following year, the University of Western Ontario created an entire department of business to support the adaptation of the business curriculum from Harvard Business School – the alma mater of several of its faculty. While Queen's won the distinction for being 'first,' it is no less important to note that their first-mover advantage was a success given how the university has come to be accepted as a 'top' school in Canada.[4] In other words, being first – by coincidence of timing or otherwise – meant that the business school at Queen's served (and continues to this day) as a blueprint for other programs to aspire.

Absence of French Perspectives in Histories of Canadian Business Education

The sense we get from tracing the early developments that etch Canadian business education history is that the narratives are immensely Anglocentric. That is, the character of these histories advances an English hegemony in business education in Canada. A brief read of Canada's history in its totality would reveal a much different, more complicated political and cultural context. Crafting the intellectual heritage of business education in Canada is a noble undertaking and those who have done so have expanded our understanding. However, what we are simply pointing out is how these extant histories – be it of individual schools (Austin, 1998, 2000), Canadian-made theory (McLaren & Mills, 2015), or use of textbooks (Richard, Deal, & Mills, 2021) – seldom is there a discussion about the (mis)placement of the French school. There is no better place to begin remedying this absence than presenting a history of 'French Canada' as is written into the history of Canadian business education.

'Diversity' that Binds Canada Together

Most histories of Canada celebrate cultural diversity and present this type of diversity as if it were universally understood, accepted, and lauded from time immemorial (Black, 2014; Ducharme, Bélanger, & Bumsted, 2017; Fleras, 2018). Sadly, that is simply not the case. There are far too many examples to choose from that offer a counter-history of diversity in Canada. Canada is a country composed of distinct regions that share common political, cultural, and economic characteristics. Take Atlantic Canada as an example. It is said that the region is characterized by the centuries-old culture of its settlers (e.g., British, Scottish, Gaelic, Black Loyalist, and French)[5] whose tastes and customs have worked together to create a tradition-oriented people (Wiseman, 2007). Each region is unique. The regional fabric that knits Quebec together is an entirely different story.

In Canada's second most populated province and the only region in North America with a French-speaking majority, Quebec and its distinct culture should be an example of the Canadian diversity narrative. This has hardly been the case, however. The history of Canada and its 'founding' is partly to blame. French and English expeditions dating back to the 15th century were responsible for the colonization of vast swaths of land and Peoples in North America. The story goes that the colony of New France – translated 'Canada' to refer to territory along the Saint Lawrence River (Richards, 2009) – was the first official settlement of Canada, having been founded by French colonist Samuel de Champlain in 1608. In the procession of time, the 'new' found country changed hands with the British and eventually, forged its own independence as a commonwealth nation. In all, French culture would not go away but, as histories demonstrate, be relegated to a distinct society vis-à-vis the Province of Quebec and to a much lesser extent, New Brunswick.[6] Herein, we conceive the idea of French management and French business education as originating in Quebec.

The historical situatedness of a distinct French culture presented primarily in Quebec gives rise to a sense of difference within Canada. Space in this chapter does not permit a more detailed discussion of Quebec nationalism and its influence in creating a problematic of 'diversity' narratives in Canada. Suffice it to say, the cultural distinctiveness of Quebec from the rest of Canada throughout history and into the present has produced a collective that desires cultural belonging to, and the recognition of, the Québécois as a distinct society. Seymour (2000, p. 227) expressed it as the desire of Québécois – the embodiment of the French 'way of life' – to legitimize the culture and politics in Quebec as 'a nation within a nation.' Many interventions have sought to quell the feeling of difference between French and English Canada. The *Official Languages Act* forms the most visible change recognizing the importance of bilingualism and biculturalism. Today, Canada is officially a French-English bilingual country. In practice, old wounds between the cultures prevent healing in the truest sense.

Canada may claim diversity as a narrative of its strength but from the way it has grappled with mistreatment of peoples other than the old English order throughout history, the ties that bind the country together are fragile. For an example of how entrenched English had become in Canada and what that means for the absence of French management in histories of Canadian business education, we turn to the Quiet Revolution in Quebec.

Impact of the Quiet Revolution on Business Education in Quebec

Two points in the contextualization of Quebec as a culture occurred exactly 200 years apart (Wiseman, 2007). First, the battle on the Plains of Abraham in Quebec City spelled the end of New France. To the victor, the British Empire, belonged the spoils – Canada – and this effectively ushered in an English imperative that remains in force to this day. The second point, the death of Quebec's long-serving premier in 1959, provided a much-needed opening for the Quiet Revolution. It is important to unpack this point in time as it represents a key formative context that influenced the evolution of French business education in Quebec.

Briefly put, the Quiet Revolution was a period of monumental socio-political and socio-cultural change beginning in the 1960s. Leading up to this point, French society in Quebec had been dominated by an English-speaking minority (mostly those whose relatives had 'conquered' New France for the British Crown). The province was exceedingly rural and agrarian, having borrowed social values from the Roman Catholic Church to arouse a pious way of life. Quebec became more industrialized following the Second World War, especially with the arrival of the television and American corporations expanding

North. Traditional lifestyles began to cede to more secular ideologies (Baum, 2014) as the influence of the Church declined in favor of the cosmopolitanism of large cities – mainly, Montreal. What this meant in terms of politics was that an opportune time had come to deliver much-needed policy change throughout the province. After the death of conservative premier Maurice Duplessis and a Liberal election victory for Jean Lesage, the provincial government began an ambitious policy of modernizing Quebec as a secular state, including a new Department of Education run by bureaucrats and not the Roman Catholic order (Thomson, 1984).

The significance of the Quiet Revolution reveals the absence of any substantiative French business curriculum. Prior to the Revolution, business subjects were slowly making their way through commercial colleges and thereafter, some university programs (i.e., Bachelor of Commerce at Queen's University). Keep in mind these changes were happening across the country but especially in Ontario – just the next province over. The opposite was happening in Quebec. Boothman (2000, p. 21) noted how this frustrated progress was given the province's 'slower pace of industrialization or clerical influence over schooling.' Until the Quiet Revolution, the responsibility of French education – be it primary, secondary, or post-secondary – fell *de facto* to the Church. Only a handful of courses loosely related to business were offered in Quebec. McGill University, for instance, had scaffolded its diploma and undergraduate business degree programs to work in tandem, but they were offered completely in English.

What the Quiet Revolution did for French business education was more indirect than anything. Instead of creating French-only programs, the Lesage government's Ministry of Education sought to prepare a skilled industrial workforce (Cuccioletta & Lubin, 2011). To keep up with industrialization within the province, there had to be a direct link between Quebec's new economic policy and employing more French Canadians in business. To achieve the Liberal's pledge to promote more French representation within managerial positions, the Ministry of Education looked to the universities in Montreal to help.

A New History of French Business Education Origins in Quebec

Remedying the absence of French management histories of Canadian business education would appear to involve offering an alternative history. We point to the Quebec provincial government having played some role in developing French business education as a start. With the Quiet Revolution underway during the 1960s, the university system appeared best positioned to fill the gap in skills training. Now that post-secondary education was decoupled from the Catholic Church – most universities subsequently received their own charter – Quebec could catch up with the rest of Canada but with one caveat: emphasis on programs being accessible in French. In other words, Quebec was interested in developing its own business school that would further its own economic interests.

Depending on whose version of history is accepted, business education in Quebec is said to have started in HEC Montréal[7] in 1907. However, McGill's diploma program in commerce began accepting students that same year. The difference here is that McGill is an English-speaking university, while HEC Montréal is French. The policy framework within the Quiet Revolution was tasked to transform the post-secondary system by training French citizens to become skilled laborers. It was important for the Liberals that they keep their promise to modernize Quebec for two reasons. First, the French-speaking base of the Liberal Party was mostly located in urban areas and yet were routinely displaced by Anglophones in securing stable employment. This meant their electoral fortunes were tied to the employability of Francophones. Second, as Quebec attracted foreign investment, that same investment was slowly brought under the control of the province (e.g., nationalizing the private utility as 'Hydro-Quebec'). In turn, once bureaucrats became involved in the daily management of these public organizations, it became evident that some business training was needed (Wiseman, 2007). Applied, undergraduate programs were needed and the schools in Montréal were the most responsive to developing fully fledged business programs akin to the rest of Canada (Tanguay, 1987).

The first French-speaking institution was The Université du Québec. It was formed in 1969 by the provincial government to improve higher education in Quebec. Emphasis on the hard sciences in the curriculum meant that students like engineers, for example, could be employable in Quebec upon graduation. The fruit of this policy move was that graduates of baccalaureate programs in science had already been gravitating toward business. Elsewhere in Canada but mostly in the US, engineers were increasingly enrolled in Master of Business Administration (MBA) degree programs (Daniel, 1998). The Université du Québec system used Montreal as its chosen site for the École des Sciences de la Gestion (School of Management Sciences). Then, as the provincial economy grew from agrarian to service-based activity, business programs also flourished. There are numerous polytechnics that grew alongside these university-based business schools.

Lastly, a new history of French business education also includes a move toward growing the French business academy. In another chapter of this book, Deal and Hartt (2024) outline the development of doctoral programs across Canada. They found that the four business schools in Montreal – Concordia University, HEC Montréal, McGill University, and Université du Québec – had teamed up to support a collaborative inter-institutional doctoral program that shared resources across each school. As a result, business programs in Quebec could keep up with the demand for senior academics by graduating their own professorate.

Now that we have laid out a version of how French business education in Quebec grew somewhat separately from the rest of Canada, it is a good idea to bring this history into the present.

Mobilizing the Past to Present

There is no denying that a historical narrative of French-Canadian business education has been neglected. Indeed, our efforts to situate the French context in Canadian business education thus far in this chapter have taken us across multiple areas of peripheral literature (e.g., cultural history, political science, and language arts, to name a few). In short, a corpus of work focusing on this very issue does not exist. We became aware of this absence a few years ago while exploring the character of Canadian management textbooks (Arseneault, Deal, & Mills, 2019).

Our work was partly motivated by our interest in the constitution of Canadian business knowledge as well as our own subjectivities. For example, our first author was raised in an English home. His formative context in childhood was the national unity crisis leading up to and following the 1995 Quebec referendum. While not bilingual, his extended martial family are descendants of early French settlers of New France (i.e., pre-confederation Canada). Our second author identifies as a French Canadian, is bilingual, and has a French heritage dating back to the settling of old Quebec. His employment at Université Laval is a testament to his interest in French management education.

The research we conducted with Canadian textbooks contributed to a nearly two-decade research project involving several colleagues interested in the way textbooks influence understandings of management theory and practice. For more on the history of management textbooks, Weatherbee (2015, 2025) offers a robust explanation of how these texts shape ideas of management over time. What drew us to study the construction of textbooks was the lack of a 'Canadian management' perspective (Doucette & Deal, 2019). In the process, we were struck with the presentation of Canada being monolithic; as if it were possible to describe the cultural mosaic as 'one thing.' Moreover, the offering of a perspective other than English intrigued us since Canada is supposed to be a bilingual country yet very little has been offered to explore the French context.

In addition to our own interest and work in the area, the impetus for this chapter also stems from Austin's (2000) *Capitalizing Knowledge*. Her book offers a first look at the evolution of Canadian business education. Two decades have since passed following this seminal work, and in that span of time, the content of Canadian business learning and education has changed and grown. At the time of Austin's book, organizations like Enron were in their heyday; often lauded as an exemplar for success in the early 21st century, only to fall into oblivion and become the driving force behind changes to teaching ethics in business schools (Beggs & Dean, 2007). Similarly, 20 years ago, tensions ran high between English and French Canada grappling with the aftermath of a narrow victory for the federalist campaign in Quebec's referendum for separation in 1995. Since then, numerous gestures have been made to recognize the importance of the French language and culture. Even at the time of writing this chapter, the issue of language equity remains at the fore with the passage of *An Act Respecting French, the Official and Common Language of Quebec. The Act* requires all businesses to generalize the use of French and has sparked new questions of Canadian diversity and equity toward New Canadians whose first language is neither French nor English. It seems that this topic of French in/exclusion persists.

We see an opportunity in the scholarship of business education in Canada to bring what we call the 'recent past' (Decker, 2022) of French business education forward to the present. Since we are interested in offering an alternative history of French in the Canadian business school past, we are problematizing the official narrative offered by Austin's (2000) work. The space and time of *Capitalizing Knowledge* is our starting point since her origin story of Canadian business schools does not fully engage with narratives about French Canada. While it is true that Pierre Harvey's (2000) chapter on the founding of HEC Montréal may represent a 'French perspective,' it falls short of going beyond the business school to problematize the broad issues of representation in the literature.

With this in mind, we set out to raise three narratives that center on the placement of French business education in Canada: (1) the situation of French representation across Canadian universities; (2) a disadvantage of business scholars mobilizing knowledge in French scholarly outlets; (3) prominence and impact of Anglocentrism that presents a conundrum for faculty in French-speaking universities. We surface these narratives through our engagement with a 'close read' (Deal, Mills, & Helms Mills, 2021) of multiple source texts: census data from Statistics Canada; journal ranking data from institutions like the Australian Business Deans Council (ABDC) and *SCImago Journal Rank* (SJR); and scholarly knowledge mobilization data from indices (i.e., Google Scholar).

Our approach seeks to surface the prominence and impact of 'doing business education' in French and the challenges of doing so compared to the rest of Canada. Let us now turn to and explore these narratives.

The Situation of French Representation across Canadian Universities

The situation of the French language in universities across Canada is interesting. In a recent article by Usher and MacLennan (2022) comparing two decades of enrollment metrics between universities in Quebec and the rest of Canada, the number of post-secondary education students in Quebec noticeably lagged all of Canada . What we feel this insight highlights is the context predating the Quiet Revolution: an overwhelming sense of an undereducated Québécois, thus justifying radical policy changes in education. Before this claim can be made and narrative crystalized, a more robust exploration of the size of 'French Canada' is needed.

We begin with data from the Statistics on Official Languages in Canada report (Statistics Canada, 2021. According to the Canadian Census, French happens to be the first official language spoken by approximately 22.8 percent (7,914,498) of Canadians – a clear and distinct minority. Going back some 20 years, from 1996 to 2016, the picture becomes a bit bleaker: over the last two decades, the number of French speakers has decreased from 24.6 to 22.8 percent. We use this insight – the current representation of French speakers in Canada (22.8 percent) – to explore whether Canada's academic institutions offering French coursework represent the narrative of French Canada's decline.

To illustrate an overview of language representation at Canadian universities, we compiled data from Universities Canada – an advocacy conglomerate of universities across the country – that captures all programs of study (i.e., Arts, Science, and Business, for example) and, more importantly, the language of instruction. This allows for a better sense of whether French is indeed underrepresented in Canada's university system. Our total student enrolment for the 78 institutions is 1,268,902. Broken down in terms of language of instruction, there are 58 institutions that conduct their program in English-only (80.4 percent); 17 institutions offering instruction in French-only (15.7 percent); and three bilingual institutions (3.8 percent).

From this, within our first narrative, we see that the French representation across Canadian universities does indeed contribute to a sense of difference. Since 22.8 percent of Canadians claim French as their first language, they are noticeably underrepresented in those engaged in post-secondary education (15.7 percent of students enrolled in French institutions). Beyond the numbers, what we believe this means is the formative context around French business education has been stuck in an ever-present (and growing) logic of Anglocentrism. That is, since the instruction of an overwhelming majority of university students is conducted in English, and this nearly matches those whose first language is English, then is there really an absence of French narrative? Could it be that since Canada is a predominately English-speaking country that the histories of business schools might be better suited to focus on more relevant issues than relitigating the divide between the French and English? We would counter this sentiment first by suggesting that the grand narrative of business education is that it concerns an English order and that this becomes imprinted on the business school narrative. It is also worth reiterating the supposed organizing principle of modern Canada. The pluralism we espouse should have room for an array of stakeholders – in the case of this chapter, business schools, and education – who engage in building a cultural mosaic inclusive and respectful of the contrasting French perspective.

Disadvantage of Business Scholars Mobilizing Knowledge in French Scholarly Outlets

The French problematic is not only concerned with the lack of representation across Canadian universities, but it also includes a structural disadvantage for business scholars: knowledge mobilization. This second narrative we surface is concerned with the economics of business scholarship. By 'economics' we are referring to scholars' knowledge creation as a form of currency in academia (Śliwa & Kellard, 2021). While it depends on several factors (i.e., institutional norms), Finch et al. (2017) note that journal articles remain the 'gold standard' of knowledge mobilization in most Canadian business schools. Therein lies a problem: a vast majority of journals in business, management, and organizational studies publish exclusively in English. This does not even take into consideration the expectation of faculty located in research-intensive institutions to publish in 'top tier' journals. These 'quality' outlets skew American, and thus, English. This is a clear disadvantage to French business scholars and is felt not only in Canada but also across the globe by non-English scholars of all stripes.

In our scan of literature, we sought to take a closer look at how journals impact factors and indices like *SCImago Journal and Ranking* to see if French business knowledge is indeed placed at a disadvantage in Canadian schools. We were curious to understand what options French business academics have in their effort to mobilize research. The idea is that if French business outlets are significantly less numerous (and impactful) than their English counterparts, French academics will be more motivated to publish in alternative languages (i.e., English). Indeed, in this type of arrangement, there are dire implications for La Francophonie and French business management education in Canada (i.e., challenge the 'diversity' ethos in Canadian business and society).

It is already well documented the struggles Canadian business scholarship takes in being published in high-profile, mainstream outlets (Coller, 2021; MacNeil & Mills, 2015; McLaren & Mills, 2008). These, of course, speak of Canadian business knowledge as being concrete. That is, Canadian knowledge is inextricably English. We set out to broaden this view by inserting the French language into the mix. To do so, we searched where French business scholarship was mobilized. Since the SCImago index is considered the broadest, we searched there for journals that they list as being 'Canadian.' What we found was not surprising: only nine Canadian-specific business journals. What did pique our interest was that among these, only one outlet – *Labour/Le Travail* – publishes in French and ranks second-lowest impact factor (0.117) among the Canadian journals. What this suggests is *Labour/Le Travail* is among the lowest ranked among our findings. It could also be that the journal often focuses on topics of labor activity which is not easily reconciled with interests of management or management scholarship writ large.

As the narrative of French exclusion in Canadian business scholarship took shape, we thought that adding more context would be helpful. We were curious about what other journals might French scholars in Canada publish in. This time we relied on Scopus-indexed journals and captured outlets that either published French scholarship or were decidedly bilingual. Our close read of the journals confirmed only 14 outlets (e.g., *Entreprises et Histoire*) in all 'Business, Management, and Accounting' categories.

That's it – only a handful of outlets across the entire breadth of business studies publish research in French.[8] Interestingly, of those journals that publish French articles, the highest-ranked outlet was the *Journal of Decision Systems* with a Scopus impact factor of 1.573. To put this into context, the *Academy of Management Journal* – which publishes exclusively in English – is arguably among the highest-ranked journals in all of business research and they consistently report an impact factor of more than 10.[9]

Because of this disregard for French business scholarship and the resulting barriers for scholars to publish in French, we explored this disadvantage narrative further by including data from the Financial Times Research Rank (McMaster University Library, 2019) and Australian Business Council Deans (Australian Business Council Deans (ABCD), 2022) indices. Unfortunately, the sense of French exclusion worsens. Using the ABCD Journal Quality list, we found 655 journals that publish in English for 'Business, Management, and Accounting' research. The highest-ranked French outlet, the *Journal of Decision Systems* (as previously mentioned), didn't even make the cut. The Financial Times list does not capture any outlet other than English journals. We believe this insight is significant because the 'journal quality game' (Butler & Spoelstra, 2020) that is so often played in business schools can only be played by those who can publish in English. Scholars who wish to be taken seriously must therefore conform to a discourse of excellence which is code for mainstream research in English. It appears that for French scholars, to be competitive and publish in high-impact journals, one must overcome the double bind of: (1) being located in a Canadian business school; and (2) wishing to mobilize one's own research in any other language but English.

A Conundrum of Anglocentrism for Scholars in French-Speaking Universities

This third narrative is a further exploration of the previous French scholarship problematic. A growing body in MOS has problematized the challenges 'periphery-based academics' (Barros & Alcadipani, 2022) face when publishing business research. Hurdles such as ontological politics and epistemological colonialism have long prevented novel, unique research from entering the mainstream (Burrell & Morgan, 1979). These are important issues that are slowly being focalized. Several publications as of late have centered on the geopolitics of management knowledge production; highlighting neglect of perspectives from the Global South, especially Brazilian contexts (Cooke & Alcadipani, 2015; Jammulamadaka, Faria, Jack, & Ruggunan, 2021; Wanderley & Barros, 2019). In all, the main argument is that the Anglocentric character of management poses a significant challenge to those who find themselves outside of English privilege. If we translate this problematic to French business schools in Canada, sadly the narrative remains.

The conundrum of Anglocentrism for French-speaking management scholars is not unique. It is a conundrum of disparity felt by anyone other than English-speaking scholars. There is, however, an especially unique aspect of this conundrum by French-speaking faculty. That is, the impact of disseminating business knowledge in French is blunted by a smaller number of outlets to publish which can produce potentially lower citation scores than publishing in English. We explore this conundrum by following the scholarly impact of business faculty in three institutions in Quebec: HEC Montréal, Université de Laval, and Université du Québec à Montréal (UQAM). The value of surfacing the narrative this way is to see what business knowledge is produced and see what this means for French faculty. What we find is a sobering picture for Francophone business scholars in Canada.

Following Aguillo (2012), we use data from the widely utilized Google Scholar to explore the efforts of French faculty in mobilizing business knowledge. Specifically, we take three prominent business schools in Quebec as a microcosm to surface the publication dilemma faced by French scholars in Canada. Using institutional profiles of faculty in the business schools across these three universities, we capture a 'recent past' of publishing and citation disparity between 2001 and 2021. We take Professor Linda Rouleau[10] of HEC Montréal as an example.

By most standards, Professor Linda Rouleau has an impressive resume. As a Francophone based in a French business school, Rouleau has succeeded in publishing her research in both English and French. Her record includes 30 articles, books, and book chapters. However, she has published only six papers in French (353 citations in total compared to 4,049 citations to her scholarship in English). As you may notice, most of her work in English is published in 'high quality' journals like the *Academy of Management Review* which, as we argued previously, do not print in any other language. This disparity in research impact between English and French may be a result of research expectations at HEC Montréal. Her institution being accredited with the Association to Advance Collegiate Schools of Business (AACSB) means publishing research in highly ranked journals (Romero, 2008). While this may be so, nonetheless, the fact remains that there appears to be a disparity between English and French insofar as what is researched, where it is published, and how many times it is cited. The former, English, being the norm.

Beyond our 'zoom in' (Deal, 2022) of Rouleau, we also offer a few more numbers from the Google Scholar data. Of the 2,338 data points we explored (i.e., scholarship produced by faculty in three French business schools), the range of citations was from 0 to 3,837. English publications were cited, on average, 69 times whereas French scholarship was cited only 13 times. About two-thirds of the data were English (65 percent) and the remaining in French (35 percent). What this suggests is yet another narrative of French disadvantage. Faced with a choice between publishing business knowledge in French – featuring a very limited range of French journals and zero 'top tier' outlets – and English – seeming countless outlets and quality journals – often the latter prevails. The most sobering of all: this is happening in French Canadian business schools, which only exacerbates the hegemonic practice of publishing business research in English. In the process, this narrative further minimizes the importance of pluralizing histories of Canadian business education.

Discussion and Conclusion

In problematizing the absence of French perspectives in history through surfacing three narratives from the recent past, we believe our work here has provided some context for the potential of alternative histories in the Canadian business education literature. We are not alone in offering such a contrast. While outside the domain of MOS but to our work, French Canadian scholars have similarly examined the language problematic atop both political science (Imbeau & Ouimet, 2012) and humanities (Larivière & Desrochers, 2015) disciplines. In either case, the absence of French scholarly knowledge followed a similar logic: research published in English is cited (on average) three times as often as papers in French. Given the impact or lack thereof in French outlets – measured by citation metrics – versus those in English journals, the pressure French Canadian scholars feel to 'publish (in English) or perish (in French)' (Coolidge, 1932) is real. As the old, worn story in business scholarship goes: publishing in high-impact journals (i.e., English) has the ability to catapult a career. Access to powerful scholarly networks, funding opportunities, and thus, increased visibility in the academic community entrench the exclusion of French business knowledge.

All is not lost, however. Some institutional norms have been sought to address this problem. For example, in 2015, the provincial granting council 'Fonds de Recherche du Québec – Société et Culture' (FRQSC) established a requirement that all scholarly journals supported by the council must feature at least 50 percent of their content in French. What remains to be seen is how these efforts have made a positive impact on incentivizing scholarship in French.

Another example is the role bilingualism has played historically in institutionalizing management education in Canada vis-à-vis the Administrative Sciences Association of Canada (ASAC) (Austin, 1998). ASAC's continued commitment to French inclusion is embodied in the way it emphasizes both official languages at the annual conference, communications, and longstanding sponsorship of the *Journal of Administrative Sciences/Revue Canadienne des Sciences de l'Administration* which publishes research in either language. These efforts are indeed commendable, but we invite the entirety of the Canadian business school to rethink our pluralism by moving beyond sympathy and toward the full inclusion of French business scholars and their knowledge. They are needed and their contributions welcomed.

If there was ever doubt about the character of business scholarship following an English ethos, hopefully, our work highlighting narratives of disadvantage in French Canadian business education serves as an exemplar of the exclusionary processes that marginalize groups[11] in MOS. Whether it be the disparities of Francophones pursuing higher education, the lack of French scholarly outlets, or a conundrum of Anglocentrism that forces French faculty to decide between publishing research in their native language or in 'high quality' (i.e., English) journals, the Canadian business school has a way to go before it can confidently say it embodies the often-espoused cultural pluralism ideal.

To conclude, we return once more to the beginning of this chapter: the history of Canadian business education has long resisted opening space for new histories that consider French perspectives. The absence of French inclusion need not continue. By working through tales of early business education in Canada through to the recent past, our intention with this research is to shed new light on the potential for a more inclusive Canadian milieu. In doing so, not only may we realize a truly vibrant, diverse cultural mosaic within the business school but also a historical narrative that is transparent as it is contextualized for all peoples.

Enfin, nous avions espéré que les recherches de ce chapitre aient pu mettre en lumière tout le travail intellectuel qui a caractérisé la formation commerciale française au Canada. Cependant, dans le processus de nos efforts, il est devenu évident qu'il n'y a pas autant de récits sur l'école française simplement parce qu'ils ne reçoivent pas la même attention au Canada anglais. Pour cela, nous espérons qu'un espace dans les études commerciales canadiennes s'ouvrira à la perspective française et que la discipline deviendra plus inclusive des voix alternatives, en particulier de la francophonie. Je me souviens.

Notes

1 The metaphor is often called upon to delineate Canada's national multiculturalism strategy with that of American public policy which holds a homogenous view of society (see Gibbon, 1938).
2 In a recent article in the *Journal of Management History*, Stephen Cummings and Todd Bridgman offer a comment about how their study of Louis Brandeis – a leader of the Progressive movement in the US – could not have been possible without Wren and Bedeian's mention of him in *The Evolution of Management Thought* (see Muldoon, Deal, Smith, & Lakshmikanth, 2022).

3 We would like to point out that, at the time, Toronto was considered the closest industrial city by proximity to Detroit – arguably, the capital of American industrialism (Hyde, 2001).
4 According to annual publications of university ratings like *QS World University Rankings* that list Queen's University within the top 10 schools for business in Canada.
5 It is important to point out that the history of Atlantic Canada predates settlement; Indigenous populations have played (and continue to play) an invaluable role in the development of the region.
6 Most Francophones in New Brunswick are descendants of the Acadian people. As a result of this, the bilingual status of New Brunswick, the only province in Canada with official bilingualism, is constitutionally enshrined in Sections 16–20 of the Canadian Character of Rights and Freedoms.
7 The HEC Montréal website suggests they are the first university-level business school in Canada: www.hec.ca/en/about/our-history/the-beginnings-of-a-proud-history/
8 This is a common issue in countries that are likewise diverse in languages spoken. For example, in many parts of Europe, it is common for authors to be working in upwards of three or more languages. The objective of business research, however, is to publish in English. This speaks to a larger bias that conflates English with rigor and quality. We believe this is what we might be experiencing in our research focusing on the Canadian context.
9 According to data from the Web of Science Journal Citation Report, 28 June 2022, the journal had a one-year impact factor of 10.979 and a five-year score of 16.178.
10 We do not nor have had any association with Professor Rouleau. Her academic record was selected at random to demonstrate the difference in scholarly impact between publishing business knowledge in English and French.
11 We would be remiss not to also recognize Black and African voices (Prieto & Phipps, 2019), Indigenous peoples (Bastien, Coraiola, & Foster, 2022), and feminist perspectives (Williams & Mills, 2017), that have faced similar neglect in MOS.

References

Aguillo, I. F. (2012). Is Google Scholar useful for bibliometrics? A webometric analysis. *Scientometrics*, *91*(2), 343–351.

Arseneault, R., Deal, N. M., & Helms Mills, J. (2021). Accounting for management and organizational history: Strategies and conceptions. *Journal of Management History*, *27*(2), 288–308.

Arseneault, R., Deal, N. M., & Mills, A. J. (2019). Reading "Canadian" management in context: Development of English and French education. *Journal of Management History*, *25*(2), 180–202.

Austin, B. (1998). The role of the Administrative Sciences Association of Canada in institutionalizing management education in Canada. *Canadian Journal of Administrative Sciences/Revue Canadienne des Sciences de l'Administration*, *15*(3), 255–266.

Austin, B. (Ed.) (2000). *Knowledge: Essays on the history of business education in Canada*. Toronto: University of Toronto Press.

Australian Business Council Deans (ABCD) (2022). *Journal Quality list*. Retrieved from: https://abdc.edu.au/research/abdc-journalquality-list/

Axelrod, P. (1997). *The promise of schooling: Education in Canada, 1800–1914.* Toronto: University of Toronto Press.
Bannerji, H. (2000). *The dark side of the nation: Essays on multiculturalism, nationalism and gender.* Toronto: Canadian Scholars' Press.
Barros, A., & Alcadipani, R. (2022). Decolonizing journals in management and organizations? Epistemological colonial encounters and the double translation. *Management Learning.* https://doi.org/10.1177/13505076221083204.
Bastien, F., Coraiola, D. M., & Foster, W. M. (2022). Indigenous peoples and organization studies. *Organization Studies.* https://doi.org/10.1177/01708406221141545.
Baum, G. (2014). *Truth and relevance: Catholic theology in French Quebec since the Quiet Revolution.* Montreal: McGill-Queen's Press.
Beggs, J. M., & Dean, K. L. (2007). Legislated ethics or ethics education?: Faculty views in the post-Enron era. *Journal of Business Ethics, 71*(1), 15–37.
Black, C. (2014). *Rise to greatness: The history of Canada from the Vikings to the present.* Toronto: McClelland & Stewart.
Boothman, B. E. C. (2000). Culture of utility: The development of business education in Canada. In B. Austin (Ed.), *Capitalizing knowledge: Essays on the history of business education in Canada* (pp. 11–86). Toronto: University of Toronto Press.
Brown, K. G., Doucette, M., & Tulk, J. E. (2016). *Indigenous business in Canada: Principles and practices.* Sydney, NS: Cape Breton University Press.
Brubacher, J. S., & Rudy, W. (2017). *Higher education in transition: History of American colleges and universities.* New York: Routledge.
Bullock, C., Richard, T. J., & Deal, N. M. (2023). Women at the margins: Tales from the agribusiness field in Nova Scotia. In A. J. Mills & N. M. Deal (Eds.), *History and business storytelling* (pp. 49–74). Singapore: World Scientific Publishing.
Burrell, G., & Morgan, G. (1979). *Sociological paradigms and organizational analysis.* London: Heinemann.
Butler, N., & Spoelstra, S. (2020). Academics at play: Why the "publication game" is more than a metaphor. *Management Learning, 51*(4), 414–430.
Coller, K. E. (2021). Americanization and the development of management studies in Canada [Doctoral dissertation, Saint Mary's University]. SMU Institutional Repository. https://library2.smu.ca/handle/01/29673
Conn, S. (2019). *Nothing succeeds like failure: The sad history of American business schools.* Ithaca: Cornell University Press.
Contardo, I., & Wensley, R. (2004). The Harvard Business School story: Avoiding knowledge by being relevant. *Organization, 11*(2), 211–231.
Cooke, B., & Alcadipani, R. (2015). Toward a global history of management education: The case of the Ford Foundation and the São Paulo School of Business Administration, Brazil. *Academy of Management Learning & Education, 14*(4), 482–499.
Coolidge, H. J. (1932). *Archibald Cary Coolidge.* Boston: Houghton Mifflin.
Cuccioletta, D., & Lubin, M. (2011). The Quebec quiet revolution: A noisy evolution. In M. D. Behiels & M. Haydey (Eds.), *Contemporary Quebec: Selected readings and commentaries* (pp. 182–197). Montreal & Kingston: McGill-Queen's University Press.
Cummings, S., Bridgman, T., Hassard, J., & Rowlinson, M. (2017). *A new history of management.* Cambridge: Cambridge University Press.
Daniel, C. A. (1998). *MBA: The first century.* Lewisburg, PA: Bucknell University Press.

Daub, M., & Buchan, P. B. (2000). Business education at Queen's, 1889–1988. In B. Austin (Ed.), *Capitalizing knowledge: Essays on the history of business education in Canada* (pp. 101–145). Toronto: University of Toronto Press.

Deal, N. M. (2022). Toward an ANTi-Microhistory approach in management and organization studies: Revisiting the socio-past of Trans Canada Airlines [Doctoral dissertation, Saint Mary's University]. SMU Institutional Repository. https://library2.smu.ca/handle/01/30890

Deal, N. M., & Hartt, C. M. (2025). From past to present: Tracing the development of Canadian doctoral programs in business. In K. S. Williams, A. J. Mills, & H. Weigand (Eds.), *Management education in Canada: Historical reflections*. Toronto: University of Toronto Press.

Deal, N.M., Hartt, C.M., & Mills, A.J. (2024). *ANTi-History: Theorization, application, critique and dispersion*. Leeds: Emerald.

Decker, S. (2022). Introducing the eventful temporality of historical research into international business. *Journal of World Business*, *57*(6), 101380.

Doucette, M. B., & Deal, N. M. (2019). CJAS constructions of Canadian pluralism. *The Workplace Review*, *25*(1), 31–54.

Doucette, M. B., Gladstone, J. S., & Carter, T. (2021). Indigenous conversational approach to history and business education. *Academy of Management Learning & Education*, *20*(3), 473–484.

Ducharme, M., Bélanger, D.-C., & Bumsted, J. M. (2017). *Interpreting Canada's past: A pre-confederation reader*. Don Mills, ON: Oxford University Press.

Dunning, P. (1997). *Education in Canada: An overview*. Toronto: Canadian Education Association.

Durepos, G., & Mills, A. J. (2012). Actor-network theory, ANTi-History and critical organizational historiography. *Organization*, *19*(6), 703–721.

Durepos, G., Shaffner, E. C., & Taylor, S. (2021). Developing critical organizational history: Context, practice and implications. *Organization*, *28*(3), 449–467.

Finch, D., Deephouse, D. L., O'Reilly, N., Foster, W. M., Falkenberg, L., & Strong, M. (2017). Institutional biography and knowledge dissemination: An analysis of Canadian business school faculty. *Academy of Management Learning & Education*, *16*(2), 237–256.

Fleras, A. (2018). Canadian exceptionalism: From a society of immigrants to an immigration society. In *Immigration, Racial and Ethnic Studies in 150 Years of Canada* (pp. 301–324). Leiden: Brill.

Fraser, G. (2007). *Sorry, I don't speak French: Confronting the Canadian crisis that won't go away*. Toronto: McClelland & Stewart.

Friedland, M. L. (2013). *The University of Toronto: A history*. Toronto: University of Toronto Press.

Frost, S. B. (1984). McGill University. For the advancement of learning, Volume II: 1895–1971. Kingston and Montreal: McGill-Queen's University Press.

Gibbon, J. M. (1938). *Canadian mosaic: The making of a Northern nation*. Toronto: McClelland & Stewart.

Gill, T. G. (2011). *Informing with the case method: A guide to case method research, writing & facilitation*. Santa Rosa, California: Informing Science.

Harvey, P. (2000). The founding of the École des Hautes Études Commerciales de Montréal. In B. Austin (Ed.), *Capitalizing knowledge: Essays on the history of business education in Canada* (pp. 87–100). Toronto: University of Toronto Press.

Hyde, C. K. (2001). 'Detroit the dynamic': The industrial history of Detroit from cigars to cars. *The Michigan Historical Review, 27*(1), 57–73.

Imbeau, L., & Ouimet, M. (2012). Langue de publication et performance en recherche: publier en français a-t-il un impact sur les performances bibliométriques des chercheurs francophones en science politique? *Politique et Sociétés, 31*(3), 39–65.

Jammulamadaka, N., Faria, A., Jack, G., & Ruggunan, S. (2021). Decolonising management and organisational knowledge (MOK): Praxistical theorising for potential worlds. *Organization, 28*(5), 717–740.

Kaplan, A. (2014). European management and European business schools: Insights from the history of business schools. *European Management Journal, 32*(2), 529–534.

Khurana, R. (2007). *From higher aims to hired hands: The social transformation of American business schools and the unfulfilled promise of management as a profession.* Princeton: Princeton University Press.

Kristofferson, R. (2005). Craftsworkers and Canada's first industrial revolution: Reassessing the context. *Journal of the Canadian Historical Association/Revue de la Société historique du Canada, 16*(1), 101–137.

Larivière, V., & Desrochers, N. (2015). *Langues et diffusion de la recherche: le cas des sciences humaines et sociales*. Découvrir, le magazine de l'ACFAS. Retrieved online from www.acfas.ca/publications/decouvrir/2015/11/langues-diffusion-recherche-cas-sciences-humaines-sociales

MacNeil, R. T., & Mills, A. J. (2015). Organizing a precarious black box: An actor-network account of the Atlantic Schools of Business, 1980–2006. *Canadian Journal of Administrative Sciences/Revue Canadienne des Sciences de l'Administration, 32*(3), 203–213.

McKeagan, D. (2014). The first fifty years of the École des Hautes Études Commerciales de Montréal: from "School of Higher Studies" to University Business School. *Historical Studies in Education/Revue d'histoire de l'éducation*, 26(1), 1–25.

McLaren, P. G., Bridgman, T., Cummings, S., Lubinski, C., O'Connor, E., Spender, J. C., & Durepos, G. (2021). From the editors—New times, new histories of the business school. *Academy of Management Learning & Education, 20*(3), 293–299.

McLaren, P. G., & Durepos, G. (2021). A call to practice context in management and organization studies. *Journal of Management Inquiry, 30*(1), 74–84.

McLaren, P. G., & Mills, A. J. (2008). "I'd like to thank the academy": An analysis of the awards discourse at the Atlantic Schools of Business Conference. *Canadian Journal of Administrative Sciences/Revue Canadienne des Sciences de l'Administration, 25*(4), 307–316.

McLaren, P. G., & Mills, A. J. (2015). History and the absence of Canadian management theory. In P. G. McLaren, A. J. Mills, & T. G. Weatherbee (Eds.), *The Routledge companion to management and organizational history* (pp. 319–331). London: Routledge.

McMaster University Library (2019). List retrieved from McMaster University Library Research Guides. https://libguides.mcmaster.ca/ft-top50

Mesny, A. (2013). Taking stock of the century-long utilization of the case method in management education. *Canadian Journal of Administrative Sciences/Revue Canadienne Des Sciences De l'Administration, 30*(1), 56–66.

Muldoon, J., Deal, N. M., Smith, D., & Lakshmikanth, G. S. (2022). The past masters: The impact of the evolution of management thought on history. *Journal of Management History*. https://doi.org/10.1108/JMH-10-2021-0057

Prieto, L. C., & Phipps, S. T. (2019). *African American management history: Insights on gaining a cooperative advantage*. Bingley: Emerald.

Reid, J. (1984). *Mount Allison University, Volume I: 1843–1914*. Toronto: University of Toronto Press.

Richard, T., Deal, N. M., & Mills, A. J. (2021). Damsels in distress: Discourses of entrepreneurship in management textbooks. *Industry and Higher Education, 35*(4), 281–292.

Richards, M. (2009). Putting Québec studies on the map. *Contemporary French and Francophone Studies, 13*(1), 81–89.

Romero, E. J. (2008). AACSB accreditation: Addressing faculty concerns. *Academy of Management Learning & Education, 7*(2), 245–255.

Russell, J. (2018). *Making Managers in Canada, 1945–1995: Companies, community colleges, and universities*. New York: Routledge.

Schwind, H. F., Uggerslev, K., Wagar, T. H., & Fassina, N. (2022). *Canadian human resource management: A strategic approach (13th ed.)*. Toronto: McGraw-Hill Education.

Seymour, M. (2000). Quebec and Canada at the crossroads: A nation within a nation. *Nations and Nationalism, 6*(2), 227–255.

Śliwa, M., & Kellard, N. (2021). *The research impact Agenda: Navigating the impact of impact*. London: Routledge.

Statistics Canada. (2021 Census). *Table 1: Population by first official language spoken and bilingualism, provinces and territories*. www.canada.ca/en/canadian-heritage/services/official-languages-bilingualism/publications/statistics.html

Tanguay, A. B. (1987). Business, labor, and the state in the "new" Quebec. *American Review of Canadian Studies, 17*(4), 395–408.

Thomson, D. C. (1984). *Jean Lesage & the quiet revolution*. Toronto: Macmillan.

Usdiken, B., & Kipping, M. (2014). History and organization studies: A long-term view. In M. Bucheli & R. D. Wadhwani (Eds.), *Organizations in time: History, theory, methods* (pp. 33–55). Oxford: Oxford University Press.

Usher, A., & MacLennan, T. (2022). *Quebec in a Nutshell*. Retrieved July 27th from https://higheredstrategy.com/quebec-in-a-nutshell/

Wanderley, S., & Barros, A. (2019). Decoloniality, geopolitics of knowledge and historic turn: Towards a Latin American agenda. *Management & Organizational History, 14*(1), 79–97.

Weatherbee, T. G. (2015). History in management textbooks: Adding, transforming, or more? In P. G. McLaren, A. J. Mills, & T. G. Weatherbee (Eds.), *The Routledge companion to management and organizational history* (pp. 112–126). London: Routledge.

Weatherbee, T. G. (2025). Textbooks as reflections of who we are. In K. S. Williams, A. J. Mills, & H. Weigand (Eds.), *Management education in Canada: Historical reflections*. Toronto: University of Toronto Press.

Williams, K. S., & Mills, A. J. (2017). Frances Perkins: Gender, context and history in the neglect of a management theorist. *Journal of Management History*, *23*(1), 32–50.

Wiseman, N. (2007). *In search of Canadian political culture*. Vancouver: The University of British Columbia Press.

Wren, D. A., & Bedeian, A. G. (2020). *The evolution of management thought* (8th ed.). Hoboken: Wiley.

5 Globalization of Management Education

Business Theory, Competency Model, and the Role of Canadian Business Schools

Vishwanath Baba and Shamsud D. Chowdhury

Definition of Globalization

Globalization is one of the most contested phenomena in the social sciences. Consistent with its complex and multifaceted nature, its definitions are rooted in the economic, political, cultural, or sociological orientations of the authors who define it. Despite these differences, globalization can be broadly split into either a platform for "accumulation and control of material wealth" (Guttal, 2007: 524) on the one hand and for promoting inequality and oppression on the other. This contrasting classification essentially mirrors the tenets of two corresponding distinct disciplines, that is, economics and sociology (Klein et al., 2022). In economics, the essence of globalization is being efficient at every step of production and distribution (i.e., supply chains, operating costs, and tariffs) and larger market shares, which again leads to cost minimization. In sociology, globalization is about power and legitimacy (Klein et al., 2022). The polarization of countries and societies leads to an imbalance in power and opportunity, which translates into structural inequality in society, a culture of fear among the disadvantaged, and degradation of the environment. Although these opposite views of globalization seem to dominate the extant literature, "the evidence on globalization's contribution to rising incomes, not only in the developing world but the developed, is overwhelming" (Coyne, 2022).

Economists have a direct stake in understanding and promoting globalization. According to the Organization for Economic Co-operation and Development (OECD), globalization is "an increasing internationalisation of markets for goods and services, the means of production, financial systems, competition, corporations, technology and industries" (OECD Glossary of Statistical Terms, 2008). It refers to an increased interdependence of the economies of individual countries brought about by the dynamics of cross-border trade of goods and services, the flow of capital, technology, people, and information. According to Parker (1998), globalization (1) draws resources from the world, (2) views the entire world as its home, (3) establishes a worldwide presence, (4) adopts a global business strategy, and (5) transcends internal boundaries (of people, process, and structure) and external boundaries of nations. When local firms realize sufficient market share at the national level, they expand overseas to build on their existing market power (Penrose, 1959).

Capitalism and Globalization

Capitalism provides the operational framework for globalization (Guttal, 2007). With respect to factors of production, globalization has pushed the boundary of ownership beyond private citizens. In pursuit of efficiency, multinational corporations (MNCs, hereafter,) locate production where costs are the lowest and investors deploy capital where returns are the highest (Economist, 2022a). This, in turn, allows for transnational mobility of people and capital, privatization, innovation, and restructuring of local and national economies to ensure and perpetuate further economic growth. As a result, since the mid-1970s, the process of globalization has accelerated considerably. An ardent search for efficiency, rationalization, value creation, and, above all, a relentless pursuit for competitive advantage among large MNCs served as a powerful push for globalization. As the Economist (2022b) reports, in the 1970s and 1980s, the global flows of foreign direct investment (FDI) were worth 0.5% of global gross domestic product (GDP), but by the mid-2000s, they were worth 5% or more. In the two decades to 2008, trade as a share of global GDP jumped from 37% to 61%. Such exponential growth in FDI flow across nations created a global marketplace for most MNCs.

Despite these positive attributes of globalization as a system of economic exchange, it is also blamed for a variety of economic and social ills (Klein et al., 2022). The inevitable results of hyper-cost efficiency are evident in massive layoffs of blue-collar workers even in highly developed countries and breakups in established supply chains. The eerie images of ghost towns in the United States following the closure of integrated steel mills vividly demonstrate the consequences of globalization. Negative externalities and the rapid flight of capital across countries and regions, which are also associated with globalization, bring devastating consequences, particularly for underdeveloped countries. Together, these consequences result in large income inequality, social unrest, populism, and nationalism (Ciravegna & Michailova, 2022). Because globalization is a natural outcome of technological, scientific, and economic progress in human activities evolving over time, significant concomitant social transformations (Guttal, 2007; Martin et al., 2018) are to be expected. Therefore, strategies to mitigate the negative consequences of globalization need to be considered carefully in view of the existing political and structural mechanisms in a country.

Globalization and Value Chain

The onset of the COVID-19 pandemic has brought about significant changes in the patterns of the mobility of people across countries, capital flow, and volume of trade involving globalization. The pandemic has also resulted in border closures and halted international trade and capital flows (Altman & Bastian, 2021; Ciravegna & Michailova, 2021). Not to put too fine a point on it, there are questions about the lasting impact of globalization. However, there is no gainsaying that the COVID-19 pandemic has caused a fundamental shift in the philosophies and strategies of large MNCs (Ciravegna & Michailova, 2021). The basic rationale for globalization has not eroded, and in a post-pandemic world, there may be an even greater need and utility for globalization (Contractor, 2022). Citing the 2020 edition of the Global Connectedness Index, based on more than 3.5 million data points on trade, capital, information, and people flows, Altman and Bastian (2021) report that the flows of trade, capital, and digital information have surpassed its pre-pandemic level by November 2020. In addition, they also note that the average distance across which countries trade has been on a rising trend since 2016, thus laying to rest concerns about a big shift from globalization to regionalization (Altman & Bastian, 2021).

The creation of value lies at the heart of competitive advantage. The value chain (VC, hereafter) refers to the idea that a company is a chain of strategically important sequential activities for transforming inputs into outputs that customers value (Porter, 1985). Because every important strategically relevant activity adds to the cost of producing a product or service, VC provides a roadmap for attaining a competitive advantage. Value is the amount that customers are willing to pay for what they buy from a firm. Therefore, the most important use of the VC lies in effective cost control, pricing, product positioning, and distribution strategies.

To sum up, the value of a product can be increased by manipulating the VC. It can be done by minimizing the cost structure through efficiency gains in all or some of the activities in the VC or through the creation of uniqueness around its products or services so that customers are willing to pay a premium for them. The latter can be done through the marketing and sales functions. In addition, realizing both ends are possible which, in turn, spurs innovation and creativity in the VC. This is where business schools can play a vital role by training and supplying competent graduates for all value-chain activities. Because COVID-19 has mandated the discharge of work and education from home, digital flows surged (Altman & Bastian, 2021) and opened frontiers of opportunities that were unavailable previously. Massive digitization, in turn, has brought about enhanced opportunities for educational institutions. Real-time problem-solving, opportunities for flexible partnerships with corporate executives, video conferencing, and digital networking among students for case discussions and brainstorming have become more accessible at little to no cost.

Large-scale digitization is also causing increasingly sophisticated and informed behavior among consumers, resulting in demands for more varied, customized, and sophisticated products.

Such opportunities in the pursuit of globalization emphasize the need for efficient international human resource professionals for MNCs. This need manifests in different ways under different contexts, such as planning for future mergers or acquisitions or for the integration of already merged activities (Sparrow et al., 2004). Moreover, the differences in the nuances of institutional environments across host countries and the human resource management (HRM) practices of the MNCs operating in those countries are also different and challenging (Chowdhury & Mahmoud, 2012). Such challenges reveal different degrees of social embeddedness in the HRM practices of different multinational subsidiaries. This also calls for very qualified and competent human resource professionals.

Consequently, the post-COVID-19 era will witness a global war for talent among MNCs. This opens additional opportunities for business schools, especially those in Canada. Covering over 9.98 million square kilometers or 3.85 million square miles in size, Canada is the second largest country in the world. However, with over 41 million people as of 2024 (Statistics Canada, 2024), Canada ranks 36th globally in terms of population. . Therefore, Canada is a small country. The very low density of the population in Canada, 4.2 people per square kilometer (Statistics Canada, 2021), substantially negates its carrying capacity. Despite this limitation, Canada is the 8th largest economy in the world and plays a major role in the global economy. The fact that the United States, the largest economy in the world, and Canada are each other's largest trading partners and the fact that many successful US MNCs have maintained operations in Canada and vice versa for decades are a contributor to this standing of Canada in the global economy. However, despite its economic prowess, Canada is the 14th most competitive nation in the world out of 140 countries. More troubling is that Canadian global competitiveness is gradually declining, a trend that does not bode well for future generations of this country.

Productivity measures the relationship between input and output. The less labor and capital are needed to produce a given output or more output is produced given a certain amount of capital and labor, the more competitive is the firm in relation to its competitors. This involves the VC which, in turn, affects every activity of a business. This implies an intricate bi-directional relationship between business schools and globalization, therefore, the globalization of management education is becoming a necessity. Prestigious business schools in other developed countries like Australia, France, the United Kingdom, and the United States are already well-entrenched in the globalization of business education (Bharadwaj, 2010). Consistent with their insight, Canadian business schools can also contribute to the enhancement of productivity gains in corporations within and beyond Canada by embracing globalization as the driver for business education and training. Before we elaborate on that process, it is important to briefly trace the development of business education in Canada so that the attempts of Canadian business schools toward establishing global linkages could be brought on a historical footing.

The Role of Canadian Business Schools

"The second half of the twentieth century was *la belle époque* for Canadian management education" (Boothman, 2000: 295). Following World War II, the traditional operations of large Canadian corporations underwent considerable changes, underscoring the need for highly specialized and well-educated professional managers capable of operating in more complex and competitive environments. The increasingly diverse demands made on managers spurred the attention of many corporate top executives, academics, business and industry representatives, and key policymakers for up-to-date and relevant management education at Canadian universities. This sense of urgency to modernize management education led to the establishment of the first executive MBA program at the University of Western Ontario (UWO) in 1948 (https://vancouver.mba/what-is-the-history-of-mba-program/). The success of UWO's MBA program prompted the establishment of other MBA programs in different parts of the country. Such establishments provided an impetus and platform for greater integration of business theories and business practices, thus connecting, to some extent, the business schools and the business world. As Boothman (2000) notes, the number of MBA programs quintupled between 1961 and 1991 and the enrollment expanded tenfold. We have now 47 MBA programs in Canada[1] and there has been a consistent increase in enrollment since 1991.[2] According to the MBA Association, the total MBA enrollment in Canada in 2019 is in excess of 5400.

In parallel with, and in response to, the outgrowth of post-secondary business education in different regions in Canada, an association of business schools, called the Canadian Federation of Deans of Management and Administrative Sciences (CFDMAS), was founded in 1969. The main purpose of CFMDAS was "to build strong links with Canadian business schools through an associate program" (Austin, 2000: 284). In 1995, the title CFMDAS was changed to the then famously known Canadian Federation of Business School Deans (CFBSD). The main mission of CFBSD was "to promote quality in management education and the professional development of business school administrators through various types of events, research and information services, and representation" (www.cfbsd.ca/). The CFBSD contributed significantly toward the standardization of teaching and program structures at different business schools in Canada. The CFBSD was collecting, disseminating, and monitoring data on faculty salaries, enrollments, graduates, and operational costs and fees at its member institutions. This allowed for benchmarking programs and courses for schools that were trying to improve their degree offerings. The publications of CFBSD strengthened Canadian management education and its global contacts (Austin, 2000). The stature of CFBSD stayed intact until June 30, 2020, when it was replaced with its current reincarnation, titled, the Business Schools Association of Canada (BSAC). According to its website, BSAC includes almost every business school in Canada and is committed to building safe and inclusive business schools across the country. It also monitors public policy and international trends relevant to Canadian industries (www.cfbsd.ca/). BSAC is dedicated to promoting the interests of its members to the Government of Canada, other agencies of Canada, and abroad. It may be apparent from this synthesis that globalization of management education per se, as we conceptualized in this chapter, was never on the list of priorities of these associations.

Concurrent with, and following the development of, some very remarkable global geo-political events (i.e., the collapse of the Berlin Wall, the overthrow of the Communist regime throughout Eastern Europe, and most importantly, the collapse of the Soviet Union) in the early 1990s, the Canadian International Development Agency (CIDA) sponsored, in collaboration with the member schools of the CFBSD, a few substantially large projects to promote management education in China, Eastern Europe, Latin America, and South-East Asia.

As a revolt against CFBSD (especially against six of its large and powerful member schools) over the control of CIDA funds, the Canadian Consortium of Management Schools (CCMS),emerged as a notable rival organization in 1989. With an initial membership of 30 business schools, CCMS claimed itself to be an "open, not elite" representative of most Canadian business schools (Austin, 2000). With CIDA's strong financial support over the years, CCMS was able to launch many international management development workshops and deliver courses in Canada, East Europe, and Latin America. In collaboration with the Administrative Sciences Association of Canada (ASAC), the CCMS also sponsored symposiums on the globalization of management education at the annual conferences of the ASAC. Though CCMS played an impressive role in the internationalization of Canadian business schools for more than a decade, it was also criticized in some quarters for cost overruns and mismanagement of CIDA funds. Some member school deans were very openly critical of how the affairs of CCMS were run by a select group of individuals at its helm. Moreover, the CIDA funding was drying out. As a result, CCMS was winding up its operations and finally went into extinction in 2004.[3]

There have been attempts for Canadian business schools to partner with other schools for the overseas delivery of programs and courses. Many have established exchange programs with business schools around the globe. A few have established formal joint programs, such as the Schulich–Kellogg program and the Smith–Johnson program. Schulich also has a campus in India. McGill has an international MBA, where they are partnering with business schools in Japan, China, and India. These were pursued more in the context of internationalization and cross-pollination of ideas and mutual learning. Exchange programs sent Canadian students to their partner business schools abroad to take courses for transfer credits and received students from abroad to take courses at Canadian campuses. All these efforts have opened Canadian business schools to the world at large, albeit quite selectively in their choices and outreach. That said, globalization, as it is defined and dealt with in this chapter, has no concrete presence in Canadian business education. There was – and still is – awareness about the international dimension of business. However, operationalization of such awareness was left to individual business schools and was not handled at a higher level, such as an association of business schools like the BSAC. This did not extend to curriculum changes toward globalization. While BSAC talked about internationalization as a desirable step for Canadian business schools to take, there was never any systematic initiative toward globalization of the curriculum or joint research sponsored at the national level as represented by the BSAC. We believe that for Canada to benefit from the current trends toward an economically integrated world, it has to undertake a fundamental change in the way our business schools train our future managers. To that end, we offer a theory, model, and strategy in what follows.

Theory of Business

Societies are human constructions driven by values and their members have recurring needs. People realize that their needs can be well met when they live and commune with each other. Communal living also creates broader communal needs and organizing helps with need fulfillment. Organizers create institutions, and social mechanisms sustain those institutions.

Society is sustained by bringing social, cultural, and economic values into alignment. Legal, political, educational, and spiritual institutions embed those values in the fabric of society. Economic institutions transact value among members of society for creating wealth. Society needs to develop mechanisms to distribute wealth, create order, preserve culture, promote health (physical, mental, and spiritual), offer education, provide infrastructure (energy, transportation, and communication), and defend itself from calamities and aggression. The polity serves to develop and entrench these mechanisms as shown in Figure 5.1. Society survives by having effective institutions that meet its complex and continuing needs. Each institution is supported by resources generated by the economic entities we call the business. The primary role of these entities is to create wealth that is to be appropriately distributed across society by the polity to keep the institutions in operation. To put it simply, the wealth generated by the economic institutions of society goes to support the society's security apparatus which includes police and military, art galleries, concert halls, churches, mosques, synagogues, hospitals, schools, courts of justice, transportation, communication systems, etc.

Globalization of Management Education 123

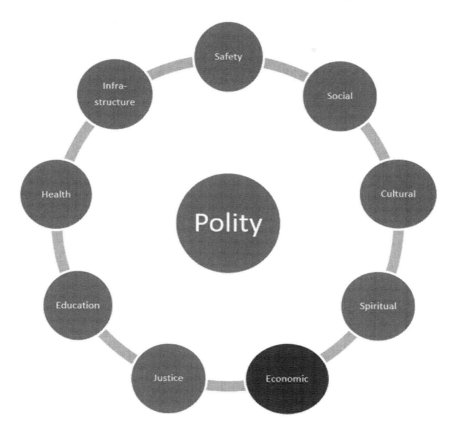

Figure 5.1 Model of society.

Arguably, the central purpose of business is to create wealth (Baba, 2018; Donaldson & Walsh, 2015). This calls for an understanding of what wealth is. By its very definition, value must precede wealth. Business generates wealth by creating value, assessing its worth, as well as optimizing, enhancing, and exchanging value while allocating the proceeds to the participants. To ensure the continuity of the process, we must analyze information, set goals and strategies, establish structures, collaborate with others, engage stakeholders in an ethical and dignified manner, understand the business environment, and operate in a socially responsible manner. These are the basic parameters of any business. The sustainability of wealth creation depends upon the coherence of these parameters. It is leadership and management that enable that coherence (Baba, 2018; Donaldson & Walsh, 2015).

124 *Management Education in Canada*

The role of business schools is to educate and train people who would carry out the mandate of business – wealth creation – effectively and efficiently. In what follows, we will elaborate on a theory of business that would enable the development of a curriculum appropriate to the Canadian context. We will deliver a model to help Canada engage the world of business globally and sustain that engagement. We will consider Canada's role in the global economy, offer suggestions on how to leverage Canadian business education, and provide guidance to business schools on how to prepare our graduates to steer such engagement and benefit from it.

Theories are both guided and constrained by assumptions. We are making our assumptions explicit to enable the reader to understand the theoretical landscape and our theorizing process. To elaborate on our model of society mentioned earlier, we believe that society is sustained by bringing social, cultural, and economic values into alignment and that legal, political, educational, and spiritual institutions embed those values in the fabric of society. We look at business as a *transaction of value* among members of society. We maintain that value precedes wealth and that the role of business is to create wealth, and that society needs to construct mechanisms to distribute wealth.

Figure 5.2 shows that to create wealth, one must not only create, assess, exchange, optimize, and allocate value as mentioned earlier but must also consolidate those processes through synergistic fusion (Baba, 2016). This process is facilitated by other supportive activities shown in Figure 5.3. The value functions cannot be consolidated effectively without a general understanding of wealth and resources. One needs to gather information to support the value functions; provide organizational space, structures, and processes; motivate and lead people; set goals and strategy; engage the stakeholders in an ethical and socially responsible way; and respond nimbly to the demands of the environment. This engagement must be effective and efficient. It is leadership and management that determine the value proposition or the brand that sustains the organization's competitive advantage. In essence, leadership and management, through leveraging the brand, consolidate the process. As the inward arrows

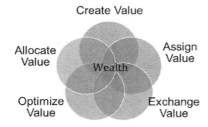

Figure 5.2 Value and wealth.

Globalization of Management Education 125

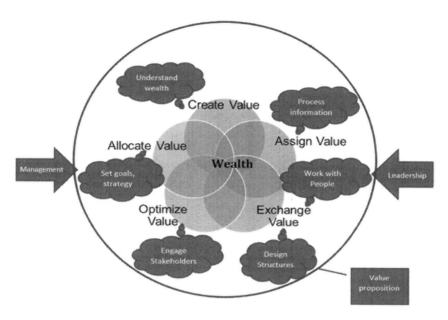

Figure 5.3 Theory of business.

in Figure 5.3 suggest, the more the consolidation, the more the functions fuse together, and the more the wealth creation (Baba, 2018).

Although we have explained components of business theory in the foregoing, we provide a formal articulation here as we believe it would facilitate the design of a program for business education.

The value theory of business shown in Figure 5.3 views the purpose of business as creating wealth for society. Wealth is created by consolidating value – increasing consolidation leads to increasing wealth creation. Organizations, through processes of production and innovation and the utilization of resources, create value in goods and services and assign worth. They exchange goods and services for money in the marketplace in a manner that optimizes value and allocates the proceeds to stakeholders. The value enhancement process is sustained by understanding wealth, processing information, working with people, designing structures, engaging stakeholders, setting goals, developing strategy, and interacting with the environment. This consolidation is carried out by leadership and management. Management extracts value through the adroit deployment of resources, while leadership provides the needed organizational direction – a vision of the future. In essence, what good management and leadership do is exert inward pressure (as shown by the arrows) in a manner

126 *Management Education in Canada*

that ensures that the various value functions cohere toward value enhancement. In other words, the more they fuse together, the larger the nexus becomes, and the larger the nexus, the greater the potential for wealth creation.

Business Program Design

This theory informs business education in all professional MBA programs, regardless of where they are offered. Surely, there are variations on the theme that establish the unique value proposition of the program, but the core program remains the same. We are focusing on the MBA program as opposed to undergraduate programs in business, as the professionalization of a manager takes place at the post-graduate level. It is also why most ranking and rating agencies focus on the MBA and not the BBA or B.Com.

In what follows, we will outline how the different components of the theory are incorporated into the design of a typical MBA program. Figure 5.4 shows the topic areas that correspond to the functions depicted in Figure 5.3.

We will also explore ways by which the components are integrated and consolidated through appropriate pedagogy to train competent business professionals. While the core components are designed to ensure managerial competence, the value proposition of the program is woven through the curriculum and signals the program's unique strength compared to other offerings. We have observed that MBA brands that harmonize with their environment and meet employer needs endure, generating substantial brand equity. The graduates

Figure 5.4 Program design.

have a unique stamp of competence and enjoy a significant competitive advantage in the marketplace. They have describable attributes that emanate from the brand proposition of the program. Professional competence is a function of knowledge and skills tempered by experience and awareness of the context. We will embed these features in our model for business education in Canada.

Curriculum Components

Although value precedes wealth, one needs to understand that wealth is to steer value functions to wealth creation. So, most programs will expose the students to micro, macro, and business economics to provide the platform for all business functions. Value creation begins with the procurement of resources through efficient supply chains and engaging in creative operations with appropriate logistics to ensure quality outcomes. Courses are designed to address these aspects within the program. The idea of value creation is entrenched by exposing the student to aspects of operations, logistics, supply chains, procurement, and quality management. The student then becomes acquainted with the theoretical aspects of production and operations and acquires the skill set needed to manage the creation of value.

Value assessment begins with an introduction to cost, financial and managerial accounting, then moves on to gaining competence in analyzing financial statements, ultimately establishing an accounting information system that incorporates notions, such as tax and insurance in measuring value. The student acquires facility in the concepts and models of accounting and picks up skills in valuation through hands-on exercises.

Value exchange begins with an understanding of exchange concepts and applications in the marketplace and systematic exposure to consumer behavior, new product development, marketing innovation, marketing analytics, and communication. The student is then introduced to the processes for sustaining the exchange through service provision, reputation enhancement, and brand management.

Value optimization is where one learns the operational meaning of efficiency and effectiveness. The student is exposed to various aspects of business analytics, including simulation and predictive modeling, to ensure all aspects of the wealth creation function are optimally coordinated. Several exercises introduce the student to real-life situations and the evolving dynamics of optimization. This component of the program introduces the burgeoning manager that it is optimization at the level of the firm and not optimization at the level of functions that contribute to organizational efficiency and effectiveness – thus entrenching firm value.

Value allocation focuses on the finance function of the firm. The student learns the basics of behavioral, social, and corporate finance and their management, along with the techniques that render them operational. The student is exposed to the role of assets, investments, options, and portfolios and learns to trade, assess, and manage risk. The value allocation also stresses the importance of financial institutions not only for the management of the firm but also in shaping the international economic environment.

While the foregoing discussion fleshes out the core functions of a business (Figure 5.2), its sustainability depends on several other tasks that must be woven into the program to ensure competency in wealth creation. Information needs to be gathered, processed, and made available to support each operation contributing to wealth creation. In an increasingly digital environment, and with greater dependence on knowledge, wealth creation depends on systems that manage information and knowledge. Consequently, the student is exposed to data mining and big data analytics and learns to leverage artificial intelligence and machine learning to facilitate evidence-based management. Business process and project management courses help the student leverage information systems toward accomplishing organizational objectives.

Employees, customers, and other stakeholders are central to any business. Therefore, it is vital to understand people's behavior and manage their presence in organizations. This involves recruitment, selection, training, and development of employees. To that end, the student learns the intricacies of organizational behavior and human resources management and consequently picks up leadership and negotiation skills. To ensure the orderly conduct of business activities, one needs to design structures and processes. Exposure to organizational and management development as well as techniques for managing change ensures that the student has the skill set to steer the organization toward its central purpose. As mentioned earlier, business is an institution of society with obligatory corporate citizenship responsibilities. So, the program introduces the student to corporate ethics and social responsibility, obligations to the environment, and productive engagement of relevant stakeholders.

Leadership at the top provides direction for the organization and the vision for its future. Management ensures that the vision is carried out by setting goals and formulating a strategy. It involves integrating all the functions that contribute to the mission of the organization and the optimal deployment of resources toward accomplishing its mission. This involves an understanding of the global environment and the roles of business and government therein. Toward the end of the program, the student is exposed to integrative courses on strategic management, innovation, entrepreneurship, corporate governance, and legal aspects of the business. Integrative case studies and business clinics round out the skills component of strategic management.

The unique value proposition that establishes the school and program brand is introduced in a multifaceted approach. A separate course such as innovation, globalization, or sustainability, for example, would be one facet. Meriting mention in each course in terms of how those ideas influence a particular subject is another facet. In a typical 20-course MBA, the program brand is a common feature regardless of the subject matter. This creates brand awareness in the minds of students and is communicated to the employer both by the program and by the students themselves at the point of hire.

A curriculum is a living entity and is constantly revising and refreshing itself to reflect current concerns. For example, there are issues of gender, diversity, and ethnicity that require consideration. Other changes to management practice as influenced by artificial intelligence, sustainability, and the grand challenges facing humankind as articulated by the United Nations also require attention in the curriculum. They show up in the content of an effective curriculum shown in Figure 5.4. We fully expect discussion of these issues in the specific courses we have identified. These topics will be variously housed and their relevance to business theory in a globalized context incorporated in courses on organizational behavior, human resource, ethics, corporate social responsibility, consumer behavior, organizational change, organizational design, management development, governance, strategy, operations management, etc. In this work, we kept our focus on a broader enveloping notion namely globalization than elaborate on how specific course content responds to the paradigmatic push.

Incorporating Globalization

With Canada's stature as a small country without large markets or a strong manufacturing base, our strategy should not depend on the size of our markets or the capacity of the economy to consume the proceeds of our intellectual labor. Our orientation to business by necessity is through global trade and our ability to innovate. Consequently, our business training should both promote globalization and benefit from it. This calls for innovative methods to implement globalization in our business curriculum so that our business graduates can engage in the world competently and confidently. Canada is a trading nation, and we argue that the globalization of our business education will give our graduates a competitive advantage in an increasingly interconnected world. Although the pandemic has exposed fault lines in our supply chains and has given rise to insularity and nationalism that has, in turn, slowed down global trade, it is impossible to eliminate interdependency in any of our industrial sectors – not in the primary industries, not in manufacturing, and certainly not in the tertiary service sector. The future will present a different type of interdependency and a different model of globalization. We believe that Canadian business education can and should set the stage for that scenario.

We suggest that courses and seminars on globalization should be an essential part of the business curriculum in all Canadian schools with relevant aspects of globalization incorporated into every course. This will be a four-step process. The first step is to create awareness of globalization. The second step is to integrate aspects of globalization into each business course, which can be done internally at the academic and institutional levels. The third step is for Canadian business schools to become advocates of globalization collectively by engaging the profession and promoting the value of globalization among employers and the broader professional community. The fourth step involves convincing international bodies of business scholarship, such as the International Federation of Scholarly Association of Management (IFSAM) and accreditation bodies of business education, such as the Association to Advance Collegiate Schools of Business (AACSB), the European Foundation for Management Development (EFMD), and the Association of MBAs (AMBA) to require accredited MBA programs to subscribe to the idea of a connected world where both labor and capital move to promote optimization of wealth creation across the globe. This can be done at the level of BSAC and the ASAC through their lobbying mechanisms. We will elaborate on the four steps in what follows.

In the classroom, it is the instructor that creates awareness of globalization. Typically, toward the end of each course, the instructor raises two questions: (1) how is the course content relevant to globalization? and (2) how would the student use the content to promote the globalization of business? These questions are raised in each course regardless of the topic, thus creating an awareness of globalization within the context of each specific subject. When the student is exposed to these questions over 20 courses that cover the entire program, awareness of globalization becomes the common thread that links the subjects beyond the central function of wealth creation, and the issue becomes one of the wealth creation through globalization.

With the integration of this awareness, the instructors become sensitized to the issue of globalization and start substantively incorporating the concept into the curriculum. This is the second step of the four-step process. Thus, the program coheres to this notion, and globalization becomes the brand of Canadian business education. This does not preclude individual school branding. In other words, within the framework of globalization, individual schools can consolidate their programs around themes relevant to their context, such as innovation, sustainability, and evidence-based management, to promote their unique brand identity. Similarly, these themes are also woven into the curriculum through similar strategies mentioned in conjunction with globalization.

The last two steps are a collective enterprise where Canadian business schools must act in unison to canvass relevant bodies to entrench the globalization mindset. The third step begins with sensitizing employers and the profession through a systematic strategy undertaken by individual business schools and BSAC. Here we include research as well. In this context, business school leadership should simultaneously encourage the incorporation of globalization in faculty research and lobby granting agencies to prioritize funding research in this area. The fourth and final step is for BSAC to lobby accreditation institutions and international umbrella organizations that coordinate national scholarly associations in management, such as IFSAM, to incorporate globalization as part of business management curricula and research. It's important to reiterate here that globalization has been subjected to a critical evaluation during the pandemic. Emerging research offers a more sophisticated optic of globalization, which adds currency to context. For this reason, we believe it is good timing to reintroduce globalization into the business curriculum and reexamine its relevance in the post-pandemic context.

Building Competence

To this point, we have discussed business curriculum as one effective entity emerging from business theory. We now want to unpack the curriculum regarding its knowledge and skill components, as we believe that competence lies in the fusion of knowledge and skills enriched by appropriate technology and experience.

Knowledge

We argue that the knowledge that professionals use in practice comes from a combination of formal, experiential, situational, and technological expertise. Formal knowledge is what is learned in the classroom, generated through research and critical scholarship, and codified in textbooks, scholarly journals, and professional magazines. Experiential knowledge comes from both the students' and teachers' lived experiences as well as from guest lecturers and real-life case studies. Situational knowledge comes from exposure to and understanding of the context in which business unfolds and its geographic, cultural, economic, political, social, and industrial concomitants. Again, the curriculum incorporates mechanisms by which this knowledge is imparted to the student. Finally, the student professional acquires facility with the prevailing technology that provides the platform for competent professional practice.

Business schools must incorporate appropriate measures in the curriculum delivery to ensure optimal exposure to these four bodies of knowledge (Baba, 2018). Here we propose that the formal knowledge provided in the classroom becomes sensitive to the issues of globalization. We have noted that this must be appropriately introduced in every course a student takes. Experiential and situational knowledge should be embellished through explicit global references and exposure to international business contexts. At the same time, technology platforms will evolve through the delivery of other bodies of knowledge and acquire currency. In addition, we recommend a stand-alone course on globalization that integrates the value functions shown in Figure 5.3 and their curricular derivatives shown in Figure 5.4. It is important to note that these four bodies of knowledge are orthogonal. They must coalesce to provide benefits in professional practice.

132 *Management Education in Canada*

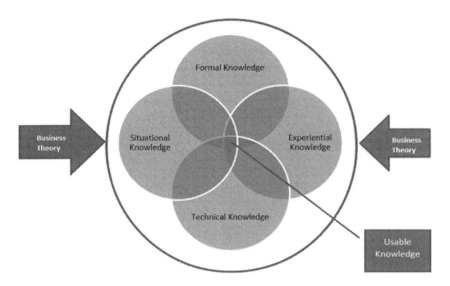

Figure 5.5 Business theory and usable knowledge.

It is business theory, as articulated earlier, that facilitates the fusion of these four bodies of knowledge. Theory helps the student understand why these four bodies of knowledge must converge to provide maximum usefulness in practice. It also illustrates that the stronger the theory, the more usable the knowledge, thus emphasizing theory-driven research. If the curriculum does not provide the theoretical push, the four bodies of knowledge may still be acquired but may not cohere to create *usable* knowledge: it is only usable knowledge that is operational in professional practice. The rest will remain dormant. Figure 5.5 shows the process by which usable knowledge is developed.

In addition, we emphasize that all four bodies of knowledge must be present in curriculum delivery. The absence of any one of these will render the resulting knowledge differentially deficient. For example, possessing experiential, situational, and technological knowledge may help students perform tasks on the job, and appropriate skill sets may be adequate in delivering competence. However, students may not understand nor be able to explain why they use these competencies without the formal knowledge they gain from textbooks and articles. In addition, this lack of understanding will worsen as the global context shifts. Similarly, in the absence of situational knowledge in a globalizing environment, when the context shifts, managers become ineffective as they are unschooled, unaware, and consequently unable to appreciate and react to the context in which they are managing. Possession of formal, situational, and technological knowledge without experiential knowledge will keep the manager guessing and unsure of how to handle certain circumstances as the demands of experiential knowledge shift from one industrial context to another.

Skill

In professional practice, knowledge is necessary, but it must be augmented with the skill to produce competence. In other words, the usable knowledge one acquires in the classroom has to be leveraged through a skill set in order to generate value. Knowledge makes professional practice effective; skills make it efficient. This is common to all professions.

Skill theory recommends four essential skill sets, which include personal skills, interpersonal skills, group skills, and organizational skills (Whetten & Cameron, 2016). Personal skills assist with analyzing and solving problems, managing one's time and stress levels, and incorporating innovative ideas in practice – each resonates with the concept of globalization. Interpersonal skills such as motivating, leading, coaching, counseling, mentoring, and communication require considerable cultural, geographic, and social sensitivity in a global context. Economic differences must also be considered when interacting with people of different backgrounds. Group skills that include training, team building, coordinating, conflict management, and project management must be nuanced in a global context for them to produce results. Organizational skills such as planning, organizing, recruitment, selection, placement, compensation, information management, and resource allocation/deployment must operationalize the globalization agenda. In essence, we recommend skill training that explicitly factors in the demands of globalization in appropriate formats that optimize each skill set outlined above.

As in the case of the four bodies of knowledge, the four skill sets are orthogonal. It is possible for individuals to possess one skill set and not the others. There needs to be a mechanism that brings these skills together to add value, which must be incorporated into the curriculum. It must build bridges between the usable knowledge gained from exposure to formal, experiential, situational, and technological expertise as well as the four skill sets.

Model of Global Competence

Competence is a multiplicative function of knowledge and skills. It can be thought of as usable knowledge that animates skill sets. Competence must be guided by management theory operating on a platform of globalization. Possession and demonstration of competence are where the scientific approach coheres with professional practice. The manager demonstrates the seven C's of competence: confidence, courage, comfort, conviction, compass, conscience, and communication. This process is enveloped by business theory to sustain itself, which, in turn, is permeated by globalization as the driving paradigm.

134 *Management Education in Canada*

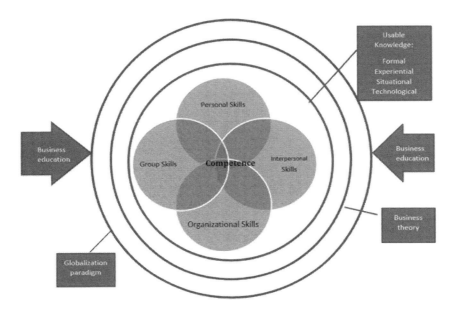

Figure 5.6 Globalization, business education, and managerial competence.

Figure 5.6 shows the interaction of knowledge and skills in the development of managerial competence and the broader roles of business theory and the globalization paradigm in developing and sustaining that competence. The inward arrows underscore the importance of the active roles that business schools play at every level of the process depicted by the concentric circles.

What we have done here is offer a working theory of managerial competence, which is an optimal combination of knowledge and skills. Codified, experiential, contextual, and technological knowledge constitute the knowledge base. The fusion of these four bodies, in turn, generates professionally usable knowledge. Paradigms such as globalization and theories of business and management facilitate the fusion. Usable knowledge contributes to managerial effectiveness. The greater the fusion, the greater the effectiveness. The personal, interpersonal, group, and organizational skills constitute the skill base. The fusion of these four skills generates a professionally valuable skill set. Usable knowledge facilitates skill fusion. Skill fusion contributes to managerial efficiency. The greater the fusion, the greater the efficiency. We argue that managerial competence is manifested by managerial effectiveness and efficiency. Our theory of competence provides a framework for designing business education, and our discussion on globalization supplies an arguably relevant envelope that guides Canadian business education.

Strategy

While business schools have developed strategies to entrench the brand paradigm, theory, and pedagogy into a unique value proposition with a competitive advantage in relevant markets, we add to that strategy to ensure that globalization is woven into their curriculum and pedagogy. In codifying knowledge that is transmitted in business school classrooms, we suggest that special attention be paid to ensure that the core body of knowledge incorporates globalization and that the theories communicated are globally portable. At the same time, they should be capable of guiding the development of context-specific models. We also suggest that research establishments and granting agencies promote the incorporation of globalization in the proposals they fund. We hope that the findings from such research are incorporated into Canadian textbooks and management training programs. We also recommend recruiting globally diverse students and faculty, using global managers and executives-in-residence for guest lectures, special seminars, and workshops, and using global case studies to provide an experiential impetus to business education. The globalization of the curriculum should be accompanied by international site visits, global exchange programs for faculty and students, international internships for students, and ongoing international partnerships in research and programming. We also recommend business faculty undertake international industry sabbaticals to bring back both experiential and situational knowledge that enriches global business education. This can also be supplemented by management development programs offered offshore. Our experience with the pandemic opened the doors to many innovative technological practices that can be utilized to entrench our schools' technology platforms in implementing our globalization agenda.

Conclusion

In this chapter, we began with an introduction to globalization and discussed its strengths and weaknesses in the context of capitalism. We argued that globalization has positively influenced both economic growth and human well-being. Consequently, we proposed that globalization may serve as a paradigmatic platform for business education. Our emphasis was on the MBA program as it is generally understood that professionalization of management takes place at this level. We offered a theory of business education that incorporates globalization as a permeating notion in generating a usable body of business knowledge that would serve as the basis for management training. We identified critical skills that contribute to managerial competence. We defined a suite of knowledge and skills and offered an integrated business education and managerial competence model that is globally relevant. We addressed the leadership role Canadian business schools should play in promoting a globalized curriculum for business education and management training and provided examples of those roles at academic, institutional, professional, and political levels. We concluded with some operational strategies for globalizing business education that Canadian business schools can implement. It is our hope that this discussion will generate interest in pushing this proposal further.

Notes

1 MBA in Canada, 2025 MBA programs in Canada https://find-mba.com/schools/americas/canada (accessed January 25, 2025).
2 Graduate Management Graduate Management Admission Council. November 2020. Demand for B-schools increases amidst global pandemic. www.gmac.com/why-gmac/gmac-news/gmac-press-releases/demand-for-b-schools-increases-amidst-global-pandemic (accessed January 25, 2025).
3 This part is based on Austin (2000) and the memories of three business school professors who participated in some activities of CCMS. According to these sources, it is also not clear when exactly CCMS went into extinction.

References

Altman, S. A., & Bastian, C. R. 2022. The state of globalization in 2021. *Harvard Business Review* https://store.hbr.org/product/the-state-of-globalization-in-2022/h06ykj?ab=at_art_idp_v1x2_s02 (accessed October 10, 2022).

Austin, B. 2020. The Administrative Sciences Association of Canada, 1957–1999. In B. Austin (ed.). *Capitalizing Knowledge: Essays on the History of Business Education in Canada* (266–294). Toronto: The University of Toronto Press.

Baba, V. V. 2018. On globalizing business training in Africa: Toward a theory of business education and managerial competence. *Africa Journal of Management*, 4(2): 137–157.

Bharadwaj, A. 2010. Globalization in management education: Challenges and strategies. *International Journal of Arts and Sciences*, 3(7): 466–477 (2010).

Boothman, B. E. C. 2000. Canadian Management Education at the Millennium. In B. Austin (ed.). *Capitalizing Knowledge: Essays on the History of Business Education in Canada* (295–356). Toronto: The University of Toronto Press.

Business Schools Association of Canada. 2022. BSAC www.bsac-aegc.ca/en/ (accessed January 25, 2025).

Chowdhury, S. D., & Mahmood, M. 2012. Societal institutions and HRM practices: An analysis of four European multinational subsidiaries in Bangladesh. *International Journal of Human Resource Management*, 23: 1808–1831.

Ciravegna, L., & Michailova, S. 2022. Why the world economy needs, but will not get, more globalization in the post-COVID-19 decade. *Journal of International Business Studies*, 53: 172–186.

Contractor, F. J. 2022. The world economy will need even more globalization in the post-pandemic 2021 decade. *Journal of International Business Studies*, 53: 156–171.

Coyne, A. 2022. With the 'Freeland doctrine', the Liberals say what's long been apparent to everyone else. *The Globe and Mail*, October 22, 2022.

Donaldson, T., & Walsh, J. P. 2015. Toward a theory of business. *Research in Organizational Behavior*, 35: 181–207. http://dx.doi.org/10.1016/j.riob.2015.10.002

Economist. 2022a June 18). Reinvesting globalisation. 443(9301):11..

Economist (2022b June 18): Chain reaction. 443(9301): 18–20.

Guttal, S. 2007. Globalisation. *Development in Practice*, 17(4–5): 523–531. http://dx.doi.org/10.1080/09614520701469492

Klein, P. G. Holmes, M. M. Jr., Foss, N., Terjesen, S., & Pepe, J. 2022. Capitalism, cronyism, and management scholarship: A call for clarity. *Academy of Management Perspectives*, 36: 6–29.

Martin, R., Tyler, P., Storper,M., Evenhuis, E., & Glasmeier, A. 2018. Globalization at a critical juncture? *Cambridge Journal of Regions, Economy and Society*, 11: 3–16

OECD Glossary of Statistical Terms (2008): http://stats.oecd.org/glossary (accessed January 25, 2025)

Parker, B. 1998. *Globalization and Business Practice: Managing across Boundaries.* London: Sage.

Penrose, E. 1959. *The Theory of the Growth of the Firm.* Oxford: Oxford University Press.

Porter, M. E. 1985. *Competitive Advantage: Creating and Sustaining Superior Performance*. New York: Free Press.

Sparrow, P., Brewster, C., & Harris, H. 2004. *Globalizing Human Resource Management.* New York: Routledge.

Statistics Canada, 2024. Population estimates quarterly https://doi.org/10.25318/1710000901-eng (accessed January 25, 2025).

Vancouver MBA. 2022, October 1. What is the history of MBA program. https://vancouver.mba/what-is-the-history-of-mba-program/ (accessed January 25 2025).

Whetten, D. A., & Cameron, K. S. 2016. *Developing Management Skills* (9th ed.). North York, ON: Pearson.

6 NIKANA'LULKWIK (Leadership)

Jeff Ward, Kristin S. Williams, and Heidi Weigand

Introduction

We write this chapter in Mi'kma'ki, the ancestral and unceded territory of the Mi'kmaq. This land is governed by the treaties of Peace and Friendship, first negotiated and signed in 1725 (Figure 6.1).

In this chapter, we offer an Indigenous perspective to contribute to our developing ideas of management education, management, and leadership. This is not to suggest such an effort has not been made before, but Indigenous perspectives on management as a discipline remains marginalized due to the legacies of colonialism and ongoing systemic racism (Gram-Hanssen, 2021; Jackson, 2013; Jorgensen et al., 2013). Traditional, Western management theories continue to dominate management practice (Holtbrügge, 2013).

We also understand that for many readers, this might be the first time you have encountered the intersection of management education and Indigenous ideas. We therefore write for a reader who might be unfamiliar with the implications of bringing together Indigenous perspectives and Western management thought. In a book about the history of management education in Canada, it is fair to characterize our chapter as a reflection on the negligence of management education to consider *Indigenous ways of knowing*, in hopes that it might inspire a more inclusive future practice.

Our chapter proceeds as follows, we begin with reflecting on our positionality as contributors and the nature of our methodological collaboration. We then share several stories from an Indigenous perspective and attempt to anchor these stories by offering contextual opportunities within Western notions of management as entry points. We are not attempting to compare Indigenous and Western perspectives on management and leadership, but rather we are trying to offer a bridge or entry point for Western scholars to contemplate the richness of Indigenous ways of knowing. We then briefly outline some of the efforts that are being made across Canada to integrate Indigenous perspectives in

DOI: 10.4324/9781003612612-7

NIKANA'LULKWIK (Leadership) 139

Illustration by Tammy Williams, Mi'kmaw Graphic Artist

Figure 6.1 Ula Kekinua'tekek ta'n telpukuiksipnek aq ta'n telsutmi'tisnek Mi'kmak'ki. Kikmanaq teluejik na l'uiknek el-tepkis-wekasikl maqmikal, tujiw klujjiew'l na saqmaq, tujiw ap miawe'k tepknuset aq n'ku'set mikwimulkwik Kisu'lkwal.
  This symbol informs us of the government and leadership in Mi'kma'ki. Our people say the seven hills represent the seven districts; the seven crosses are the seven district chiefs, while the moon and sun in the centre are there to remind us of Creator. Membertou First Nation, Heritage Park.

management education and we cite the business case for such efforts by outlining the Indigenous business footprint in Canada. We conclude with a reflection on the Calls to Action from the Truth and Reconciliation Commission (TRC) as it relates to business practice. Please see this as an invitation to respect what you will learn. Acknowledge it as a gift and share it selflessly with others so that they may also benefit.

Methods

This chapter includes stories within stories that are both allegory and autobiographical (Leskelä-Kärki, 2008). It also draws on storytelling methods and specifically postcolonial storytelling methods, which recognize the "web of complex relationships and entangled genealogies, which comprise both colonisers and the colonised/neocolonised" (Jorgensen et al., 2013, p. 45). Drawing on story-in-the-making ideas we seek to activate the process of materialization, to disrupt the reified narrative representation that currently exists in management studies (Boje, 2001). We are placing at the centre Indigenous voice and epistemology (Simonds & Christopher, 2013).

As the writer, I (Kristin Williams) bring my epistemic stance as a feminist critical historiographer. I write polemics of the heart, often learning and sharing emotionally, and writing emotionally affective and affecting text (Ferguson, 1986; Williams, 2020). Jeff Ward brings his traditional practices of storytelling to share Indigenous ways of knowing and Indigenous perspectives on leadership and management. Our third author, Heidi Weigand, though sitting in the background in this text, brings her experience of being betwixt and between, as a Western woman living in an Indigenous community and Indigenous family context and working with Indigenous leaders; she has a familiarity with two-eyed seeing and helped us navigate and sense-make.

We see our efforts as a practice of collaborating and sharing and learning. Me as writer and learner, Jeff as storyteller and teacher, and Heidi as interpreter and guide. Jeff also wants our readers to know that the stories he shares are not his own. They have come to him through personal teachings, from experience with his community, from his ancestors, through prayer and from Elders. This knowledge is passed, and he is now a knowledge sharer with a sacred responsibility to share what he has learned.

The result of our collaboration is something that is difficult to label, but we embrace it from a decolonizing standpoint (Reyes Cruz & Sonn, 2011), that engages in critical thinking and reflexivity, for inspiration and emancipatory action.

A Meeting

I first met Jeff Ward several years ago at Membertou First Nation. Jeff's spirit name is Dancing Son. He is a Mi'kmaw knowledge keeper and sharer. He grew up in Metepenagiag Mi'kmaq Nation in what we now commonly call, Red Bank, New Brunswick. He is a leader in the White Eagle Sundance, a lodge keeper, drum keeper and maker, and a conductor of ceremonies, talking circles and justice circles. At the time of writing this chapter, Jeff served as General Manager of Membertou Heritage Park.

In 2018, I was attending a youth conference at Membertou First Nation, hosted by In.Business: A Mentorship Program for Indigenous Youth in my capacity at the time as President and CEO of Junior Achievement of Nova Scotia, an organization that offers entrepreneurial education to youth. In.Business provides young leaders with the opportunity to work with Indigenous business mentors and facilitates business learning. Our two organizations shared much in terms of mission and purpose, and I wanted to learn more.

I quickly developed an appreciation for the experience that In.Business offers. It is much more than just mentorship and business education. Imbedded in the programme were opportunities to connect Indigenous youth with their traditions, history, culture, and language. This connection is seen as central to identity and without identity, youth could not be expected to explore their potential. How are youth to see themselves as enterprising individuals if they do not know who they are? This resonated with me as a significant oversight in our traditional approaches to management education.

Jeff started his lesson that day with a smudging ceremony. He lit the sage and fanned the smudge with an eagle feather and smoke billowed out. This was not something that I had ever experienced before, but Jeff explained what I was to do and explained what the ceremony was for. Smudging is a purification process – a cleansing. Invited, I fanned the smoke over my head to have positive thoughts. I fanned the smoke over my eyes to see good in everything. I fanned the smoke over my mouth to say only positive things. I fanned the smoke over my ears to hear good things from others. I fanned the smoke over my heart to create positive emotions. I fanned the smoke over my body for health and good energy.

As I sat down with my young companions from the In.Business programme, our conversation went in many directions and we spoke about many things. One young woman referred to another young woman as "cousin". I remarked that it was lovely that they were related. The young woman gently let me know that they were not actually biological cousins, but because they did not know all of their relations, nor their true name, it was customary to call each other "cousin". In the context of the lessons we were receiving about tradition, history, culture, and language, the significance dawned on me anew. In my young companions, I was seeing the vestiges of colonialism, of residential schools, of the Sixties Scoop, of historical trauma, and lost generations. These young people were trying to recognize their place and the place of others. I was starting to understand what it means to say, "all my relations".

One of our group activities was making dream catchers. These are symbols of oneness and identity in many Indigenous cultures, though many associate dream catchers with the Anishinaabe Peoples. As my fingers struggled with the fine work of weaving thread and beads in intricate strokes, my companions giggled as I scrunched up my face in concentration. In an act of solidarity and inclusion, my companions surprised me by saying that they had not made dream catchers before either. I was genuinely surprised. This was another tangible example of lost connection to culture. As my companions were connecting with their own traditions, I was connecting with each of them. I felt honoured and privileged. I was constantly reminded that I was experiencing something very special and sharing in a sacred cultural activity of so much importance, not all of it visible to me.

Since 2018, Jeff and I have found ourselves in intersecting circles of peers and colleagues. Another formal opportunity came about with a leadership series offered through the Atlantic School of Theology in 2020, where both Jeff and I were invited as speakers and panellists to offer our perspectives on leadership. In this space, we saw the ideas of spirituality, of compassion and connection infused into our ideas about what leadership can be. Spending time with Jeff was broadening my ideas. This intersection of management, leadership, and management education has shaped our relationship and is the foundation of this chapter. It is ultimately the reason I sought out Jeff to provide a perspective that I felt was so integral to this book, and I was so delighted that he agreed to be a part of the project.

Our Conversation

In our conversation, and to build out the ideas for this chapter, Jeff shared with me some key lessons that we believe hold value to management education and practice. This, understandably, cannot be an exhaustive list, it is merely a beginning. These lessons include (1) what constitutes our ideas of wealth, (2) the role of Elders (3) ceremony, (4) leadership, and (5) the medicine wheel. Underpinning these ideas are the values inherent in the seven sacred teachings. We share these lessons in story form and we also share what contemporary views within management and organizational studies have to say that might relate to these ideas and serve as entry points to broader management education discourse. However, at times, the contrast between Western thought and Indigenous perspectives are stark and contrary. Again, we are not attempting to compare ideas or conflate them, but we are hoping to help make connections for readers about where Indigenous perspectives might begin to *take up space* and *occupy* the practice of management, and the education of managers and leaders. We do believe that they will disrupt some ideas of what readers might consider to be the purview of management thought.

Wealth

The concept of wealth in economic terms is tied to wealth creation by *making money* or *adding value* (Enderle, 2009). In the context of globalization, it highlights the difference between countries who have a favourable economic situation and those who do not, and these ideas influence our notions of value and social order. Wealth often does not consider environmental harm, population health, poverty, nor the economic responsibility of organizations to create wealth while also taking social responsibility for the implications of said wealth and the pursuit of maximization (Enderle, 2009). Wealth is a fundamental concept within economics and business and considers the "total amount of economically relevant private and public assets including physical (or natural), financial, human, and 'social' capital" (p. 288). These conceptions of wealth permeate our notions of business, profit (purpose) and how individuals work together in an organization and how we teach leaders to manage organizations.

This concept of wealth has always bothered me because it supplants the health of communities for profit. So, I ask Jeff what his views of wealth are.

> *My cousin passed away. Todd Ward. And he was young at the time. It was very tragic. It was tough on all of us. But I remember, as a family, we're walking up front [in] the line walking to the graveyard. And this line of people went right to the graveyard, and right around the church. And there were still people as far as you could see. And I looked back [and] they said that this is what matters ... he had a big heart. And he did. He had a very big heart. And he was a big man too. But he you know, he was such a nice kind, kind, person, kind boy, kind man. And that's [how] we measure wealth. When it comes back to the values, you know, that love and humility, courage, respect, truth, wisdom, and honesty. So those are the seven key teachings. When you have those seven sacred teachings, it leads to true wealth. Money is not wealth to us.*

The Indigenous view of wealth is not monetary. It is based on relationships and values like generosity, responsibility, and reciprocity. *Indigenomics* is the idea that "the way we see the world shapes the way we treat it" and it points to a sharp contrast between an Indigenous world view and that of a profit-centric, Western world view (Hilton, 2021). Indigenous knowledge is ancient knowledge. Even so, we would argue it is more relevant and important today, than ever. Famed environmentalist, David Suzuki, has been arguing for decades that our constructs like economics need to shift:

> *The way we see the world shapes the way we treat it. If a mountain is a deity, not a pile of ore; if a river is one of the veins of the land, not potential irrigation water; if the forest is a sacred grove, not timber; if other species are biological kin, not resources; or if the planet is our mother, not an opportunity – then we will treat each other with greater respect. This is the challenge, to look at the world from a different perspective.*
>
> (Suzuki et al., 2008, p. 11)

Elders

An Elder is form of leadership in an Indigenous community that is not achieved based on age or title but instead it is based on a community's perception of contribution and as a holder of traditional knowledge. Elders are leaders driving positive change through traditional knowledge, often serving as advisors, or helping to act. They are not static, but dynamic. Mentors in a business context play a vital role in management education and practice. Perhaps it is easy to see the potential similarities between mentors and Elders, but there are important distinctions. Mentorship can be defined as a developmental relationship in organizations, between someone with less experience and someone with more experience (Maynard-Patrick & Baugh, 2019). Whereas Elders play a vital role in sharing, preserving, and protecting traditional knowledge, culture, and language. As I saw in the In.Business programme, Elders and mentors share space in the education of youth about their past and their futures.

I ask Jeff if he can tell me a little bit more about his experience with Elders.

It was important to earn trust before I was given responsibility. I earned that trust at a young age by working with the Elders in my community. I worked with my uncles at the church. I worked with my uncle at the school. I worked with my other uncle doing community events, picking up the garbage, cutting firewood, delivering firewood. I did anything that I was asked to do. People see me doing a lot of things. I got stronger and more knowledgeable as I grew. In our language, that describes somebody who's into everything like a squirrel. What I learned from my Elders from a very young age is that you learn by doing and showing love and taking care of others. It becomes part of you. Each lesson leads to another.

Indigenous Elders' social participation contributes to individual and community wellness (Viscogliosi et al., 2020). The "teaching of traditional knowledge and practices involves sharing values, culture and collective identity, notably through Indigenous elders' participation in education, community development, and intergenerational relationships" (p. 668). Decolonial work involves promoting opportunities for reclamation, healing and acknowledging our history (Quayle & Sonn, 2019). Amplifying the voices of Elders can not only reveal historical trauma but can share expressions of resilience, of resistance, and survival; to understand oppression and how experience frames current social realities (Quayle & Sonn, 2019). The message for contemporary managers and organizations is that organizations are the product of organizing around a shared goal, which is an expression of human activity and human experience, and these ideas cannot be disentangled from social history.

Ceremony

Organizations and organizational activities are full of "rites" of passage, "rituals", and symbols. As Jeff explained the significance of ceremony, it occurred to me that this might be how to bridge our understandings, but it is a tenuous bridge. In Western notions of business, rites, rituals, and symbols are a way to communicate corporate identity and often are used as a way to express values and shared beliefs among a collective group (with empowering properties) (Zhu, 2017). Conveying symbolism as an outwards expression of a business can be achieved through branding and logos and other material activities, but inwardly it is also a mechanism to create boundaries and control, regulating "internal solidarity and external identity" (Durkheim, 1915 as cited in, Zhu, 2017, p. 42). Workplace rituals are also ways to communicate organizational culture, create comradery, efficiency, effectiveness, and retention. Rituals communicate symbolically, the values that a business either has or hopes to espouse (Erhardt et al., 2016). Some research also purports that rituals decrease performance anxiety and regulate emotions in the routines of work (Brooks et al., 2016).

When I talk with Jeff about rituals in a management context, he shares with me a much richer teaching about ceremony from an Indigenous perspective.

> *Wisdom is in ceremony. For instance, the Sundance represents the cycle of life with the tree of life in the middle. We sing and we pray. It is medicine. There is no negativity. From sunrise to sunset, we're praying, and prayers get answered. Ceremony teaches you. It brings you back to the time that you only knew love. Just like those drums. The heartbeat [his hand over his heart begins to drum]. The heartbeat of Mother Earth. The heartbeat of your mother. It is the same sound that we've all heard. Even if we speak different languages, there are things that transcend language, like laughter, tears, and our heartbeat.*

I am struck by several things in Jeff's story. One is that ceremony is medicine. It is a way to heal from trauma (Nyman, 2012). It is not a way to control. It is a way to clear your mind and heart and spirit; restoring balancing, cultivating relationships, and nurturing creativity (Nyman, 2012). The rituals of business have the pretence of connection and belonging but are practices of regulation and control. They are not about *love*. Additionally, the rituals of business lack an important connection to knowledge and wisdom. Ceremony is a way to teach, convey knowledge with the stories of experiences and wisdom, while also honouring our connections to each other and our past (Nyman, 2012). Ceremony is the manifestation of culture and Indigenous values of belonging and identity (Chung, 2018; Wilson, 2008).

Leadership

There are several theories of leadership and many traits and behaviours that describe leaders of business. In management education, leadership, as a subject, is taught in business schools typically starting in undergraduate courses on organizational behaviour. Management defines leaders as having the capacity to exert influence and inspire achievement in an organizational context (Johns & Saks, 2017). Business students and would-be managers learn that leaders have innate traits like *intellectual ability*, but also exhibit behaviours like *consideration*. Leadership behaviours are understood on a spectrum of rewarding to punishing, resulting in satisfaction through to dejection. Leaders can adopt various communication strategies to increase quality and accountability (White, 2017). There are situational theories of leadership which consider how a leader manages contingencies (Fiedler's Contingency Theory). Leadership has also been theorized in terms of the attainment of goals (House's Path-Goal Theory). Leadership studies have also considered the loci of leadership (e.g., follower, collective, context) (Hernandez et al., 2011). And finally, leadership has also been studied in terms of the effects of leader engagement with followers, and this participation level has implications for effectiveness and efficiency.

There is hardly a dearth of leadership scholarship, but the ways in which leadership has been studied and taught leaves much room for criticism, including conceptual ambiguity and what constitutes management's responsibilities and how to achieve leadership performance, motivation and creativity (Marshall et al., 2011; Mittal & Dhar, 2015; Zoghbi-Manrique-de-Lara & Viera-Armas, 2019). Critical scholars, like myself, engage with debates about power and aspects of leadership beyond function and skills. Critical scholars are also interested in how leadership perpetuates racism (Walter et al., 2017; Winters, 2020), silences organizational actors (Calás & Smircich, 1991), the relationships between patriarchy and leadership (Rohmann & Rowold, 2009), intersectionality (Lugar et al., 2020), the ethics of care (Johansson & Edwards, 2021), and more.

My questions for Jeff relate to how he learned to be a leader and what behaviours are valued in his Indigenous culture.

Leaders go in first. They take the risk. We protect our children because they are the future. A leader gives the ingredients and teaches the lessons. [he smiles] My Elder said, "I want you to go home and make bread. Not right away. But you know when you get home learn to make bread and make bread. Okay?" So about six months later, I thought, geez, I can't make bread. William said to make bread. So, one day, I got all the ingredients out and told Stephanie Elaine, honey, "I'm going to make bread". I made the bread, and it was the best bread I have ever eaten in my life. It was warm and delicious, and I said to my wife "this is amazing!". I called William and said, "hey, I made bread" He said, "who's this?". I said, "it's me!". He said: "Oh, yeah, you made bread, hey! Well, you will never be hungry". But there was so much to it. The ingredients, kneading the dough, letting it rise. That's like a ceremony. It isn't instant. There is so much to it. Ceremony connects you to wisdom and it connects you to lived experience and that is what leadership is about. Leadership is love, community, prayer. Leadership as it relates to the seven sacred teachings, connects us to our ancestors and their teachings and instructions for a full and healthy life.

The dominant Western views and tools of leadership are grossly inadequate for considering postcolonial and anti-colonial leadership perspectives and approaches. They unwittingly preserve the ideological precepts of capitalism, colonialism, racism, and patriarchy and do not engender sincere engagement with the excluded and marginalized (Nkomo, 2011). Additionally, Western views of leadership and their representations deny agency, representation, and mechanisms for resistance for many (Nkomo, 2011). Whereas, Indigenous perspectives on leadership prioritize values like humility, altruism, generosity, cultural authenticity (Haar et al., 2019). Indigenous leadership practices are inherently relational, focusing on collectivism versus individualism, whilst honouring agency (Gram-Hanssen, 2021). Management education tends to focus on the "I" in leadership and the collective nature of leadership is not well studied. The collective locus leadership theories, however, can help bridge an understanding with the Indigenous focus on the collective (Hernandez et al., 2011), where relationships amongst group (or community) members are the most important.

The Medicine Wheel

Organizational rules are a framework to guide and understand organizational action (Mills & Murgatroyd, 1990). Rules govern behaviour and are both formal and informal, gendered and hierarchical (Mastracci & Bowman, 2015). They create social realities and inform meaning-making for organizational actors (Mastracci & Bowman, 2015). Rules, though durable, are also constantly being rewritten (Morley, 2018). Rules can also help elevate lower-power individuals in an organizational context (Portillo & DeHart-David, 2009).

The medicine wheel has deep spiritual meaning as a powerful symbol of cycles: day and night, directions, seasons, birth, life, and death. The medicine wheel has the capacity to teach many concepts, illustrate, and share philosophy. These ideas spoke to me of a "cosmic order" but also of knowledge (the product of experience). Rules within organizations attempt to communicate the accumulated wisdom of organizational actors, but they are a shallow representation of the wisdom of the medicine wheel. However, I believe that this loose connection serves to onboard these insights, so I ask Jeff to tell me about the medicine wheel.

> The medicine wheel is about people. People need medicine. Just as it is important to recognize our sameness it is also important to recognise our difference. The danger of saying we are all one colour is that we are disrespecting people's culture, language, or upbringing and who they are. So, when we are standing in a circle, you are standing side by side equally, but the medicine wheel also acknowledges our differences. There are many different ways that this concept is expressed, all reflecting the importance of wholeness and balance and the significance of the number four: four seasons, four directions, four elements, four aspects of our nature and four life stages. There is no beginning and no end. And though the meaning may vary according to a specific region or Elder or spiritual advisory, it helps us understand ourselves and that the human capacity to develop is infinite.

What organizational rules tend to do is treat organizational actors within hierarchal orders as the same or similar; protecting a select few to occupy freer positions (while also curtailing resistance) (Bonilla-Silva, 2021). It is challenging for organizations to honour both sameness and difference. In organizing people, rules are cloaked as justice-seeking strategies, suggesting the means to achieve equality (not necessarily inclusivity or equity) (Williams & Mills, 2019). However, what makes discrimination systemic is rules (the maintenance of individual-level behaviours that are routinized and practiced as rules) (Bonilla-Silva, 2021).

The medicine wheel provides a conceptual framework to create a culturally relevant and ethical space for engagement and growth; simultaneously demonstrating interconnectedness, interrelatedness, and balance (Rieger et al., 2021). It is based on the values of mutual trust and respectful processes as well as relationships, reciprocity, and reconciliation. It is one way that Indigenous Peoples govern collaboration. The medicine wheel honours the four quadrants of intellectual, spiritual, physical, and emotional wellbeing, as well as our sameness and our difference (Rieger et al., 2021). It both denotes roles, but also forms of action. It's a paradigm that helps "situate or make sense of the varied and often interconnected processes experienced" (Tanner et al., 2022, p. 2836).

The Seven Virtues

As I stated in the beginning, there are seven sacred teachings that underpin Jeff's knowledge sharing. He describes these as both teachings, but also natural laws left by ancestors, like original instructions, conveyed in an origin story. These seven teachings include honesty, humility, wisdom, love, respect, truth, and courage.

I ask Jeff to explain the seven sacred teachings to me. He tells me that he uses the animal world to help represent the seven sacred teachings because it is a way to acknowledge that we must live close to the earth and in harmony with it.

> ***Love** is represented by the Eagle as to feel love is to know the creator. The Eagle can take your prayers to the creator. We must first love ourselves before we can love another person. It is the most powerful medicine.* ***Humility*** *is represented by the wolf. The wolf is in a pack and as such we honour the commitment to family: to provide, protect, share, and guide. We must never think that we are above or more important than anyone else. This sacred teaching cannot be taught it can only be role modeled.* ***Courage*** *is represented by the bear, who is gentle by nature but protective of their young. The bear reminds us to honour our Elders who know the medicines. It takes courage to make change and to have the moral and mental strength to over cover fears that prevent us from living.* ***Respect*** *is represented by the buffalo and reminds us to acknowledge our ancestors and call upon them for help and direction, and to seek forgiveness. A buffalo faces the storm head on.* ***Truth*** *is represented by the turtle, and it is the oldest symbol. As the oldest symbol it ensures that the laws are not lost and that we remain faithful. The turtle also represents Turtle Island [North America].* ***Wisdom*** *is represented by the beaver, and it reflects the idea of building a community with all the gifts that people are given. The beaver must use his teeth to build his dam, and we must use our gifts as well. The final sacred teaching is* ***honesty****, and it represented by the Sabe, which means to walk tall and to have integrity. It represents the promises we keep to the creator and to ourselves. It is the highest honour to be an honest person.*

Throughout this chapter I have found entry points in the management and leadership literature, but I will not do so here. The seven sacred teachings transcend these ideas and are about the human experience, about faith, about community, and about love. We bring ourselves into organizations and if we can honour the sacred teachings, my impression is that organizations would be very different places. If we built organizations like a community, we would have the capacity to be very different kinds of leaders.

Making Connections

The incorporation and adoption of Indigenous perspectives in management education requires the inclusion of Indigenous Peoples. The In.Business programme mentioned at the start of this chapter was created in 2014 to help facilitate business mentorship in five regions across Canada and to help encourage Indigenous youth to study business (Bourassa, 2017). By 2025 it is estimated that there will be over 600,000 young Indigenous Peoples entering the workforce and in many parts of Canada, Indigenous youth are some of the fastest-growing populations throughout Canada (Bourassa, 2017). However, there is considerable work to be done to equalize the opportunities for Indigenous youth and to empower them to seek business futures.

You might ask, where is this intersection of business education and Indigenous knowledge happening? The First Nations University of Canada is a unique Canadian institution that specializes in Indigenous knowledge and post-secondary education in a culturally supportive environment. In addition to non-business degrees, they offer a degree in Indigenous Business & Public Administration that emphasizes "a unique First Nations perspective in the fields of business management and public administration". In Eastern Canada, the Purdy Crawford Chair in Aboriginal Business is housed in the Shannon School of Business at Cape Breton University. Established in 2010 to promote the interests of Indigenous Peoples to study business at the post-secondary level. The university also houses Unama'ki College, "the vibrant heartbeat of Indigenous education at CBU for more than 40 years". The college embraces the knowledge and wisdom and traditions of the Mi'kmaq People. In the West, the Ch'nook Indigenous Business Education initiative resides in the UBC Sauder School of Business at the University of British Columbia, with a mission to develop "leadership and management skills for business success and economic independence for Indigenous leaners, leaders and entrepreneurs". In the Alberta School of Business, at the University of Alberta, a course is offered to undergraduate and graduate students to learn and explore the "challenges facing Indigenous entrepreneurs and business". In central Canada, the Indigenous Business Education Partners, within Asper School of Business at the University of Manitoba links Indigenous undergraduate and graduate students with networking opportunities, tutoring, bursaries, and scholarships with a "dedicated team". There are also universities offering various Indigenous business training, such as a partnership between the Centre for Business Venturing at Smith School of Business at Queens University and Splayan Education Group (an Indigenous company that recruits Indigenous knowledge keepers and sharers to create and deliver "Indigenized training programs in community") announced in 2021. This initiative provides specialized training in business applications, proposal writing, and Indigenous leadership. And while this does not put Indigenous perspectives on par with Western notions of business and economics, a growing imperative suggests that neither business nor management education can continue to ignore the value of Indigenous perspectives, Indigenous business cases, Indigenous business, and Indigenous leaders (Lewingson, 2021). The most recent initiative we could find is at the University of Victoria's Peter B. Gustavson School of Business that announced "the world's first custom MBA in Indigenous Reconciliation" (July 2022).

The Government of Canada has several programmes which support Indigenous business development, including access to capital, opportunities, procurement, and partnership initiatives. However, with our history in Canada, we have work to do. The current support does not address what was stolen through unceded land and lost generations. The Indian Residential Schools Settlement Agreement, the largest class-action settlement in Canadian history, began to be implemented in 2007 (Government of Canada, 2022). One of the elements of the agreement was the establishment of the TRC of Canada. The TRC spent six years hearing from more than 6,500 witnesses to engage and educate the Canadian public about the history and legacy of residential schools. In 2015, 94 Calls to Action were presented in a final report. The Calls to Action span child welfare, education, health, language and culture, and justice. On behalf of Indigenous Peoples, they seek equity in the legal system, self-determination in spiritual matters, education for reconciliation and training for public servants. With respect to business, the Calls for Action ask for meaningful consultation, informed consent, equitable access to jobs, training, education and intercultural competency, conflict resolution, and human rights training for management (National Centre for Truth and Reconciliation, 2022). At the core of Truth and Reconciliation is a process of healing relationships, public truth, and the creation of a more equitable and inclusive society.

Despite past and present injustices, the footprint of Indigenous business in Canada is significant and this reinforces the need to support Indigenous business with managers, leaders, and human talent, in addition to providing the aforementioned supports, while also addressing the legacies of colonization, which have left Indigenous Peoples suffering institutional and systemic racism, more heavily represented in incarcerated populations, foster care, as well as disproportionally impoverished and isolated. The business profile of Indigenous-owned companies is Canada is significant: there are over 50,000 Indigenous-owned companies in Canada, contributing over $30 billion to the Canadian economy, and 24% Indigenous-owned small and medium-sized enterprises (SMEs) in Canada export to varying degrees (EDC, 2020).

Conclusion

As I pen this conclusion, it is April 2022. Jeff is in the news today. He has been asked for his opinion on the papal apology. He says, "recognition is the start of healing. That's the first spark" (Ayers, 2022b). Jeff's mother is a survivor of residential schools (Ayers, 2022a). He wants our society to change as a whole and for Indigenous Peoples to have "unconditional acceptance" (Ayers, 2022b). He has every reason to be angry and sad and yet, he is hopeful. I think that our purpose in writing this chapter is to create a spark as well. A spark of reflection, a spark of connection – the belief we can be better by doing better.

Jeff shares with me his final thoughts:

Maw glu'lg goqwei Lnueiei gepmite'tmg.
It's really good to respect things pertaining to our people.

Acknowledgement

Jeff would like to acknowledge his wife Stephanie, his children Tyler, Tanaysha, Oonig, and Shaya. His grandson, Elijah. His parents, Yvonne Paul-Meunier and Sylvester Ward and Joe Meunier, Grandparents: Gregory Peter-Paul (seventh son of the seventh son) Bertha Sewell, Former Chief William Ward and Mary Veronica Caplin Ward. All my Uncles and Aunties and Cousins, and Ancestors. My Sundance Chiefs William Nevins, Keith Chief Moon, Danny Ward, Arnold Joe, and My White Eagle Sundance Family. Uncle George Paul, Albert Lightening, Dr. Jesse Morris, Paul Brisk, Pauline Bernard, Jane Meader, Katy McEwen, Todd Vassallo, and many more.

References

Ayers, T. (2022a, March 26). Why a 400-year relationship between Mi'kmaq and Catholic Church is under pressure. *CBC News*, 1–11. www.cbc.ca/news/canada/nova-scotia/some-m-ikmaw-react-strongly-to-pope-francis-apology-1.6405426

Ayers, T. (2022b, April 1). Papal apology for residential school abuses draws strong reaction from Mi'kmaw leaders. *CBC News*, 1–5. www.cbc.ca/news/canada/nova-scotia/some-m-ikmaw-react-strongly-to-pope-francis-apology-1.6405426

Boje, D. M. (2001). *Narrative methods for organizational & communication research*. Sage Publications.

Bonilla-Silva, E. (2021). What makes systemic racism systemic? *Sociological Inquiry*, *91*(3), 513–533. https://doi.org/10.1111/soin.12420

Bourassa, C. (2017). In.Business: A National Mentorship Program for Indigenous Youth (Issue March). www.cbu.ca/indigenous-initiatives/in-business-program (January 30, 2025).

Brooks, A. W., Schroeder, J., Risen, J. L., Gino, F., Galinsky, A. D., Norton, M. I., & Schweitzer, M. E. (2016). Don't stop believing: Rituals improve performance by decreasing anxiety. *Organizational Behavior and Human Decision Processes*, *137*, 71–85. https://doi.org/10.1016/j.obhdp.2016.07.004

Calás, M. B., & Smircich, L. (1991). Voicing seduction to silence leadership. *Organization Studies*, *12*(4), 567–601. https://doi.org/10.1177/017084069101200406

Chung, S. (2018). Education is ceremony: Thinking with stories of Indigenous youth and families. *LEARNing Landscapes*, *11*(2), 93–108. https://doi.org/10.36510/learnland.v11i2.949

EDC. (2020, June 19). Building trust with Canada's Indigenous business community. 1–10. www.edc.ca/en/article/building-relationships-with-indigenous-businesses.html (January, 30, 2025).

Enderle, G. (2009). A rich concept of wealth creation beyond profit maximization and adding value. *Journal of Business Ethics*, *84*(3 Suppl.), 281–295. https://doi.org/10.1007/s10551-009-0205-y

Erhardt, N., Martin-Rios, C., & Heckscher, C. (2016). Am I doing the right thing? Unpacking workplace rituals as mechanisms for strong organizational culture. *International Journal of Hospitality Management*, *59*, 31–41. https://doi.org/10.1016/j.ijhm.2016.08.006

Ferguson, M. (1986). Feminist Polemic: British women's writings in English from the late renaissance to the French Revolution. *Women's Studies International Forum, 9*(3), 451–464.

Government of Canada. (2022). *Crown-Indigenous Relations and Northern Affairs Canada: Reconciliation.* Truth and Reconciliation Commission of Canada. www.rcaanc-cirnac.gc.ca/eng/1450124405592/1529106060525

Gram-Hanssen, I. (2021). Individual and collective leadership for deliberate transformations: Insights from Indigenous leadership. *Leadership, 17*(5), 519–541. https://doi.org/10.1177/1742715021996486

Haar, J., Roche, M., & Brougham, D. (2019). Indigenous insights into ethical leadership: A study of Māori Leaders. *Journal of Business Ethics, 160*(3), 621–640. https://doi.org/10.1007/s10551-018-3869-3

Hernandez, M., Eberly, M. B., Avolio, B. J., & Johnson, M. D. (2011). The loci and mechanisms of leadership: Exploring a more comprehensive view of leadership theory. *Leadership Quarterly, 22*(6), 1165–1185. https://doi.org/10.1016/j.leaqua.2011.09.009

Hilton, C. A. (2021). *Indigenomics: Taking a seat at the economic table.* New Society.

Holtbrügge, D. (2013). Indigenous management research. *Management International Review, 53*(1), 1–11. https://doi.org/10.1007/s11575-012-0160-1

Jackson, T. (2013). Reconstructing the Indigenous in African management research: Implications for international management studies in a globalized world. *Management International Review, 53*(1), 13–38. https://doi.org/10.1007/s11575-012-0161-0

Johansson, J., & Edwards, M. (2021). Exploring caring leadership through a feminist ethic of care: The case of a sporty CEO. *Leadership.* https://doi.org/10.1177/1742715020987092

Johns, G., & Saks, A. M. (Eds.). (2017). *Organizational Behaviour: Understanding and Managing Life at Work* (10th ed.). Pearson.

Jorgensen, K., Strand, A., & Boje, D. (2013). Towards a postcolonial-storytelling theory of management and organisation. *Philosophy of Management, 12*(1), 43–66. https://doi.org/10.5840/pom20131214

Leskelä-Kärki, M. (2008). Narrating life stories in between the fictional and the autobiographical. *Qualitative Research, 8*(3), 325–332. https://doi.org/10.1177/1468794108093628

Lewington, J. (2021, November 19). Business schools launch 'overdue' efforts to Indigenize curricula. *The Voice of Clean Capitalism: Corporate Knights.*

Lugar, C. W., Garrett-Scott, S., Novicevic, M. M., Popoola, I. T., Humphreys, J., & Mills, A. J. (2020). The historic emergence of intersectional leadership: Maggie Lena Walker and the Independent Order of St. Luke. *Leadership, 16*(2), 220–240. https://doi.org/10.1177/1742715019870375

Marshall, S. J., Orrell, J., Cameron, A., Bosanquet, A., & Thomas, S. (2011). Leading and managing learning and teaching in higher education. *Higher Education Research and Development, 30*(2), 87–103. https://doi.org/10.1080/07294360.2010.512631

Mastracci, S., & Bowman, L. (2015). Public agencies, gendered organizations: The future of gender studies in public management. *Public Management Review, 17*(6), 857–875. https://doi.org/10.1080/14719037.2013.867067

Maynard-Patrick, S., & Baugh, S. G. (2019). The role of felt obligation to mentor in mentor performance: An exploration of generalized reciprocity in mentoring.

Career Development International, *24*(7), 619–635. https://doi.org/10.1108/CDI-11-2018-0286

Mills, A. J., & Murgatroyd, S. J. (1990). *Organizational rules: A framework for understanding organizational action*. Milton Keynes England.

Mittal, S., & Dhar, R. (2015). Transformational leadership and employee creativity. *Management Learning*, *53*(5), 894–910.

Morley, T. (2018). Making the business case for diversity and inclusion. *Strategic HR Review*, *17*(1), 58–60. https://doi.org/10.1108/shr-10-2017-0068

National Centre for Truth and Reconciliation. (2022). TRC Website. https://nctr.ca/about/history-of-the-trc/trc-website/

Nkomo, S. M. (2011). A postcolonial and anti-colonial reading of "African" leadership and management in organization studies: Tensions, contradictions and possibilities. *Organization*, *18*(3), 365–386. https://doi.org/10.1177/1350508411398731

Nyman, S. (2012). *Indigenous ceremony and traditional knowledge: Exploring their use as models for healing the impacts of traumatic experiences*. University of Victoria. www.collectionscanada.gc.ca/obj/thesescanada/vol2/BVIV/TC-BVIV-5875.pdf

Portillo, S., & DeHart-David, L. (2009). Gender and organizational rule abidance. *Public Administrative Review*, *69*(2), 339–347.

Quayle, A. F., & Sonn, C. C. (2019). Amplifying the voices of Indigenous elders through community arts and narrative inquiry: Stories of oppression, psychosocial suffering, and survival. *American Journal of Community Psychology*, *64*(1–2), 46–58. https://doi.org/10.1002/ajcp.12367

Reyes Cruz, M., & Sonn, C. C. (2011). (De)colonizing culture in community psychology: Reflections from critical social science. *American Journal of Community Psychology*, *47*(1), 203–214. https://doi.org/10.1007/s10464-010-9378-x

Rieger, K. L., Bennett, M., Martin, D., Hack, T. F., Cook, L., & Hornan, B. (2021). Digital storytelling as a patient engagement and research approach with First Nations women: How the medicine wheel guided our Debwewin* journey. *Qualitative Health Research*, *31*(12), 2163–2175. https://doi.org/10.1177/10497323211027529

Rohmann, A., & Rowold, J. (2009). Gender and leadership style: A field study in different organizational contexts in Germany. *Equal Opportunities International*, *28*(7), 545–560. https://doi.org/10.1108/02610150910996399

Simonds, V. W., & Christopher, S. (2013). Adapting western research methods to indigenous ways of knowing. *American Journal of Public Health*, *103*(12), 2185–2192. https://doi.org/10.2105/AJPH.2012.301157

Suzuki, D., McConnell, A., & Mason, A. (2008). *The sacred balance: Rediscovering our place in nature* (3rd ed.). Greystone Books.

Tanner, B., Plain, S., George, T., George, J., Mushquash, C. J., Bernards, S., Ninomiya, M. M., & Wells, S. (2022). Understanding social determinants of First Nations health using a four-domain model of health and wellness based on the medicine wheel: Findings from a community survey in one First Nation. *International Journal of Environmental Research and Public Health*, *19*(5). https://doi.org/10.3390/ijerph19052836

Viscogliosi, C., Asselin, H., Basile, S., Borwick, K., Couturier, Y., Drolet, M. J., Gagnon, D., Obradovic, N., Torrie, J., Zhou, D., & Levasseur, M. (2020). Importance of Indigenous elders' contributions to individual and community wellness: results from a scoping review on social participation and intergenerational solidarity.

Canadian Journal of Public Health, 111(5), 667–681. https://doi.org/10.17269/s41997-019-00292-3

Walter, A. W., Ruiz, Y., Tourse, R. W. C., Kress, H., Morningstar, B., MacArthur, B., & Daniels, A. (2017). Leadership matters: How hidden biases perpetuate institutional racism in organizations. *Human Service Organizations Management, Leadership and Governance, 41*(3), 213–221. https://doi.org/10.1080/23303131.2016.1249584

White, B. J. (2017). A leadership and professional development teaching and learning model for undergraduate management programs. *Journal of Higher Education Theory and Practice, 17*(4), 57–74.

Williams, K. S. (2020). Finding Viola: The untrue, true story of a groundbreaking female African Nova Scotian entrepreneur. *Culture and Organization*. https://doi.org/10.1080/14759551.2020.1833207

Williams, K. S., & Mills, A. J. (2019). The problem with women: A feminist interrogation of management textbooks. *Management and Organizational History, 14*(2), 148–166. https://doi.org/10.1080/17449359.2019.1598436

Wilson, S. (2008). *Research is ceremony: Indigenous research methods*. Fernwood Publishing.

Winters, M. (2020). Black fatigue: Racism, organizations, and the role of future leadership. *Leader to Leader, 2020*(98), 7–13. https://doi.org/10.1002/ltl.20539

Zhu, Y. (2017). Creation of corporate identity: The role of rites and symbol in management. *International Journal of Business Anthropology, 7*(2), 39–64.

Zoghbi-Manrique-de-Lara, P., & Viera-Armas, M. (2019). Does ethical leadership motivate followers to participate in delivering compassion? *Journal of Business Ethics, 154*, 195–210. https://doi.org/10.1007/s10551-017-3454-1

7 The Ubuntu Mindset

Learning to Manage and Lead Better Together, the Africentric Way

George Frempong and Raavee Kadam

Introduction

Canada is home to diverse cultures and communities that have given the country its distinctive reputation of being a very inclusive and welcoming society. One such prominent community, the Black community, accounts for 3.5% of Canada's total population and 15.6% of the population defined as a visible minority (Statistics Canada, 2022). The first recorded Black person to arrive in Canada was Mathieu Da Costa from Africa in 1608. Historical records describe him as an interpreter of the Mi'kmaq language to the governor of Acadia (Library and Archives Canada, 2022). Since then, there has been a steady stream of migration of Black people into Canada via Africa, Europe, the Caribbean, and the United States (Library and Archives Canada, 2022). While a majority of the Black population can trace their roots in Canada back to many generations, others have immigrated in recent decades. Since the early 1600s, Black Canadians have contributed to Canada's growth and development and are indispensable to the country's culture and heritage. Despite the contributions of people of African descent to the diversification and strengthening of this country, the depth of Black underrepresentation in social, legal, and educational institutions has sustained over the years. Within the higher education landscape also, data has consistently indicated a significant achievement gap amongst Black learners as compared to other students. To address the same, the Scarborough Charter on Anti-Black Racism and Black Inclusion in Canadian Higher Education called for bold, decisive, and transformative action by post-secondary institutions to combat anti-Black racism and foster Black inclusion in higher education. Amongst other action items, the charter emphasized "decentring epistemic Eurocentrism" and "acknowledging the role that institutions of higher education have played in constructing the bodies of knowledge about historically excluded groups and acknowledging the ethical responsibility to give voice to alternative ways of knowing while supporting community capacity building" (Inter-Institutional Advisory Committee, 2021, p. 5). While Canadian universities and colleges

DOI: 10.4324/9781003612612-8

have committed to furthering the equity, diversity, and inclusion agenda and are taking extensive measures to bring about a change in institutional policies, practices, and structures, true transformation can happen when teaching and learning also reflect the diverse knowledge systems of the communities that call Canada their home.

Business schools and colleges in Canada endeavour to foster educational excellence and prepare students for an increasingly complex global work environment. They play a pivotal role in enabling future managers to realize their full potential and thrive in their workplaces. However, Eurocentric and Anglo-American thought processes and philosophies have played a central role in shaping what is taught and learned in business schools. The dominant focus on teaching Western management theories has led to the exclusion of other knowledge systems and alternative worldviews from the praxis of management education. The absence of these knowledge systems from business schools has led to "institutional barriers that are systematically reproduced, often through the isomorphic tendencies of business schools that recreate common values and knowledge production standards" (Doucette, et al., 2021, p. 473). Emphasizing the significance of other knowledge systems, Breidlid (2009) indicates that "any pedagogical act is a symbolic act of violence, since it more or less takes for granted that a certain knowledge system and certain pictures of how the world is perceived (hegemonic discourses) are more legitimate than others" (p. 118). The myopic focus on Western thought processes has led to the development of managerial thought and practice that is predominantly informed by "primacy of individualism, self-interest, and the pursuit of wealth creation through profit maximization and economic growth" (Woods et al., 2022, p. 84). As we contemplate the future of business schools in the post-pandemic era, Indigenous values and multiple perspectives play a prominent role in reiterating the relational nature of humankind, which has become highly evident during the Covid-19 pandemic. This makes the role of the business schools even more critical in providing counter-narratives rather than a monolithic emphasis on Western knowledge. The inclusion of different Indigenous knowledge systems can act as a catalyst in education to "empower communities to participate in their educational development since it respects diversity and acknowledges the challenge of the hegemony of Western Eurocentric forms of universal knowledge" (Saurombe, 2021, p. 30). We introduce the Africentric philosophy of Ubuntu that provides a way to address some of the individualistic ethics that form the basis of most theories in management (Lutz, 2009) and provides alternative perspectives to Western managerial thought and practice.

The Black ways of knowing, being, and doing are highly diverse and encompass the rich culture and traditions of Black communities from across the globe (Hailu & Tachine, 2021). Africentric knowledge systems have a rich heritage that has shaped and defined the way of life for Black people for centuries.

Integrating this Black expertise and knowledge in higher education has the power to enhance our shared knowledge that can inform our thought processes and the actions we take. This chapter focuses on one such philosophy of Ubuntu that is pervasive in the African continent and can be adopted within the praxis of management education to train future managers and leaders to develop people-centred mindsets. Ubuntu as a management philosophy can help integrate new perspectives of organizational and people management within management education that differ from the individualistic and utilitarian thinking of Western management philosophies (Mutwarasibo & Iken, 2019). According to van der Colff (2003), "values such as Ubuntu should not only be seen as African values but also human values that are important in establishing both an enabling organizational culture and a set of skills and competencies valued in most organizational contexts" (p. 257). The principal argument of this chapter is the inclusion of Africentric knowledge systems in management education in Canada "as a way to infuse Western conceived theories of management with Indigenous ontologies" (Mangaliso et al., 2021, p. 1). Dei and Kempf (2011) contend that Africentric teachings such as Ubuntu are "rooted in a worldview that espouses social responsibility, community belonging, mutual interdependence, respect for self, group and community, authority and the duties of citizen responsibility" (p. 1). Similarly, Horwitz (2012) states that African Indigenous thought systems reflect high collectivism and group solidarity tendencies, which are especially important as organizations worldwide continue to recover from the aftermath of the Covid-19 pandemic and work towards building a resilient and sustainable future. This chapter makes a case for the inclusion of Africentric theories and practices to enrich global management scholarship and expand the current management discourse by bringing together Western and African intellect. The next part of the chapter focusses on understanding the concept of Ubuntu and how it has been (and can be) applied within the study of management and leadership.

Ubuntu as a Defining African Philosophy

The philosophy of Ubuntu underlies the beliefs, values, and practices of the various African societies and forms the core of most traditional African cultures (Woermann & Engelbrecht, 2019). According to Gade (2011), Ubuntu is an African philosophy, an ethic, or a worldview that first emerged in written sources during the second half of the 1900s. Nussbaum (2003) defines Ubuntu as an "underlying social philosophy of African culture" and one of "the inspiring dimensions of life in Africa" (p. 1). The concept of Ubuntu is found in the African Bantu languages and is derived from the Bantu Nguni languages of Zulu, Xhosa, Swati, and Ndebele (Ncube, 2010). It shares its roots with the word "*bantu*", which means "people" and denotes the importance of community and connection (Ngomane, 2020). Ubuntu is commonly referred to by an African aphorism that exists in almost all African languages of South Africa – "*umuntu ngumuntu ngabantu*" (Mangaliso et al., 2021) or the Sotho version, "*motho ke motho ke batho*" (McDonald, 2010), which translates to the basic idea of Ubuntu – "I am, because we are and since we are, therefore I am" (Mbiti, 1989, p. 106). In other words, human beings achieve humanity through their relations with other human beings, or likewise, a person is a person only through other persons (Pérezts et al., 2020). Tauetsile (2021) mentions the different equivalents of Ubuntu found in different sub-Saharan African states, such as "in Tanzania, it is called Ujamaa; in Botswana, it is known as Botho; in Ghana, it is referred to as Biakoye; in Zimbabwe, Nunhu, in Uganda Abantu and popularly referred to as Omoluabi and the Yoruba of Nigeria" (p. 248). Furthermore, in Rwanda and Burundi, it means human generosity, whereas in parts of Kenya, "*utu*" means that every action by an individual should be for the benefit of the larger community (Ngomane, 2020). According to Hailey (2008), though the term Ubuntu is commonly found in the Nguni languages of Southern Africa, there are words with a similar meaning found throughout sub-Saharan Africa. For example, "botho (Sesotho or Setswana), bumuntu (kiSukuma and Kihayi in Tanzania), bomoto (Bobangi in Congo) and gimuntu (kiKongo and giKwese in Angola), umundu (Kikuyu in Kenya), umuntu (Uganda), umunthu (Malawi), vumuntu (shiTsonga and shiTswa in Mozambique)" (Hailey, 2008, p. 3). Though the concept of Ubuntu might be known by different words in different parts of Africa, they all embrace the same central value of humanity. According to Karsten and Illa (2005), "Ubuntu expresses an African view of the world anchored in its own person, culture, and society which is difficult to define in a Western context" (p. 613) and emphasizes the common bond of humanity and being connected to one another (Nansubuga & Munene, 2020). The Ubuntu concept sees human potential and attributes the success of individuals to their interactions and relations with others (Ngambi, 2011).

Two of the prominent icons in the history of South Africa – Nelson Mandela and Desmond Tutu – not only embodied Ubuntu but also taught millions to discover that same spirit within themselves. On the occasion of Nelson Mandela's 100th birthday, the former president of the United States, Barack Obama, while speaking in Johannesburg, South Africa, quoted that Madiba "*understood the ties that bind the human spirit*" (The White House – Office of the Press Secretary, 2013). He further added:

> there is a word in South Africa – Ubuntu – that describes his greatest gift: his recognition that we are all bound together in ways that can be invisible to the eye; that there is a oneness to humanity; that we achieve ourselves by sharing ourselves with others and caring for those around us.
>
> (p. 1)

160 *Management Education in Canada*

Nobel Peace laureate and the late Archbishop Emeritus Desmond Tutu, in his book *No Future without Forgiveness* (Tutu, 1999), talked about Ubuntu being:

> the very essence of being human. Ubuntu speaks particularly about the fact that you can't exist as a human being in isolation. It speaks about our interconnectedness. You can't be human all by yourself, and when you have this quality – Ubuntu – you are known for your generosity. We think of ourselves far too frequently as just individuals, separated from one another, whereas you are connected and what you do affects the whole world. When you do well, it spreads out; it is for the whole of humanity.
>
> (p. 31)

Highlighting this collectivist aspect of the African philosophy as opposed to individualism found in Western societies, he further reiterated that Ubuntu is not "I think therefore I am, but rather "I am human, therefore I belong, I participate, I share" (Tutu, 1999, p. 31). Ubuntu can be defined as "humanness, a pervasive spirit of caring and community, harmony and hospitality, respect and responsiveness that individuals and groups display for one another" (Mangaliso, 2001, p. 24). It is about the larger network of relationships within which an individual is situated and forms connections with others. Ubuntu highlights interdependence and interconnectedness as central values to human existence and asserts that the relationship between an individual and the community is important, interdependent, and mutually beneficial (West, 2014). Desmond Tutu's granddaughter and author Mungi Ngomane, in her book *Everyday Ubuntu: Living Better Together, the African Way*, writes, "Ubuntu refutes the notion that a person can ever be self-made, because we all are interconnected. We should not be fooled by the myth of self-made individual, as no one exists in true isolation" (Ngomane, 2020, p. 25).

According to Broodryk (2002), Ubuntu has been in Africa as long as the human race and the core values are "similar to the '*assegais*' (Zulu word for spear), which are used to defend brotherhood, manage society and guide interpersonal relations" (as cited in Poovan et al., 2006, p. 18). These core values of the Ubuntu philosophy can be derived from the Collective Fingers Theory given by Mbigi (1997) in his book titled *Ubuntu: The African Dream in Management*. Referring to the fingers on our hand, he stated that "a thumb although it is strong cannot kill aphids on its own; it would require the collective cooperation of the other fingers" (Mbigi, 1997, p. 33). So similarly, for an individual to accomplish a collective goal, they would need the collective support and cooperation of other individuals. The five fingers represent the five core values of Ubuntu as identified by Mbigi (1997), namely, compassion, dignity, respect, solidarity, and survival, which are "interdependent and synergetic and need to come together to build and maintain the collective culture" (Hailey, 2008, p. 12). Although different researchers talk about the diverse values of Ubuntu, all those values essentially signify the collective way of African life (Poovan et al., 2006). In the book *Understanding South Africa*, the author Johanne Broodryk (2007) states the eight different values of Ubuntu, namely, compassion, forgiveness, responsibility, honesty, self-control, care, love, and perseverance. Some other fundamental values of Ubuntu, as stated by different scholars, include "humanness, dignity, empathy and compassion for others" (Mangaliso, 2001, p. 31). Furthermore, Mangaliso et al. (2021) talk about values such as "harmony and solidarity, reciprocity, respect for elders, collaboration, mutual concern, compassion, consultation, and consensus" (p. 5) that form the central tenets of Ubuntu. Also, practising Ubuntu is about one's adherence to "collective trust, deference to rank and seniority, sanctity of reciprocity and good social and personal relations" (Horwitz, 2012, p. 2943). A central point of departure in the concept of Ubuntu as compared to Western thinking is the relational way of thinking about "being" (Asamoah & Yeboah-Assiamah, 2019). Ubuntu emphasizes the relationality among individuals and addresses the interconnectedness and interdependency among individuals and their communities (McDonald, 2010). Ubuntu can be understood as "in and by relationships" (Pérezts et al., 2020, p. 732) and with the idea that "altruism is the highest form of self-interest and by serving others well, one ultimately serves one's own best interests" (Mangaliso et al., 2018, p. 4). Thus, the nature of Ubuntu is more collectivist and communitarian, with an emphasis on relationality and solidarity with the group, and humanity as the underlying principle. As Broodryk (2007) states, "humanity finds fulfillment only in community with others" and Ubuntu as a philosophy places communal interests above that of the individual (McDonald, 2010).

Ubuntu as a Management Philosophy

As a management philosophy, Ubuntu has been gaining rapid prominence with extant research recognizing its usefulness in managing and leading people and organizations. Several scholars have studied business ethics, leadership, employee behaviour, team dynamics, knowledge management, etc. through the lens of Ubuntu. Ubuntu's focus on relationships and communal values provides a mindset that can help organizations build an inclusive culture where every individual is valued. Lutz (2009) suggests that the way Ubuntu philosophy places the community at the centre could help global management more adequately address issues pertaining to the common good. Similarly, Mangaliso et al. (2018) state that Ubuntu as an African philosophy offers an excellent way to incorporate the African thought system into management practices in the field of human relations, which is premised on the "centrality of the collective as a prerequisite for corporate success" (p. 4). Along similar lines, Mutwarasibo and Iken (2019) indicate,

> Ubuntu is a strong community and relationship-based concept of management which could help organizations to develop deeper consideration for the

people who work with them and provide a basis on which to build a culture of empowerment and productive teamwork in the workplace.

(p. 16)

Proponents of Ubuntu suggest that the communal nature of the philosophy makes it an excellent choice for the alignment of organizational practices and routines and that an Ubuntu-driven mindset within an organization can have a positive impact on the culture of the organization. Mangaliso et al. (2021) state that "Ubuntu-mediated management operates through a distinctive set of values and beliefs that manifest themselves in a number of contextual factors to affect organizational outcomes" (p. 8). The core values of Ubuntu can serve as guiding principles for the organizational context and can have a positive impact on individual and organizational factors that impact performance. According to Ncube (2010), although Ubuntu is more than a cultural practice of the Bantu people, as a leadership philosophy it "balances the past (by learning from it), the present (by examining immediate and pressing concerns), and the future (by providing a vision)" (p. 78). Furthermore, Ubuntu which stresses the importance of connectedness, interpersonal relationships, and values such as harmony and care has significant relevance in the business sphere (West, 2014) for better people management. Though Ubuntu might be an African philosophy, its basic beliefs and ethos have a global appeal for leading and managing people and organizations effectively (Msila, 2008).

In his book titled *Ubuntu: Shaping the Current Workplace with (African) Wisdom*, the author Vuyisile Msila (2015) demystifies the concept of Ubuntu and explains its meaning for everyday corporate life and organizations. He talks about the five Ps in Ubuntu philosophy:

- People-centredness: Ubuntu emphasizes the role of the people within the organization. Without an interest in people, Ubuntu cannot be realized.
- Permeable walls: Communication in the organization is not restricted and the walls are not opaque. All the members can communicate with one another without fear.
- Partisanship: One of the most positive factors of the Ubuntu philosophy is loyalty. People communicate freely and they are made to feel closer to the organization.
- Progeny: Ubuntu leadership promotes collective decision-making. However under this, effective leadership is respected, and the leader is respected.
- Production: When the above characterizes the organization, production is guaranteed. The organization prospers when its members enjoy respect, loyalty, and good leadership (p. 15).

A distinctive feature of the Ubuntu philosophy according to Pérezts et al. (2020) is that it "refuses to submit to binary alternatives and mutually exclusive solutions" (p. 737) that characterize Western ways of thinking and its application for resolving business ethical dilemmas and contradictions. Similarly, Horwitz (2012) contends that African Indigenous thought systems reflect a high level of collectivism and group solidarity tendencies that can be integrated into management thought for a more people-centred managerial practice and emphasize group decision-making and interdependence (Mbigi, 1997). Celebrating the spirit of community and solidarity, an Ubuntu-based management mindset includes the voices of all individuals in an organization (Mbigi & Maree, 2005) and cultivating such a mindset can be a source of competitive advantage for organizations as it emphasizes the social well-being of all (Mangaliso et al., 2018). In a review of Africentric management practices, Jackson (2004) suggests that the Ubuntu mindset could be a critical element for developing a culturally appropriate humanistic management style, where employees are not just resources for an organization but are respected and valued. Similarly, Hailey (2008) signifies the importance of Ubuntu for management by stating that organizations that reflect Ubuntu principles are characterized by humanity and team spirit, which in turn can give a business its competitive advantage. Ubuntu-driven management practices have the ability to shape the organizational culture and positively impact interpersonal relationships within the organization. Thus, "engaging Ubuntu within the context of work and organizations emphasizes the need to draw on traditional African collective solidarity, community networks/ relationships and social sensitivity in evolving new approaches to leadership and management practice" (Iwowo, 2015, p. 7).

Ubuntu for Leadership and Management

According to Lutz (2009), the starting point for applying the Ubuntu philosophy in a management context would be to recognize the firm as a community and not a mere collection of individuals. The author suggests viewing the company "not as a mere collection of individuals, but as a collective, which is linked to a variety of other communities through a network of relations" (p. 318). Once the organization is understood as a community, the goal of management is to pursue the common good for all the stakeholders associated with the organization and not just a small section of individuals (for instance shareholders). According to Mutwarasibo and Iken (2019), Ubuntu envisages the "company as a collective and acknowledges the interdependency of all actors involved in the achievement of the company's goals" (p. 22). Woermann and Engelbrecht (2017) build upon the Ubuntu concept to conceptualize stakeholders as relation holders, emphasizing the relationality and interconnectedness among each individual associated with the organization and the moral responsibility of the organization due to the relations it has and not because of the benefits derived from the relationships. Malunga (2006) recommends ritualizing some of the organizational practices in the workplaces with the core values of Ubuntu to encourage collective ownership, emphasis on people and relationships, participatory decision-making and leadership, loyalty, and effective conflict resolution. According to Mbigi and Maree (2005), harnessing Ubuntu within the organization can enable individuals to develop a sense of belonging and solidarity with the shared practices of the organization.

Ubuntu-based management literature features leadership more prominently as one of the aspects of organizational behaviour where Ubuntu can be applied. Van der Colff (2003) applies Ubuntu to the development of leaders in African organizations and discusses how it helps to create ethical organizational cultures. Malunga (2006) suggests the use of African resources, value systems, and beliefs in leadership development initiatives and suggests the potentiality of Ubuntu as a positive contribution to leadership development initiatives. Malunga (2009) points out that the principles of Ubuntu as a leadership philosophy emphasize collectivism and relationships over material things, including ownership of opportunities, responsibilities, and challenges, where leadership and decision-making are participatory, transparent, and democratic. Ncube (2010) argues that Ubuntu as a worldview perspective or guiding philosophy for transformative leadership shares characteristics that qualify it as a leadership philosophy and holds promise for progressive and ethical change for Africa. Similarly, Hoffmann and Metz (2017) demonstrate that Ubuntu leadership is about mutuality and communal relationships based on harmony and fellowship. Abebe et al. (2020) operationalize Ubuntu as a leadership concept and examine its contribution to employee and organizational outcomes in African countries above and beyond those of the Western leadership styles. Drawing on the central Ubuntu idea, Pérezts et al. (2020) suggest that a core goal of ethical leadership is to work towards the greater good of others. The authors further conceptualize leadership not as the traditionally defined masculine stereotypes, but as humility, relationality, and the interconnectedness among individuals with the single pursuit of the common good for all (Pérezts et al., 2020). Moreover, Fourie et al. (2017) suggest reclaiming African values, such as Ubuntu, and discuss the several values and implications of Ubuntu for leadership development that could "form a foundation for a new type of leadership" (p. 240).

Furthermore, a growing body of research has applied the Ubuntu ethic within the context of business ethics to humanize business practices (Woermann & Engelbrecht, 2019). Hailey (2008) suggests that many recognize Ubuntu for its ethical dimension and strong moral overtones. Similarly, Woermann and Engelbrecht (2019) talk about how the African ethic of Ubuntu can contribute to ethical thinking in general and provide an alternative to stakeholder theory specifically where the focus is on benefits from and for each group of stakeholders. The authors suggest that adopting an Ubuntu mindset helps the organization to focus on people and relationships, instead of primarily focusing on profit maximization or on individual wealth. They further suggest that an Ubuntu-inspired business would not focus on profit maximization as its primary aim but would envision the common good of all stakeholders associated with the organization and aim to establish harmonious relationships based on shared identity and goodwill. Naude (2019) questions whether an Indigenous African ethic, as expressed in Ubuntu, may serve as an example of how to decolonize Western knowledge and provide an alternative to bringing in different ways of knowing within the ambit of managing organizations. Metz and Gaie (2010) argue that the African ethic of Ubuntu is distinctive from Western approaches in two ways – firstly, it is essentially relational, and secondly, the communal way in which it defines positive relations with others. Such a conception of ethics guides what the majority wants, or which norms become dominant in the organization since the focus is on the betterment of the community rather than one's self-interests.

According to Karsten and Illa (2005), "given its communitarian nature and focus on interdependence and harmonious human relationships, Ubuntu as a philosophical approach has, first and foremost, the potential to shape the habitus of managers and thus their performative attitude when interacting with others" (p. 616). Nansubuga and Munene (2020) cite a paradigm shift due to Ubuntu-driven people management methods characterized by democracy, collaboration, and reciprocity that promote productive knowledge and knowledge management systems. Tauetsile (2021) highlights differences between the Western and Ubuntu concept of teamwork suggesting that in Ubuntu-driven teamwork, the need for collectivism and the common good is more important than just working together for the benefit of the organization. Ubuntu can be a source of competitive advantage as it emphasizes social well-being and favours solutions that are preferred by a wider group of employees (Mangaliso, 2001). Similarly, Gade (2012) suggests that an Ubuntu mindset can help strengthen group identity and compassion provided the group members believe in interconnectedness with each other.

Given the extant scholarship that talks about adopting the Ubuntu mindset within the praxis of management and leadership, we next look into how Ubuntu formed the foundation of one of the biggest transformative crusades in the history of Black people.

Ubuntu for Transformative Change: The Story of South Africa

The greatest application of Ubuntu has been in the history of South Africa with Nelson Mandela leading the revolution that transformed the entire nation in its fight against apartheid. Nelson Mandela and Desmond Tutu used the concept of Ubuntu to lead South Africa to a peaceful post-apartheid transition, showing us how to act with peace, compassion, and integrity rather than vengeance or retaliation (Global Citizen, 2018). Ubuntu was used as a "political discourse by the South African Truth and Reconciliation Commission, where it became interrelated with forgiveness as the preferred mode of interaction between victims and perpetrators in the process of reconciliation and nation-building" (Stuit, 2016, p. 39). We now briefly look into the history of South Africa as documented by the Apartheid Museum in Johannesburg, South Africa (Apartheid Museum, 2022) which illustrates the apartheid movement and transformation of South Africa to a democracy.

In 1910, South Africa had become a Union, and racial segregation was an official policy of the Union which laid the foundation for the practice of apartheid. The Union implemented 148 apartheid laws from 1949 to 1971, affecting every facet of people's lives. Life during this period was rife with injustices as Black South Africans saw apartheid hardened into persistent and systemic racism. Through the years 1959 and 1960, violence broke out in various South African cities in protest of the practices of the Union. To further strengthen the segregation policy, "homelands" were created by the Union to forcibly remove Blacks from their homes and settle them into the "homelands" as per their ethnic identity. These mass removals of almost three and a half million Blacks from 1960 to 1964 led to many losing their livelihoods and with no future to look forward to. Eventually, a new generation of Black youth, with leaders such as Bantu Stephen Biko, posed the first challenge to the apartheid regime and gave voice to the Black Consciousness Movement in South Africa. As the fight against apartheid continued, several supporters and leaders were executed under terrorism laws. The day of 16 June 1976 was a significant turning point in South African history when Soweto school children took to the streets to demonstrate against the introduction of Afrikaans as a medium of instruction in Black schools. This movement marked the beginning of a new, renewed, and much bigger struggle against apartheid in which nearly 1000 school children were killed. The decade of 1980 was characterized by the strongest outburst of civic and student unrest that the nation had ever known, with Nelson Mandela continuing to be imprisoned. The date 11 February 1990 was a historical moment. Nelson Mandela was released from the Victor Verster prison after spending 27 years in prison. While violence continued in several parts of the country, South Africa stood on the verge of a new era. After lengthy and complex negotiations with the government, the first-ever democratic elections were held on 27 April 1994, where all South Africans could vote irrespective of their skin colour. These elections were the beginning of a new nation that had no place for segregation and apartheid. On 10 May 1994, after almost three and a half centuries of colonialism and apartheid, Nelson Mandela became the country's first-ever democratically elected president. In July 1995, the new government passed a law to establish the Truth and Reconciliation Commission under the leadership of Desmond Tutu. The Commission's purpose was to lay the foundation for reconciliation among the offenders and victims of apartheid and aimed at helping South Africans come to terms with their past. Desmond Tutu maintained that the nation could deal with the past and seek reconciliation by and through Ubuntu. Ubuntu was at the heart of the Truth and Reconciliation Commission (Truth and

Reconciliation Commission, 2003) and was quoted in the amnesty section of the report:

> The adoption of this Constitution lays the secure foundation for the people of South Africa to transcend the divisions and strife of the past, which generated gross violations of human rights, the transgression of humanitarian principles in violent conflicts and a legacy of hatred, fear, guilt and revenge. These can now be addressed on the basis that there is a need for understanding but not for vengeance, a need for reparation but not for retaliation, a need for Ubuntu but not for victimization.
>
> (p. 3)

Through the spirit of Ubuntu, President Nelson Mandela and Archbishop Desmond Tutu provided leadership and managed a potentially explosive crisis leading to a transformative change and the birth of "the rainbow nation" where Black and White people decided to work better together for the survival and prosperity of South Africa. We argue that the sustainability of this change will require policies and practices with an Ubuntu mindset supporting the development of inclusive community settings, systemics of education, workplaces and development systems that leave no one behind.

In Canada, the release of the Truth and Reconciliation Commission's (TRC) report and Calls to Action (2015) generated discussions on how the Canadian post-secondary education system should function to address racial injustices and provide opportunities for all students to succeed. The discussions promote the need to embrace Indigenous knowledge and teaching methods in classrooms to bring about tangible change. This change, we contend, will be transformative when universities affirm the critical role of Indigenous knowledges in the development of human capabilities and inclusive systems. This role will require reflective engagement with how Indigenous knowledges, as conceptualized in the past, should inform the present and future educational development agenda to work for all. We next present how the Africentric Indigenous knowledge of Ubuntu can serve as an inclusive pedagogical tool to address racial injustices and humanize learning environments in higher education.

Ubuntu for Transformative Pedagogical Change

Eurocentric views continue to inform the pedagogical practices in universities across the globe, including Canada. Letseka (2014) claims that these views undermine and dismiss the credibility of Indigenous knowledges and often lead to what Ndlovu-Gatsheni (2018) describes as "epistemic violence" where in curriculum, including pedagogy, Indigenous and other minority students in higher education are marginalized and dehumanized. In addressing this problem, researchers (e.g. Blignaut 2021; Chilisa 2016; Maistry 2021) have proposed "epistemic freedom" through intentional processes to decolonize and transform the learning environment of higher education institutions. Likewise, in the field of management education, there have been persistent calls to decolonize business schools, and for a shift from the prevalent mainstream economist paradigm to a more humanistic approach to management if businesses are to become "agents of world benefit" (Laszlo, 2019, p. 85). Worline and Dutton (2022) state that the

> emphasis in management education on power as a form of domination, social exchange as the sole mode of interacting, and the relative absence of relational views of human nature have informed a global managerialism that now dehumanizes those who profess it as well as those who study it.
>
> (p. 36)

With several other scholars emphasizing similar views, Pirson (2017) recommends humanistic management as a much-needed alternative paradigm for those seeking to organize and manage in a sustainable way in the face of several global crises. Humanistic management promotes the dignity and well-being of each person as two of its central tenets and emphasizes the relationality of human beings to help us not only achieve our goals but also serve the common good (Melé, 2016). Recognizing and fostering this relationality in the management classroom is critical to developing managers and leaders who are more compassionate, humanistic, and accountable to the society in which they exist. Creating a relational environment in the classroom can form a "social infrastructure of connectedness that creates conditions for the development of respect and self-respect, trust and self-trust, and esteem and self-esteem for those within that infrastructure" (Honneth, 2004, as cited in Worline & Dutton, 2022, p. 34).

One way in which business school educators can introduce the relational approach to learning is by embracing the Ubuntu pedagogy. Following Ukpokodu (2016) and Ngubane and Makua (2021), we advocate for Ubuntu pedagogy – teaching and learning with an Indigenous Ubuntu philosophical mindset where the humanity of learners drives the learning processes. The Ubuntu pedagogy proposed by Ukpokodu (2016) has six main guiding principles. The first principle, recognition of self and others, is about the acknowledgement of our humanity and the humanity of others and how our interactions and engagement with others are critical to the learning processes that help us to develop our identity and sense of belonging, and to become fully human. The second principle, building positive relationships, places emphasis on how love and respect for each other and our humanity build relations of trust to share knowledge and to develop inclusive and effective learning environments. The third principle, getting students to work cooperatively, encourages and promotes team spirit. The fourth principle talks about nurturing the student's mind through participative and interactive learning. The fifth principle recommends teaching from a position of love and care that will not only empower students but also bring about a positive change among them. And finally, the sixth principle mentions utilizing students' linguistic resources to promote meaningful learning and collective meaning-making.

We started the chapter by providing a detailed account of the Ubuntu philosophy and demonstrating its significance in serving as a powerful educational and cultural instrument to guide development through human interaction and relationship building amongst African Indigenous people for centuries. This historical account is often excluded and oppressed in formal educational institutions preventing intergenerational Indigenous knowledge transfer. We agree with Ramose (2002) and Ukpokodu (2016) that educational institutions such as universities can play a critical role in addressing this injustice through Ubuntu pedagogy. The pedagogy employs the "Ubuntu philosophical values of compassion, care, cooperation, respect and dignity" (Ukpokodu, 2016, p. 155) to guide the development of inclusive learning environments where students from diverse backgrounds and cultures learn to value each other's cultures, opinions, and ideas, and to learn how to learn better together. Ukpokodu (2016) further states that the fundamental assumption of the Ubuntu pedagogy is that students (as human beings) "naturally aspire to feelings of compassion and care, dignity and respect" (p. 155) and are more likely to be successful in a learning environment that "affirms, validate[s] and treat[s] all students as dignified human beings" (p.155). Another critical aspect of the Ubuntu pedagogy is the intentional development of a learning culture where students "perceive each other as significant others who bring unique backgrounds, experiences and prior knowledge to build on and towards the development of new knowledge" (Ngubane & Makua, 2021, p. 5). Additionally, Ubuntu pedagogy recognizes individual and collective needs and dependence on each other as exemplified in the Ubuntu maxim "*umuntu ungumuntu ngabantu*" (a person is a person through other people). Ukpokodu (2016) argues that teachers embracing Ubuntu pedagogy provide all students, irrespective of their cultural, linguistic, social, or economic class, religion, gender, and sexual orientation, with equal opportunities to develop and exercise their full capacities.

Concluding Remarks

One of the critical lessons from the Covid-19 pandemic and the aftermath is how vulnerable we are as humans and the urgent need for inclusive systems that provide opportunities for us to learn better together and leave no one behind. Developing these systems presents challenges, including a mindset to drive transformative change. While much of the Ubuntu scholarship originates from Africa and talks about Ubuntu from the perspective of management and leadership in African organizations and educational systems, a small (e.g. Lutz, 2009; Ncube, 2010) but a growing area of management education scholarship has now started talking about its application as a universal philosophy. While much work needs to be done outside the African continent, we attempt to use this chapter as a way to showcase the history and understanding of the Ubuntu philosophy to readers in a Canadian context. We have not attempted to trace the origin of Ubuntu, which we believe is a very difficult task since all Indigenous knowledges have existed since times immemorial. We have rather endeavoured to introduce the readers to the Africentric concept of Ubuntu, and how it offers unique perspectives on people-centric management and organization practices and management educational pedagogy. We argue that this Ubuntu mindset has implications for the current leadership and management practices as we recover from the Covid-19 post-pandemic. It is a new way of thinking about inclusivity in our quest to achieve common goals. As an Africentric idea, Ubuntu sees potential in all humanity and can bring out the best in every individual. If employed in education, it can impact thought processes and create a mindset shift. The Ubuntu mindset of leaving no one behind can also have implications on how we develop management courses, how management and leadership is taught, and how we provide training to our future managers so that they can bring out the best in the people that they lead and manage. Ubuntu reminds us that "no one is an island", and whatever an individual does affects those surrounding them. Ubuntu teaches us to be inclusive and exhibit kindness, compassion, support, and solidarity towards one another (Mnyaka & Motlhabi, 2005). It is through such acts that positive results can be produced for employees as well as organizations. Ubuntu-driven management and leadership practices can mobilize all stakeholders around a common goal (Bekker, 2007) for the betterment of the organization as well as the community.

We share the view that, given the current diversity, equity, and inclusivity policy in workplaces in Canada, we need a better understanding of different ways of knowing to effectively manage diverse employees in increasingly multicultural and multilinguistic workplaces. This requires the incorporation of Indigenous ontologies and adjusting the Western-derived principles of management to benefit organizations operating in highly competitive business environments (Mangaliso et al., 2018). Furthermore, following Asante (1991), we claim that Africentricity is about how the African Indigenous ways of knowing, when centred in developing systems, can significantly improve the success and participation of people of African ancestry in these systems as well. We need to reimagine the future of business education that integrates different ways of knowing to enhance our shared knowledge and create global managers capable of leading a culturally diverse workforce. The assumption is that perspectives from different knowledge systems produce a more comprehensive understanding of sustainable development interventions (Doucette et al., 2021). Managers who embrace the values represented in alternative epistemologies offer the best promise for improving organizational effectiveness in various parts of the world. Mutual respect for different ways of knowing and recognizing the intellectual contributions of diverse communities is essential to building trust, understanding, and sharing. Our globalizing world needs a management mindset that places value on the interconnectedness of the human race for the betterment of all. Ubuntu sees "community rather than self-determination as the essential aspect of personhood" (Nussbaum, 2003, p. 22). We argue that Africentric knowledge systems and values such as Ubuntu are universal and can be adapted to lead better and manage people and organizations. Ubuntu teaches us that all people belong to a single community and this helps us develop a global identity to become truly global citizens.

Furthermore, our discussion on how Ubuntu knowledge can play a significant role in transforming higher education pedagogical practices invokes critical thinking for developing learning environments that provide opportunities for all students to work together better, in an Africentric way. From Ubuntu, every student has the potential and capability to succeed when learning environments acknowledge their humanity and provide opportunities for genuine interactions and support. This Africentric Indigenous understanding is fundamental to human development, and we argue that an educational paradigm and teachers with an Ubuntu mindset (Frempong & Kadam, 2022) offer unique possibilities for inclusive learning environments. In their editorial for "Historical reflections at the intersection of past and future: celebrating 50 years of management learning", Durepos et al. (2020) claim that "the greatest source of inspiration for management learning for the future, is their use of history, reflexivity, new perspectives and theory to think differently" (p. 13) and allowing for "a space for learning about different ways of knowing and learning" (p. 12). We hope our chapter has provided a voice and insights through inspiration from Ubuntu on how we should think about humanity and human development to inform transformative pedagogical practices relevant to scholars, practitioners, and students in the management learning field.

References

Abebe, M. A., Tekleab, A. G., & Lado, A. A. (2020). Multilevel perspectives on leadership in the African context. *Africa Journal of Management, 6*(3), 145–160.

Apartheid Museum. (2022). Segregation. Retrieved from Apartheid Museum: www.apartheidmuseum.org/exhibitions/segregation

Asamoah, K., & Yeboah-Assiamah, E. (2019). "Ubuntu philosophy" for public leadership and governance praxis: Revisiting the ethos of Africa's collectivism. *Journal of Global Responsibility, 10*(4), 307–321.

Asante, M. K. (1991). The Afrocentric idea in education. *Journal of Negro Education, 60*, 170–180.

Blignaut, S. E. (2021). Transforming the curriculum for the unique challenges faced by South Africa. *Curriculum Perspectives, 41*(1), 27–34.

Breidlid, A. (2009). Culture, indigenous knowledge systems and sustainable development: A critical view of education in an African context. *International Journal of Educational Development, 29*, 140–148.

Broodryk, J. (2002). *Ubuntu: Life lessons from Africa.* Pretoria: Ubuntu School of Philosophy.

Broodryk, J. (2007). *Understanding South Africa – The uBuntu way of living.* South Africa: Ubuntu School of Philosophy.

Chilisa, B. (2016). *Indigenous research methodologies.* 2nd edn. London: Sage.

Dei, G. S., & Kempf, A. (2011). The evolution of multiculturalism. Toronto Star. Retrieved from: www.thestar.com/opinion/editorialopinion/2011/11/28/the_evolution_of_multiculturalism.html

Doucette, M. B., Gladstone, J. S., & Carter, T. (2021). Indigenous conversational approach to history and business education. *Academy of Management Learning & Education, 20*(3), 473–484.

Durepos, G., Maclean, M., Alcadipani, R., & Cummings, S. (2020). Historical reflections at the intersection of past and future: Celebrating 50 years of management learning. *Management Learning, 51*(1), 3–16.

Fourie, W., van der Merwe, S. C., & van der Merwe, B. (2017). Sixty years of research on leadership in Africa: A review of the literature. *Leadership, 13*(2), 222–251.

Frempong, G., & Kadam, R. (2022). Educational paradigm with Ubuntu mindset: Implications for sustainable development goals in education. In D. Ortega-Sánchez (Ed.), *Active learning – Research and practice for STEAM and social sciences education.* IntechOpen.

Gade, C. B. (2011). The historical development of the written discourses on Ubuntu. *South African Journal of Philosophy, 30*(3), 303–329.

Gade, C. B. (2012). What is Ubuntu,? Different interpretations among South Africans of African descent. *South African Journal of Philosophy, 31*(3), 484–503.

Global Citizen. (2018). *What is the spirit of Ubuntu? How can we have it in our lives?* Global Citizen. Retrieved from: https://www.globalcitizen.org/en/content/ubuntu-south-africa-together-nelson-mandela/

Hailey, J. (2008). *Ubuntu: A literature review.* London: Tutu Foundation, 1–26.

Hailu, M. F., & Tachine, A. R. (2021). Black and indigenous theoretical considerations for higher education sustainability. *Journal of Comparative & International Higher Education, 13*(3), 20–42.

Hoffmann, N., & Metz, T. (2017). What can the capabilities approach learn from an Ubuntu ethic? A relational approach to development theory. *World Development, 97*, 153–164.

Honneth A (2004). Recognition and justice: Outline of a plural theory of justice. *Acta Sociologica, 47*(4): 351–364.

Horwitz, F. M. (2012). Evolving human resource management in Southern African multinational firms: Towards an Afro-Asian nexus. *International Journal of Human Resource Management, 23*(14), 2938–2958.

Inter-Institutional Advisory Committee. (2021). *Scarborough Charter on anti-Black racism and Black inclusion in Canadian higher education: Principles, actions and accountability.* National dialogues and action for inclusive higher education and communities. Retrieved from www.utsc.utoronto.ca/principal/sites/utsc.utoronto.ca.principal/files/docs/Scarborough_Charter_EN_Nov2022.pdf

Iwowo, V. (2015). Leadership in Africa: Rethinking development. *Personnel Review, 44*(3), 408–429.
Jackson, T. (2004). *Management and change in Africa while.* London: Routledge.
Karsten, L., & Illa, H. (2005). Ubuntu as a key African management concept: Contextual background and practical insights for knowledge application. *Journal of Managerial Psychology, 20*(7), 607–620.
Laszlo, C. (2019). Strengthening humanistic management. *Humanist Management Journal, 4*, 85–94.
Letseka, M. (2014). Ubuntu and justice as fairness. *Mediterranean Journal of Social Sciences, 5*(9), 544–551
Library and Archives Canada. (2022). *Black history in Canada.* Government of Canada. Retrieved August 2022, from: www.bac-lac.gc.ca/eng/discover/immigration/history-ethnic-cultural/Pages/blacks.aspx
Lutz, D. W. (2009). African Ubuntu philosophy and global management. *Journal of Business Ethics, 84*, 313–328.
Maistry, S. (2021). Curriculum theorising in Africa as a social justice project: Insights from decolonial theory. In K. G. Kehdinga & B. K. Khoza (Eds.), *Curriculum theory, curriculum theorising and theories: The African theorising perspective* (pp. 133–147). Leiden: Sense.
Malunga, C. (2006). Learning leadership development from African cultures: A personal perspective. *PraxisNote, 25*, 1–13.
Mangaliso, M. P. (2001). Building competitive advantage from Ubuntu: Management lessons from South Africa. *Academy of Management Perspectives, 15*(3), 23–34.
Mangaliso, M. P., Mangaliso, N., Knipes, B. J., Ndanga, L. Z., & Jean-Denis, H. (2018). Invoking Ubuntu philosophy as a source of harmonious organizational management. Academy of Management Annual Meeting Proceedings *April 2018* (pp. 1–25). Chicago: Academy of Management.
Mangaliso, M. P., Mangaliso, N., Ndanga, L. Z., & Jean-Denis, H. (2021). Contextualizing organizational change management in Africa: Incorporating the core values of Ubuntu. *Journal of African Business.* 10.1080/15228916.2021.1984817
Mbigi, L. (1997). *Ubuntu: The African dream in management.* Knowledge Resources.
Mbigi, L., & Maree, J. (2005). *Ubuntu, the spirit of African transformation management.* Knowledge Resources.
Mbiti, J. S. (1989). *African religions and philosophy.* Oxford: Heinemann.
McDonald, D. A. (2010). Ubuntu bashing: the marketisation of 'African values' in South Africa. *Review of African Political Economy, 37*(124), 139–152.
Melé, D. (2016). Understanding humanistic management. *Humanist Management Journal, 1*, 33–55.
Metz, T., & Gaie, J. B. (2010). The African ethic of Ubuntu/Botho: Implications for research on morality. *Journal of Moral Education, 39*(3), 273–290.
Mnyaka, M., & Motlhabi, M. (2005). The African concept of Ubuntu/Botho and its socio-moral significance. *Black Theology, 3*(2), 215–237.
Msila, V. (2008). Ubuntu and school leadership. *Journal of Education, 44*, 67–84.
Msila, V. (2015). *Ubuntu: Shaping the current workplace with (African) wisdom.* Knowres Publishing.

Mutwarasibo, F., & Iken, A. (2019). I am because we are – The contribution of the Ubuntu philosophy to intercultural management thinking. *Interculture Journal: Online-Zeitschrift für interkulturelle Studien, 18*(32), 15–32.

Nansubuga, F., & Munene, J. C. (2020). Awakening the Ubuntu episteme to embrace knowledge management in Africa. *Journal of Knowledge Management, 24*(1), 105–119.

Naude, P. (2019). Decolonising knowledge: Can Ubuntu ethics save us from coloniality? *Journal of Business Ethics, 159*, 23–37.

Ncube, L. B. (2010). Ubuntu: A transformative leadership philosophy. *Journal of Leadership Studies, 4*(3), 77–82.

Ndlovu-Gatsheni, S. (2018). *Epistemic freedom in Africa: Deprovincialization and decolonization.* London: Routledge.

Nelson, B., & Lundin, S. (2010). *Ubuntu!: An inspiring story about an African tradition of teamwork and collaboration.* Crown Currency.

Ngambi, H. (2011). RARE leadership: An alternative leadership approach for Africa. *International Journal of African Renaissance Studies – Multi-, Inter- and Transdisciplinarity, 6*(1), 6–23.

Ngomane, N. M. (2020). *Everyday Ubuntu: Living better together, the African way.* HarperCollins.

Ngubane, N. I. & Makua, M. (2021). Intersection of Ubuntu pedagogy and social justice: Transforming South African higher education. *Transformation in Higher Education, 6*(0), a113.

Nussbaum, B. (2003). Ubuntu: Reflections of a South African on our common humanity. *Reflections: The SoL Journal, 4*(4), 21–26.

Pérezts, M., Russon, J.-A., & Painter, M. (2020). This time from Africa: Developing a relational approach to values-driven leadership. *Journal of Business Ethics, 161*, 731–748.

Pirson, M. (2017). *Humanistic management: Protecting dignity and promoting well-being.* Cambridge: Cambridge University Press.

Poovan, N., du Toit, M. K., & Engelbrecht, A. S. (2006). The effect of the social values of Ubuntu on team effectiveness. *South African Journal of Business Management, 37*(3), 17–27.

Ramose, M. B. (2002). The philosophy of Ubuntu and Ubuntu as a philosophy. In P. H. Coetzee, & A. P. J. Roux (Eds.), *Philosophy from Africa: A text with readings* (pp. 230–238). Cape Town: Oxford University Press.

Saurombe, A. (2021). The teaching of indigenous knowledge as a tool for curriculum transformation and Africanisation. *Journal of Education, 138*(1), 30–39.

Statistics Canada. (2022). Black History Month 2022... by the numbers. Statistics Canada. Retrieved August 2022, from: www.statcan.gc.ca/en/daily/by-the-numbers/black-history-month

Stuit, H. (2016). Ubuntu and common humanity in the South African Truth and Reconciliation Commission. In *Ubuntu strategies* (pp. 39–82). New York: Palgrave Macmillan.

Tauetsile, J. (2021). Employee engagement in non-Western contexts: The link between social resources Ubuntu and employee engagement. *International Journal of Cross Cultural Management, 21*(2), 245–259.

The White House – Office of the Press Secretary. (2013). *Remarks by President Obama at Memorial Service for Former South African President Nelson Mandela*. Retrieved from The White House – President Barack Obama: https://obamawhitehouse.archives.gov/the-press-office/2013/12/10/remarks-president-obama-memorial-service-former-south-african-president-

Truth and Reconciliation Commission. (2003). *Truth and Reconciliation Commission of South Africa report.* South Africa: Formeset.

Truth and Reconciliation Commission of Canada. (2015). *Truth and Reconciliation Commission of Canada: Calls to action.* Available at www2.gov.bc.ca/assets/gov/british-columbians-our-governments/indigenous-people/aboriginal-peoples-documents/calls_to_action_english2.pdf

Tutu, D. (1999). *No future without forgiveness.* New York: Doubleday.

Ukpokodu, O.N. (2016). *You can't teach us if you don't know us and care about us: Becoming an Ubuntu, responsive and responsible urban teacher*. New York: Peter Lang.

van der Colff, L. (2003). Leadership lessons from the African tree. *Management Decision, 41*(3), 257–261.

Weir, D. T., Mangaliso, M. P., & Mangaliso, N. A. (2017). Some implications to the intercultural approach to international human resource management: Ubuntu and Ummah. *Academy of Management Annual Meeting Proceedings* (pp. 1–6). Briarcliff Manor, NY 10510

West, A. (2014). Ubuntu and business ethics: Problems, perspectives and prospects. *Journal of Business Ethics, 121*(1), 47–61.

Woermann, M., & Engelbrecht, S. (2019). The Ubuntu challenge to business: From Stakeholders to relationholders. *Journal of Business Ethics, 157*, 27–44.

Woods, C., Dell, K., & Carroll, B. (2022). Decolonizing the business school: Reconstructing the entrepreneurship classroom through Indigenizing pedagogy and learning. *Academy of Management Learning & Education, 21*(1), 82–100.

Worline, M. C., & Dutton, J. E. (2022). The courage to teach with compassion: Enriching classroom designs and practices to foster responsiveness to suffering. *Management Learning, 53*(1), 33–54.

8 Embracing "SANKOFA" at Dalhousie University

Heidi Weigand, Binod Sundararajan, and Kristin S. Williams

Introduction

As we write this chapter, we recognize that African Nova Scotians are a distinct people whose histories, legacies, and contributions have enriched that part of Mi'kma'ki for over 400 years. We also acknowledge that despite the 1619 project (Goggins, 2019), the memorizing of important lost Civil Rights Canadian actors such as Viola Desmond (Williams, 2020), and mainstream social media campaigns supporting Black business there is considerable neglect on the value of Black, Indigenous, and Persons of Color (BIPOC) economic activity and influence, business, and consumerism and this requires the business school to address Black History (Phipps & Prieto, 2021). The Black History of Nova Scotia is a complex one. African Nova Scotian Affairs reports that Black Loyalists arrived in the province as refugees between 1782 and 1785, with further exiled groups arriving from Jamaica (Maroon) in 1796. The War of 1812 brought a significant migration between 1813 and 1816. Late arrivers, as they are called, arrived in the early 1900s. The Black community of Nova Scotia thus spans enslaved, Loyalist, Maroon, and refugees (Hamilton, 1999).

> We look back in order to move forward, so that we can create a more welcoming, just and equitable place for us all.
>
> (Baylis et al., 2019, p 8)

In this chapter, we offer insights into Dalhousie's history of anti-Blackness, settler origins, and establishment on slave-compensation money from the West India trade. We share findings from the September 2019, Report on Lord Dalhousie's History on Slavery and Race, a critical window into Dalhousie's past, undertaken in scholarly inquiry, and inviting us [all staff, faculty, students, leadership, and the board] to acknowledge and respond. "It fills a gap in Nova Scotian history, and demonstrates our willingness to look backward and reconcile our past with our future" (Cooper et al, 2019, p 4). We believe that Dalhousie is the first (if not one of the first) Universities in Canada to commission an accounting

DOI: 10.4324/9781003612612-9

of its early intersections with the legacies of slavery and make such a report public. We also offer two emic perspectives from Dalhousie University Faculty of Management. As insiders, we are deeply committed to fostering a culture of learning steeped in cultural diversity and we have had the opportunity to apply these values to teaching and governance. We share our own stories of advocating for change in administration, research, teaching, service, and in our curricula. Our third author has collaborated with the African Nova Scotian community to advocate and educate in and outside of academia. She brings her knowledge of the literature and methods and writing to this chapter. We also share how the faculty is responding to the call for change and creating awareness of the injustices perpetrated on the African Nova Scotian and Mi'kmaq communities. Though we acknowledge that there remains much work to be done, we hope to inspire our readers with our learning to nurture a climate of inclusion in the faculty. We hope that the changes we are making help the faculty to grow, to become a welcoming pavilion for all people and specifically those from historically marginalized communities. Specifically, we are keen to create pathways for members of these communities to be part of the post-secondary process.

Our chapter opens with a reflection that begins with our positionality as authors. We then outline our methodological approach. To contextualize the conversation about change, we share two documents. First, we share insights from the Report on Lord Dalhousie's History on Slavery and Race. From the report, we surface Lord Dalhousie's anti-Blackness mindset, the history of the institution's establishment, the call for change, and the recommendations. Then we share excerpts from the Dalhousie Strategic Plan. The plan is a narrative of how the faculty and the institution respond to the need for transformation. The plan acknowledges how knowledge is produced, shared, consumed, and most importantly valued by academia, professionals, and our emerging leaders and our students. As this is a chapter about management education, we also wanted to share stories of success and change in action. To do so, we share three mini cases. The first case shares the strategic change embraced by the Faculty of Management to address equity, diversity, inclusion, accessibility, and decolonization (EDIAD) to help Indigenous and African Nova Scotian faculty, staff, students, and communities address the recommendations in the Lord Dalhousie Report on anti-Blackness and racism. The EDIAD pillar is led by one of our authors. The second case is the Faculty of Management Promise Scholars Program, designed to support and nurture students with financial resources, work and internship experiences, and dedicated, personalized academic and career mentoring. The third case is the development of a collaboration course by one of our authors for Master of Business Administration students in leadership grounded in Indigenous and Afrocentric values and principles. These demonstrate the actions within our scope and act as indicators of hope and inspiration for other academics and institutions to enact similar changes. In a book about the history of management education in Canada, our chapter reflects on how one institution is demonstrating leadership in acknowledging historical wrongdoings to create a more welcoming, just, and equitable place for us all.

Methodology

Our first author identifies as a Western woman living in an Indigenous community in Mi'kma'ki with her husband and children. In her research, she brings an epistemic stance as an ethnographer grounded in participatory action research with Indigenous and African Nova Scotian communities. Heidi's ontological lens is Two-Eyed Seeing which endeavors to co-create new knowledge from Western and Indigenous perspectives in partnership with Indigenous peers (Hatcher et al., 2009). Her research, teaching, and service to the community are centered around driving change, inspiring others to engage with the change through their lens, and co-creating a bright, mutually beneficial future.

Our second author brings his own intersectional identity as an immigrant, educator, and university leader with post-colonial lived experiences in India, the Middle East, and other parts of the developing and developed world. He is immensely grateful for the opportunity to live, reside, and thrive in Mi'kma'ki, the unceded and ancestral lands of the Mi'kmaq. His research experience focuses on relationships, as recently acknowledged by a Mi'kmaq Elder at our faculty's retreat. He honors the relationship to the land we are grateful to settle and live in, the relationship to the people who occupy our workspaces, the relationships to and between the learners who come to our institution of higher education to learn and grow, the relationship to ethical ways of doing things. These values all form the central motifs of his research endeavors. These have taken the form of networked reciprocity of Harriet Tubman and the Underground Railroad Movement to free slaves (Young, Sundararajan, & Stewart, 2009) and those of Irish immigrants to Halifax (Sundararajan et al, 2015). They have also emerged in a work Binod has engaged in around student-peer learning relationships when grappling with ethics and responsible actions, group dynamics, fatigue during the pandemic, and other relevant works in the domain of the scholarship of teaching and learning.

Our final author is both an academic and community leader, bridging the interests of scholarship, advocacy, and community education. She identifies as anti-racist ally, working closely with the African Nova Scotian community to help uncover lost histories of organizational actors and leaders. Her writing is polemical, feminist, historical, and rooted in critical management studies. Her advocacy work has ensured that remarkable leaders, like Viola Desmond, are now recognized not just for their contributions to Civil Rights, but to early Black business and Black female entrepreneurship (Willaims, 2020, 2022, 2024).

Our collaboration is based on a foundation of respect for our shared vision for change, diverse experiences and identities, and our commitment to enact change. We are all present members of the Faculty of Management (as of 2022).

When we came together to write this chapter, our first and second authors were keen to share some promising steps toward transformational change. Our third author was keen to anchor these steps in the university's acknowledged racist history and the 2019 Report on Lord Dalhousie's History of Slavery and Race. What emerged was more of an approach than a method. We decided to construct our chapter as a teaching and learning piece, in which practitioners could see how we were thinking and planning and put into practice commitments to inclusivity. Teaching and learning papers prioritize illustrating how integration happens and how it can be replicated. Some examples of strategies to teach about diversity are derived from a teaching framework used with youth but are also applicable to adults called the Teaching Tolerance Anti-Bias Framework (Chiariello, 2016). The framework embraces four anchor points of anti-bias education: identity, diversity, justice, and action. All four of these elements must be present in the teaching to help students become social justice advocates. A common theme in the stories shared by teachers is to demonstrate a commitment to go beyond teaching about diversity and to instead focus on social justice and change agendas to help students move to action and inclusivity (Berlach et al, 2011). Some teachers express the importance of positionality and identity. For example, a White male who acknowledges his privilege can build trust between the teacher and the students. Understanding one's positionality and how that can influence our interpretation of a story or situation creates a safe learning space for diverse opinions to be expressed. The emphasis is on action and helping students to see the role they can play when faced with situations rooted in prejudice or discrimination (Fernandez et al., 2022, Anderson et al., 2019).

It Starts with an Apology

Today, on behalf of Dalhousie university, I apologize to the people of African descent in our community, reads the statement. "We regret the actions and views of George Ramsay, the ninth Earl of Dalhousie, and the consequences and impact they have had in our collective history as a university, as a province and as a region".

(Then President, Richard Florizone university response, 2019, para 10)

To understand the relative importance of past president Florizone's apology, we need to look back at the history of Dalhousie university, and its historical beginnings grounded in the West Indies slave trade money.

Dalhousie Report on Racism and Focus on Change

In 2015, the Black Faculty and Staff Caucus met with then-President Richard Florizone and Kevin Hewitt, Chair of the Senate, to address the dramatic rise in anti-Black racism around the Dalhousie University Campus. Students were experiencing racism in the classrooms and racist graffiti was becoming common on campus. In addition, Black faculty members and staff had concerns about the opportunities to advance in the university, and frustration was expressed over the lack of Black and African content in the school curricula. When reflecting on Dalhousie's history, Lord Dalhousie, the 9th Earl of Dalhousie, was acknowledged to be racist. The Black Faculty and Staff Caucus called for Dalhousie to examine and acknowledge their connections to slavery, the slave trade, and anti-Blackness. For a Black community member, Dalhousie was an unwelcoming campus.

In 2016, a scholarly panel was established with Dr. Afua Cooper, a leading scholar in historical slavery and racism, as the Chair to lead the development of the Report on Lord Dalhousie's History on Slavery and Race. The focus was to discuss reconciliation and how to enact this in the university's culture. The report focused on reflection on Dalhousie's history of racism and the historical beginnings of the university as grounded in the West Indies slave trade and benefiting from slave trade money. The information also provides insights on moving forward by acknowledging the history and making decisions about the type of environment we want to create at Dalhousie to nurture a welcoming environment for students and faculty to feel safe, valued, and respected. A vital element in the change is the comprehensive focus on weaving Afrocentric values and perspectives into the university policies, research, and curricula.

The report revealed insights into Lord Dalhousie's influence and overt racist attitudes toward the emancipated African Americans who came to Halifax after the War of 1812. The Crown had promised them their freedom, but instead, they faced perspectives that abolition would be "injurious to the southern slave society and Black people as a whole" (Lord Dalhousie Report, p 12). The report uncovered that the Halifax circle was pro-Confederate, and many wealthy families benefited from West Indian slave-compensation money. As a result of the report, many recommendations were presented to help transform the university. We believe that Dalhousie was the first university in Canada to take part in this self-reflection examination of its colonial and racist history and racist legacies. The goal was to engage in progressive practices to help students feel welcome. Initiatives such as the creation of the Black Student Advising Centre and a transition year program to help students succeed at university as they navigate their programs, finances, and social changes were enacted.

> Dalhousie University must be a place where everyone feels valued and respected. Where diversity, equity, and inclusion are core values in our mission of teaching and learning, research, and service to our communities. Where we challenge racism and its systemic legacies within our own walls and in our broader community.
>
> (Cooper et al, 2019, p 17)

Dalhousie Strategic Plan – Fulfilling Our Third Century Promise

In 2021, Dalhousie entered its five-year strategic plan to reach a much higher level of inclusion, service, and impact on its goals to eliminate barriers to full participation, belonging, and success. The Third Century Promise, Si'st Kasqimtlnaqnipunqekl Teli L'witmasimk in Mi'kmaq, focuses on building on Dalhousie's knowledge and success over the past two centuries to guide Dalhousie University in the Third Century Promise. The promise is,

> To give our collective best, continually push the limits, ensure that opportunities and benefits are equitably available and attainable, and rededicate ourselves to be the lever of economic and social uplift of our *diverse* communities.
>
> (Emphasis added, Strategic Plan, p. 2)

There are five pillars in the strategic plan and 37 action items. The five pillars are, (1) exceptional student experience, (2) inclusive excellence, (3) high-impact research, (4) civic university with global impact, and (5) foundation for inclusion and distinction. We begin by reviewing pillars two and four of the university's five-year Strategic Plan (2021–2026). Specifically, these action items point to meaningful engagement with Indigenous Peoples, the African Nova Scotian community, and government partnerships.

Pillar 2 Inclusive Excellence

This pillar emphasizes nurturing our talent, removing barriers, and seeking the most accomplished and promising individuals, with special attention placed on the Mi'kmaq and African Nova Scotian communities.

> We will invest in developing a more welcoming, inclusive, and caring culture for all, regardless of one's background and circumstance, emphasizing wellness, accessibility, respect, and support for all members of our communities.
>
> (strategic plan, p. 9)

Specific actions emphasize the commitment to growing the knowledge and practices that cultivate an environment of support. Activities include the development of leadership curricula steeped in EDIAD training and mentorship, prioritizing, and advancing the diversity and inclusion strategy with a commitment to an anti-racist culture and support mechanisms for students, faculty, and senior leaders. In addition, actions have been identified to review targeted hiring initiatives when necessary to ensure significant improvements in recruiting

African Canadian and Indigenous faculty and staff and a commitment to retaining African Nova Scotia and Mi'kmaq faculty and staff.

Pillar 4 Civic University with Global Impact

Essential to this discussion is pillar four which considers the importance and enactment of meaningful and authentic inclusion, equity, and diversity with respect to the Mi'kmaq and the African Nova Scotian communities. Actions 3, 4, and 5 specifically address the need for deep and meaningful partnerships with the Mi'kmaq, the African Nova Scotian community, and the government to improve access and success for students, faculty, and staff from underrepresented communities. This includes the respect for "contemporary scholarship and wisdom of Mi'kmaq Elders, knowledge holders, and scholars (p.13)". Emphasis is also placed on creating safe and welcoming learning and research spaces on campuses by working with the community to understand the unique and specific needs of Mi'kmaq and African Nova Scotian community members.

Several texts and studies have documented the treatment of the Mi'kmaq and African Nova Scotians at the hands of White settlers and the huge gaps in health, education, progress, prosperity, and economic and entrepreneurial opportunities, created because of the historical and contemporary injustices perpetrated on these communities. In recognizing these events and past actions, we note the role that the university could have played in being a beacon of hope and a leader. However, Dalhousie has historically been noticeably absent and often complicit in perpetuating the injustices in the context of slavery of peoples of African descent and the marginalization of both Mi'kmaq and African Nova Scotians. The plan outlines an imperative that the university take specific actions to ensure that our shared history is not forgotten and students in the post-secondary education space are given every opportunity to learn about this neglected history (Baylis et al., 2019, pp 88–89).

The Report on Lord Dalhousie's History on Slavery and Race states explicitly:

> As part and parcel of Black Atlantic Canada, the historical and geographical space created and defined by the intersections and interactions of slavery and colonialism, Canada and Nova Scotia are not only implicated by this history but are also obligated to acknowledge and address the consequences and ongoing legacy.
>
> (Cooper et al, 2019, p 86)

Such actions require (in part) that textbooks provide accurate histories of the injustices perpetrated on enslaved persons and acknowledging the complicity of the university in either ignoring or even partaking in the benefits accruing from the slave trade. The path forward is one of recognition, reconciliation, and recompense. While this report, conducted by a team of scholars, recommends the recognition of the colonial and post-colonial aftereffects on the African Nova Scotian communities, recommendations are equally applicable to the Mi'kmaq community, who also bore of the harms of brutal colonial occupation.

The field of management education needs to evolve to acknowledge these injustices and marginalization of these communities, while also recognizing the great contributions of members of these communities to management. While historical accounts largely focused on predominantly White workers migrating from Europe, to work in American and Canadian industries, scant attention has been paid by historians, management experts, and others to the plight of the marginalized communities that lived in the midst and at the edges of the growing early 20th century cities. Building on Young et al (2009), with slavery legally abolished in the US and Canada, and with the growing demand for workers, we suggest that organizations need every person to be part of the growing industries on either side of both the World Wars. However, both Dalhousie University and industries in Nova Scotia did not adequately respond by ensuring that African Nova Scotians, freed slaves, and free Black persons were provided sufficient means and access to employment, better living conditions, and a chance to prosper.

The Role of the of One Faculty of Management in Driving Inclusive Change

Among the several recommendations from the Lord Dalhousie Panel report, in this chapter, we will focus on what the Faculty of Management has sought to do in recent times around creating awareness of the injustices perpetrated on the African Nova Scotian and Mi'kmaq communities historically and presently. Our efforts reflect some of the activity the university has undertaken to nurture a climate of inclusion in the faculty, as the university seeks to become a welcoming place for people from historically marginalized communities. Significantly, these efforts are also focused on creating pathways for members of these communities to be part of the post-secondary experience.

Racism and Our Response

Racism presupposes that people of different backgrounds, ethnicities, cultures, etc. possess vastly different abilities. The process of colonization seeks to subjugate those deemed as "others" by force, and convert, exploit, and make disappear any cultural uniqueness of these cultures. Furthermore, any competing narratives are quashed and a narrative of uncivilized people, requiring acculturation and re-education in the norms of the dominant culture (Schwartz et al, 2010), is allowed to seep into public memory and documented histories. The issue then faced by modern educators is not just one of creating pathways into the minds of students about pre- and post-colonial histories (as prevalent) but includes the opening of the minds of the students to alternate narratives and histories that reveal the extent of the atrocities perpetrated on the subjugated communities and the economic cost of any reparations that can and should be made. Many historical corporations and family businesses have been built on or have benefitted from slavery and indentured labor and resulted in profits that did not account for the cost of forced labor. Management education is often focused on industries, cost of goods sold, breakeven analysis, return of investment, examples of legendary company leaders turning corporations from bankruptcy to profitability. Critical scholars are reconstructing our understanding of history and addressing the amnesia of labor identities left out of mainstream history (Cooper, 2000; Knight, 2004; Jones, 2021).

However, management education and textbooks in the post-secondary space have yet to fully reconcile themselves to acknowledging the contributions of BIPOC in the growth of industry, government, governance, and intellectual contributions in both industry and academia. To that extent, much effort is needed from academics and university administrators to create the spaces for learning, curating new resources and sharing of this knowledge, and concurrently creating the welcoming and nurturing spaces for BIPOC persons (students, faculty, staff) in the university milieu. This is important, for it does not end with attracting, selection, and recruitment, which has led to tokenism, but retention and ensuring the success of BIPOC persons to live and thrive in the post-secondary environment, through to career success.

Creating Welcoming Environments

When one works to create an environment that is welcoming of everyone, particularly those who have been historically marginalized, care needs to be taken that those who occupy the spaces learn to be welcoming and nurturing. Because BIPOC persons have been underrepresented in the university and post-secondary ecosystem, they will be reticent to enter these spaces as they do not see enough of others like them in these spaces. According to Dalhousie Census Report (2019), 1.5% of the student body in this faculty comprises undergraduate and masters level students self-identifies as Indigenous and 2% as African Ancestry (Black). At the staff level 9% identify as Indigenous and zero as Black, with Indigenous faculty representation also at zero in this particular faculty, and less than 5 faculty self-identifying as Black. These statistics help to emphasize the importance of taking action. Faculty, staff, and students occupying these spaces need to be open to embracing and celebrating all things around equity, diversity, accessibility, and decolonization. Only then will people of diverse backgrounds begin to feel more comfortable in these spaces and feel that they too belong. One key caveat is that all are welcomed because we celebrate their uniqueness and do not seek to have them conform to the dominant narrative for them to acquire a sense of belongingness in the post-secondary spaces.

As academic leaders, faculty, staff, and students who have had the historical privilege and access to higher education, it behooves us to be ever watchful of our language, our behavior, our actions, and our follow-through, when we set out to enact any strategic initiatives that will endeavor to make for a welcoming space in the post-secondary arena for members of marginalized communities. It is also important that we do not approach this with an air that conveys to everyone that we have deigned to create these welcoming spaces and that members of marginalized communities need to recognize our greatness and benevolence and therefore, be grateful. Rather, as we begin the process of reconciliation and decolonization, we seek the input of community leaders and engage in conversations with community groups and aspirant members. With this feedback, we also will need to make changes to curriculum that will take into aspect the contributions of BIPOC people in the growth of management education and look to weave into course materials (or re-write), conceptually and contextually, scenarios that involve management problems that deal with gender equality, reducing inequalities, justice and reconciliation, and equitable work and educational environments, all of which are stated United Nations Sustainable Development Goals. In the next sections, we will describe several efforts that are underway in the Faculty of Management at Dalhousie University. In so doing, we also recognize the imperfectness of these efforts as they are necessarily processes of "becoming" with ongoing efforts of critical appraisal, evaluation of our assumptions, values, and actions and working collaboratively to employ a more reflexive way of doing management education (Cunliffe, 2004).

Three Mini Cases in Dalhousie University's Faculty of Management

As we set out on our strategic journey, the commitment to drive change came easily. However, enacting that change required conversations, work plans, and agreement on how best to move forward. Building from the Lord Nelson Report, we were grateful for faculty, staff, student, and community input on what to change. We present three mini cases demonstrating forward movement on our strategic planning goals and initiatives. We also follow these cases with challenges as the path is full of ebbs and weaves to navigate the complexity of EDIAD and the unique needs of every community and every person.

We start with our EDIAD lens in our Faculty of Management strategic planning process with a direct commitment led by the second author, who leads the EDIAD Strategic Pillar. Next, to demonstrate how we have embraced the unique Indigenous and African Nova Scotian student experience, we share the inception and growth of the Promise Scholar's program in 2020. Our third case supports our commitment to engage Mi'kmaq Elders and knowledge holders, and African Nova Scotia cultural knowledge experts in our course design and content development. Our first author shares how she worked with community to develop an MBA leadership course with an objective to develop our leader's awareness of the benefits of various cultural practices and to create a learning space rich in Indigenous and African Nova Scotian traditions and inspired by neglected wisdom.

Case 1: EDIAD Commitment – Make It Clear We Need to Drive Change

In case 1, we aim to share how our faculty has embraced EDIAD as a core pillar in our Faculty of Management Strategic Plan (2021–2026) to demonstrate our commitment to our university strategy and our BIPOC faculty, staff, students, and communities.

In the last three years, there have been very specific efforts in the faculty to create welcoming and nurturing environments for BIPOC persons to feel embraced and celebrated. While developing our strategic plan, we recognized the importance of committing to the change, but a big part of the challenge was creating awareness on a broad scope that is meaningful, avoiding tokenism, and recognizing that EDIAD shows up differently for everyone. As the faculty crafted the strategy, the Lord Nelson Report's perspectives, lessons, and recommendations stayed at the center of our commitment to change.

Our three strategic initiatives helped to prepare our community to navigate a changing world and labor market by offering a model management curriculum. We emphasized the value of experiential learning, especially work-integrated learning; literacy, attitude, and skills development; relevant content; and a commitment to the United Nations' Sustainable Development Goals. Strategic initiative three seeks to specifically address the creation of welcoming and nurturing environments for historically marginalized communities, redress the lack of representation, and move beyond tokenism. This is a significant challenge and worth investing energy and effort. The strategic initiatives led to the formation and implementation of nine clusters that are intended to work in concert with one another. Cluster 1: Support Inclusion and Reconciliation is stewarded by our second author (Dr. Sundararajan), the Director of the Business School. The mandate is to prepare a three-year work plan to design and implement critical EDIAD programs and practices in the faculty.

Equipped with this mandate, the EDIAD cluster, as it has been named, has met to explore who should be involved in deciding what constitutes a welcoming environment, and what measures should be adopted. To this extent, the group reviewed third-party diversity metrics like MESH/Diversity (a method to measure, track, and improve DEI efforts) and invited speakers from the community to share in our EDIAD journey, so we can work toward establishing a baseline to measure progress. These metrics broadly fall under two categories, metrics for diagnosis and metrics for tracking progress. The diagnosis metrics explain how our recruitment and retention efforts are working. This includes compensation elements, engagement activities, legal and regulatory factors (e.g., grievances and lawsuits), and our partner and stakeholder engagement efforts. The progress metrics help assess if we are heading in the right direction toward achieving our stated goals. Our goal is to establish baselines and work toward a more inclusive and welcoming workplace using the United Nations Foundation commitment to diversity.

> We actively work to increase diversity, advance equity, and facilitate inclusion in a work environment welcoming to all where everyone feels valued and are empowered to do their best work regardless of age, sex, gender identity, disability, race, ethnicity, nationality, origin, religion, sexual orientation, or any other identity. We hold ourselves accountable to challenge our biases and to dismantle racists and discriminatory systems and structures.
> (*Organization Diversity*, n.d., para 5)

Concurrently, efforts are underway by the newly established standing committee on EDIAD to educate faculty members on Universal Design for Learning (a framework for expanding access to education through inclusive learning experiences) and a refresh in the faculty's Masters program that seeks to signal outwardly how EDIAD, and United Nations Sustainable Development Goals (UNSDGs) are embedded across the curriculum. This program refresh includes new courses on Environmental, Social, and Governance (ESG) and EDIAD, a new, under-construction Equitable Admissions Policy, the removal of barriers to admission like the standardized testing as an entry requirement, and the admissions committee undergoing unconscious bias training. To address recruitment and retention goals initiatives include targeted hiring positions, creating an internal inclusion survey, and increasing undergraduate student diversity by designing new equitable admissions policies for all programs associated with this faculty. While these initiatives are underway, faculty and staff need more support in learning to do things differently, including the language they use while teaching and conducting research. Other efforts to improve the feeling of belonging from members of historically marginalized communities include many visible and invisible activities spanning the experience in our buildings and classrooms, and in interactions with teaching and administrative staff through celebratory cultural events on campus.

This first case is rooted in Dalhousie University's aim to foster reconciliation between the university and the African Nova Scotian community in response to the Lord Dalhousie Report. The efforts also address some of the calls to action for Truth and Reconciliation with our Indigenous communities. The actions take the form of structural change at all levels of the university.

In case 2, we present a program to support Black and Indigenous students to become leaders and mentors in Nova Scotian communities.

Case 2: The Promise Scholars Program – Develop and Nurture Diverse Talent

Case 2 highlights an award-winning program started by the Faculty of Management in 2020 that all university-level institutions adopted in the Atlantic region to support Indigenous and African Nova Scotian youth post-secondary education. This program directly responds to recommendation 11 from the repair section of the Lord Nelson Report to provide resources to support African Nova Scotian students and Black faculty and staff.

> Establish financial aid for African Nova Scotians enrolled in undergraduate and graduate programs at Dalhousie University to support recruitment and retention, as previously articulated in the Bombay-Hewitt and Belong Reports.
>
> (Baylis et al, 2019, p. 92)

In 2020, the Faculty of Management created the Promise Scholars program at Dalhousie. It offers financial aid and wraparound support at the undergraduate and graduate level. The promise is to support Black and Indigenous students to become leaders and mentors in the Nova Scotian communities. As noted in the Lord Nelson report, Dalhousie did not have a welcoming environment for Black, Indigenous and People of Color. Our collective futures require us to attend how we have excluded and prevented racialized students, especially Black and Indigenous students, from fulfilling their potential (aka promise). Promise Scholars are given support with financial resources, academic mentoring, work and internships experiences, and personal and career coaching as these youth are significant contributors in the private sector, not-for-profit, government, small business, and in their communities.

In spring 2021, Promise Scholars grew to include all business schools across Atlantic Canada, with 13 universities in four provinces working together. The Atlantic Credit Unions also joined forces as the initiative aligned with its strategic goal to improve financial inclusion and resilience of Atlantic Canadians and create a more equitable and diverse business community. In addition, the *Atlantic Business Magazine* became a partner to help raise the profile of the regional initiative in their print and web magazines. Most significant was their reach to Top 50 CEOs past and present to support the Promise Scholars program. With the expansion to a regional program, business leaders could choose the university of their choice to partner with and grow the inclusion agenda in their community. In 2022, the *Atlantic Business Magazine* named the Atlantic Promise Scholars initiative its 2022 Top CEO Charity of Choice for its regional impact through the participation of all university-level business schools in the region and focused on the growth and development of Black and Indigenous students into leaders.

Moving beyond the borders of Atlantic Canada, the faculty initiative grew into an international campaign with donors from around the world. As a result, in Fall of 2022, Dalhousie's Faculty of Management quadrupled its intake of Promise Scholars students for undergrad and doubled its intake for graduate programs. The focus on encouraging diversity in business will make the region stronger. Diversity in the profession strengthens communities and increases innovation in the workplace, overall profits, and employee performance and satisfaction. If our classrooms and boardrooms include representation from our diverse community, our businesses and organizations will become stronger and more sustainable.

This leads us to case 3, where we share a new course development built on Afrocentric and Indigenous ways of knowing and doing in one of our Master of Business Program in Leadership.

Case 3: A Curriculum Beyond Inclusion – It's About Community

Our last case involves developing a new course steeped in Indigenous and Africentric values and principles for the MBA-Leadership program. For this case, our first author provides a personal narrative of the curriculum change's approach and rationale behind the course content design.

In July 2020, I joined the Faculty of Management at Dalhousie University, specializing in Indigenous and African Nova Scotian research contexts. I have over twenty years of working in Indigenous communities with opportunities to work with the Indian Act Section 82 c Chief and Council system and the Mi'kmaq Grand Council, a hereditary Chief and leadership body. I am grateful for the experience to engage in community activities with my Mi'kmaq partner, children, and extended family members and friends. Through these different lenses as a facilitator-researcher and a new non-L'nu community member, I have embraced a Two-Eyed Seeing (Hatcher et al, 2009) approach to my work and life. I must state that I can never understand the experience of a Mi'kmaq community member and the historical traumas and experiences. Still, I am blessed to experience the collective practices of a community that cares for one another. These sharing and caring are concepts are entirely different from what I understood growing up in a Eurocentric world. It is not about give and take, but instead, it is about supporting and learning together. In the following paragraphs, I will describe the rationale and design for developing a collaboration course in our master's program in our Faculty.

My goal when creating the "Building Collaborative Capacity" for the master's students was to share the different perspectives on collaboration and leadership from Western, Indigenous, and Afrocentric lenses. The course unfolds across three modules, with several lessons within each module. This course's overarching goal is to turn tensions between stakeholders and ideas into opportunities for innovative growth through collaboration. Students are introduced to various theories and practices that act as drivers for collaboration in contemporary organizational contexts, shifting away from routine and conventional gathering methods. In the second and third modules, students explore a diverse range of collaborative approaches and apply them to resolve complex problems in the society.

Module one introduces collaboration theory to students and quickly moves them into seeing how traditional collaboration strategies are infused into organizational practices. COVID-19 has demonstrated a need to be innovative in how we engage employees in the workplace, and we are faced with the complexity of virtual and in-person spaces and contexts. We explore systemic discrimination, racism, and unconscious bias and explore "othering" to help open our minds and embrace dialogue in our collaborative practices.

As the educator and facilitator, I help move the students toward understanding how Afrocentric leadership approaches can be employed in everyday contexts. I bring in community leaders to share their knowledge and first voice accounts. This approach to applying Afrocentricity is consistent with traditional African human development enshrined in concepts like Sankofa – the traditional proverbial bird reminding us to look back and pick the jewels we might have missed in our development journey (Small et al, 2020); Ubuntu – "I am because you are:" and the famous African proverb "It takes a village to raise a child" (Ngomane, 2019). These values are also consistent with the inclusive government policy rooted in the cultural relevance of learners that the Nova Scotian government is currently pursuing (Frempong, n.d.).

In the final module, I guide the students toward understanding how Indigenous leadership approaches can be employed in everyday contexts. Students learn about three Indigenous collaboration concepts. The first is "Two-Eyed Seeing", a decolonizing paradigmatic approach which focuses on the ability for traditional knowledge and Western knowledge to be combined and used as a vehicle for knowledge development within Indigenous communities and beyond. The second is "Netukulimk", a complex cultural concept that encompasses Mi'kmaq sovereign laws and guides individual and collective beliefs and behaviours in resource protection, procurement, and management to ensure and honour sustainability and prosperity for the ancestor, present and future generations. The third is a "Sharing Circle" led by an Elder rooted in acknowledging past traumas to Indigenous communities and recognizing the importance of Truth and Reconciliation in our organizational practices.

Central to the delivery of these modules is that students engage in sharing circles with Elders from the Mi'kmaq community in Nova Scotia and learn the practices of Ubuntu and Sankofa in classroom exercises with African Nova Scotia leaders and scholars from Dalhousie and the community. The new curricula aim to create a space where all students can engage in learning that has diverse sources of knowledge and practice imbued with cultural values and principles. The feedback has been exceptional, and in the final reflections of the course, when I ask what students will take back to their workplaces, it is the Indigenous and Afrocentric practices that almost unanimously are valued as the most helpful and insightful elements of the course.

In my journey as a scholar, I will continue to share these practices with a very important commitment: it is not my place to teach these concepts, instead it is my role to facilitate the engagement of community experts to share their wisdom and knowledge with students. My hope is to inspire faculty colleagues to embrace other teaching and learning methods to create a more diverse and welcoming environment for our students.

It's a Long Journey – Stories of Three Challenge Areas

It is also important to share the challenges we face implementing our strategic plan and EDIAD work plan. We share three challenges that we continue to face for our readers to consider as they implement their own strategies.

Challenge #1 Recruitment

To be candid, our recruitment efforts have fallen short of meeting candidate expectations. Though offers have been approved and been made to BIPOC candidates and even non-Canadian citizens, Dalhousie has been unable to always meet expectations of rank, salary, and tenure expectations. This speaks to Dalhousie relative difficulty in competing for top diverse talent and capitalizing on the associated benefits. Part of the challenge around the rank and promotion is our very biased tenure and promotion process that places weight on a candidate having progressed through a North American tenure and promotion process, as opposed to similar processes from elsewhere in the world. The challenges here are archaic institutional processes and our own biases that seem to rear their ugly head even when we have purported to change and effect changes.

When recruiting persons of African Nova Scotia descent or Mi'kmaq or Indigenous backgrounds, we must change our hiring processes entirely to recognize the unique benefits associated with hiring diverse local candidates who may not necessarily have pursued the typical academic path. Such change is slow but the work that Dalhousie is undertaking (and the values we are committed to) is bringing the issues to light. We do not want to lose the opportunity to spot, recruit, and retain talented individuals who can lead us to a more inclusive approach to management education.

Challenge #2 Retention

The challenges around retaining talented people from traditionally marginalized communities are greater than retaining those from more privileged backgrounds.

It is easy to thrive in an environment where your opinions are seen to matter, your voice is heard, and you feel welcome. In such spaces, faculty and staff can quickly acquire a sense of belonging. This can also be driven by the visibility of colleagues like themselves, thriving in the same environment.

For those from the traditionally marginalized communities, it becomes several orders of magnitude harder, as they seek to find a place for themselves in the workplace. For some perspective on this experience, our second author recounts his own experience in the faculty, where he has just entered his 15th year as an academic.

My education is in communication and rhetoric, with an engineering background. This already set me apart from the majority, who were PhDs in a different discipline. Hired as a probationary tenure-track assistant professor, primarily to teach first year Business Communication courses in the Bachelor of Commerce program, I had to work extremely hard to convince my colleagues that I was multi-talented and multi-skilled and equipped to teach and research in a range of areas. What kept me going was the belief that some of my senior colleagues had in me. They became my mentors. To them goes the credit for putting up with my uniqueness, which I have never subjugated. I fought the urge to be silent, instead expressing myself honestly and completely. I was also given opportunities to engage in developmental and formative conversations that involved the School and the Faculty. These conversations helped me feel connected to strategic work. In retrospect, I recognize my privilege even as person of colour. These faculty mentors joyfully participated as co-applicants in my tri-council grant awards. They recommended me for leadership roles. They cheered me on when I expanded my teaching skills in many allied areas in the faculty. As a result, I developed the confidence to teach across many faculty programs, and this has resulted in my becoming the first person of colour to hold the role of Director of the Business School.

I value the journey as much as I value my mentors and colleagues and the lessons that I have learned about what it takes to retain someone. The key to this is recognizing the value someone brings, allowing them to be their own true selves and express themselves without fear of ridicule or recriminations. It also requires continuously ensuring that the environment is healthy and devoid of maliciousness, gaslighting, micro-aggressive behaviour, and celebrating everyone's contributions.

The challenge is that this is easier said than done, as everyone is battling their own conscious and unconscious biases. I believe that the way to overcome this challenge is for faculty, students, and staff to continuously engage in dialogue around EDIAD, promote first voice accounts from those from traditionally marginalized backgrounds. The stories that we tell, about our lived experiences can both inform how to move forward and celebrate our collective successes. I believe that my experience can also be a potential model for those following in my footsteps.

It is our perspective that mentorship and sponsorship are central to developing the necessary connective tissue for diverse faculty and staff to feel a sense of belonging. Though it remains an unofficial practice requiring significant commitments of time and resources, it is clearly a critical driver for change.

Challenge #3 Cross-Cultural Events

The Faculty of Management has never had or conducted any cross-cultural events apart from the now morphed International Student Success Program that conducted annual Lunar New Year events. However, change is afoot. Driven by student societies with the faculty, the faculty is now poised to host the first every student-run cross-cultural event.

The student societies have each also created a VP-EDI role in their executives. In our post-COVID reality, we are looking forward to relaunching the Lunar New Year celebration alongside a new effort to develop similar events in celebration of Mi'kmaq and African Nova Scotian communities and to celebrate additional high holidays such as Kwanzaa and Eid. These initiatives are seen as tangible efforts to celebrate our diversity, to promote inclusivity, and to educate all of us.

Conclusion

The field of management (and management education) exists in a pluriverse of globalized development. We wish to be at the vanguard when tackling the worlds wicked problems (of reducing inequalities, reducing discrimination based on any physical, psychological, mental, or spiritual aspect, alleviating poverty and food insecurity, valuing the relationships we have with the land we have settled in, cherishing the life above land, life below water, respecting the treaties of friendship and peace, and recognizing the loss of culture due to slavery). As a faculty engaged in management education, we need to ensure that all who come to seek management education depart as evolved, ethical, and transcendent leaders able to tackle any challenges in this ever-present VUCA (volatility, uncertainty, complexity, and ambiguity) world.

In a book about the history of management education in Canada, our chapter reflects on how one institution is acknowledging historical wrongdoings and the ongoing legacies of racism. We provide knowledge and practices (and challenges) through the presentation of three mini cases to help other schools address the considerable neglect of the value of BIPOC economic activity and influence, business, and consumerism in our society. Among the several recommendations from the Lord Dalhousie Panel report, we focused on what the Faculty of Management has sought to do recently to create awareness of the injustices perpetrated on the African Nova Scotian and Mi'kmaq communities. In addition, we provided insights as to how we are working to nurture a climate of inclusion in the faculty that is still in a state of *becoming*. The faculty's work is creating more inclusive pathways in the post-secondary process. We encourage educators, business schools, and management faculty across Canada to look at our shared history and our shared responsibilities. We acknowledge that there remains much work to do, but we hope to inspire our readers with the learning we have done and continue to do.

References

Anderson, J., & Boyle, C. (2019). Looking in the mirror: Reflecting on 25 years of inclusive education in Australia. *International Journal of Inclusive Education*, *23*(7–8), 796–810.

Baylis, F., Cameron, D. C., Francis, M. A., Lovejoy, P., Tillotson, S., Whitfield, H. A., ... & Saney, I. (2019). Report on Lord Dalhousie's History on Slavery and Race.

Berlach, R. G., & Chambers, D. J. (2011). Interpreting inclusivity: An endeavour of great proportions. *International Journal of Inclusive Education*, *15*(5), 529–539.

Chiariello. (2016). Social justice standards: The teaching tolerance anti-bias framework. *Montgomery, AL: Southern Poverty Law Center*.

Cooper, A. (2000). Constructing black women's historical knowledge. *Atlantis*, *25*(1), 39–50.

Cunliffe, A. L. (2004). On becoming a critically reflexive practitioner. *Journal of Management Education*, *28*(4), 407–426. https://doi.org/10.1177/1052562904264440

Dalhousie University. (2019). *Dalhousie Community Equity Data Report*. Dalhousie-Community-Equity-Data-Report-2019.pdf

Fernandez, C. C., & Benner, A. D. (2022). Psychological resources as a buffer between racial/ethnic and SES-based discrimination and adolescents' academic well-being. *Journal of Youth and Adolescence*, *51*(4), 599–613.

Frempong, G. (n.d.). *DBDLI Research: Vision, Community Participation and Collaboration*. Delmore Buddy Daye Learning Institute. Retrieved January 8, 2023, from https://dbdli.ca/wp-content/uploads/DBDLI_Research_Document_web.pdf

Goggins, S. (2019). Reshaping public memory in the 1619 project: Rhetorical interventions against selective forgetting. *Museums and Social Issues*, *14*(1–2), 60–73. https://doi.org/10.1080/15596893.2019.1992832

Hamilton, S. (1999). Naming names, naming ourselves: A survey of early black women in Nova Scotia. In S. Bristow, P. Brand, D. Carty, L. Cooper, AP. Hamilton (Eds.), *We're Rooted Here and They Can't Pull Ups Up: Essays in African Canadian Women's History* (pp. 13–40). University of Toronto Press.

Hatcher, A., Bartlett, C., Marshall, A., & Marshall, M. (2009). Two-eyed seeing in the classroom environment: Concepts, approaches, and challenges. *Canadian Journal of Science, mathematics and technology education*, *9*(3), 141–153.

Jones, N. H. (2021). Our democracy's founding ideals were false when they were written. Black Americans have fought to make them true. In *The Best American Magazine Writing 2020* (pp. 359–382). Columbia University Press.

Knight, M. (2004). Black Canadian self-employed women in the twenty-first century: A critical approach. *Canadian Women's Studies*, *23*(2), 104–110.

Ngomane, N. M. (2019). *Everyday ubuntu: Living better together, the African way*. Random House.

Organization Diversity. (n.d.). unfoundation.org. Accessed Jan 31, 2025. https://unfoundation.org/organization-diversity/

Prieto, L. C., & Phipps, S. T. (2021). Why business schools need to address black history: It's time to decolonize the business curriculum. *Harvard Business Review Live*. Retrieved from https://hbsp.harvard.edu/inspiring-minds/why-business-schools-need-to-address-black-history

Schwartz, S. J., Unger, J. B., Zamboanga, B. L., & Szapocznik, J. (2010). Rethinking the concept of acculturation: Implications for theory and research. *American Psychologist*, 65(4), 237

Small, P. F., Barker, M. J., & Gasman, M. (2020). Sankofa. *Sankofa: African American Perspectives on Race and Culture in US Doctoral Education, 1*.

Sundararajan, M., & Sundararajan, B. (2015). Immigrant capital and entrepreneurial opportunities. *Entrepreneurial Business and Economics Review, 3*(3), 29.

Williams, K. S. (2020). Finding Viola: The untrue, true story of a groundbreaking female African Nova Scotian entrepreneur. *Culture and Organization, 27*(5), 365–385. https://doi.org/10.1080/14759551.2020.1833207

Williams, K. S. (2022). *Historical Female Management Theorists: Frances Perkins, Hallie Flanagan, Madeleine Parent, Viola Desmond*. Emerald Publishing.

Williams, K. S. (2024). Re-storying Canadian Entrepreneur and Civil Rights Leader, Viola Desmond (1914–1965): A Polemic of the Heart. In A World Scientific Encyclopedia of Business Storytelling Set 1: Corporate and Business Strategies of Business Storytelling Volume 4: Diversity and Business Storytelling (pp. 71–96).

Young, N.M., Sundararajan, B., P. Stewart & Stewart, M. L. (2009, Dec). Even superheroes need a network: Harriet Tubman and the rise of insurgency in the New York State Underground Railroad. *DuBois Review, 6*(2), 397–429.

9 From Past to Present
Tracing the Development of Canadian Doctoral Programs in Business

Christopher M. Hartt, Nicholous M. Deal, and Ellen C. Shaffner

Introduction

There is no shortage of work exploring the origins of management as a discipline. That is because the formal study of management is relatively new; a long past but a short history (Wren & Bedeian, 2024). Indeed, the hallmark of a maturing field like management is often measured by the coverage (i.e., breadth and depth) of scholarship contained within it (Śliwa & Kellard, 2021). More than anything, management is a vast, multidisciplinary field. Part of any field's maturation process, especially that of a field as new as management, is the development and entrance of new scholars to said field.

The development of management as a discipline, and with it, the development of an academe within which scholars may specialize, is primarily rooted in the history of American business schools. In fact, most narratives about management and the history of management learning and education center in the United States (US) (Cummings et al., 2017). This focus on the US was one reason for Barbara Austin's (2000) book, *Capitalizing Knowledge: Essays on the History of Business Education in Canada*. Austin's text sought to place the Canadian model of business education on the map and show how the development and production of the management field through education occurred differently between the two countries. However, Austin's alternative history of the business school does not focus on the way in which business and/or management doctorates have impacted the field in Canada. Our chapter picks up this thread and is concerned with the development of a Canadian management discipline (McLaren & Mills, 2015), specifically through doctoral programs in business and management in Canada over the past 60 years.

Our chapter unfolds as follows: first, we provide background and context on the development of Canadian business schools. We draw on narratives of vocationalism, warfare, and neoliberalism to understand the impetus for business education in Canada. We then outline our method for exploring the more specific case of doctoral business education, reviewing how we employ non-corporeal actant theory to trace the changing contexts that co-create doctoral business

DOI: 10.4324/9781003612612-10

programs in Canada. Our analysis reveals an origin story of the PhD in management across Canada, and we discuss the ways in which the non-corporeal actants (NCAs) of tradition, legitimacy, replication, and rigor impact that origin story from past to present. We end with a consideration of how our investigation of the development of doctoral business education in Canada points to a need to challenge the status quo of management education in Canada.

Canada and the Business School

The story of the Canadian business school begins similar to that of its counterpart in the US. Just as the education landscape in the US had morphed from commercial and propriety colleges to the newly founded business schools at Wharton, Dartmouth, and Harvard (Spender, 2005), Canada underwent an evolution of its own in the early 20th century. First, the model of commercial schools had spilled over into Canada starting in the late 19th century. Boothman (2000a) reports that by 1915, 28 of these schools were teaching stenography in downtown Toronto with some 2000 stenographers graduating annually. What made these schools popular was the fact that curriculum within the public secondary education could not keep up with the growing prestige of corporate employment and what that entailed: technical training of skills like bookkeeping, for example. Over time, however, these private colleges met the same fate as their American counterparts: an overcrowded marketspace gave the university a point of (slow) entry (Russell, 2018). In Canada, universities used existing curriculum to build business programs and thus business education initially comprised political sciences, languages, pure sciences as well as accounting and economics. The latter eventually became known as 'employable disciplines' (Römgens et al., 2020). The use of existing, established curricula to build and market a business-appropriate education offered a metaphorical backdoor for universities to sneak into a new and rapidly growing sphere of influence.

The Backdoor of Early Canadian Business Curricula

The metaphoric 'backdoor' of early business curricula involved an array of subjects that took decades to meld together. Innis (2017) writes that political science and economics in particular gave legitimacy early to Canadian business training. At the turn of the 20th century, two Canadian universities moved to include these subjects within their respective social science faculties: Queen's University and the University of Toronto. The rationale behind such moves was to reorient the neo-classic character of higher education toward a modern, industrializing Canada. At Queen's, curriculum began to shift toward topics involving social utility (Neatby, 1978).

The applied nature of economics made for an easy association between an old guard of philosophical idealism and the practicalities of a new commercial world. Even as political economy departments began to take hold in other Canadian institutions, those small classes in private colleges were still churning out bookkeepers and secretaries. Bookkeeping courses had been offered in only a smattering of Canadian universities in the late 19th century but offered as a standalone elective. Around the time professional accounting credentials were being introduced in Canada, the university responded by incorporating more accounting courses. This move was made to distinguish accounting as a 'learned profession' apart from the technical side of bookkeeping (Richardson & Kilfoyle, 2012). The logic was meant to be straightforward: private institutes would train bookkeepers' techniques of recording financial transactions while the university could educate professional accountants who process and synthesize financial information.

Subject areas in political science, economics, and accounting all played a role in the development of business studies within Canadian universities. However, if the 'backdoor' was built around these, then the opening of that door to business curricula and soon thereafter, business schools, can be attributed to engineering faculties. Administrative practices (e.g., time-motion studies used to improve work methods) had already been part of American engineering programs when, in 1906, the University of Toronto made the first step in Canada toward involving employment topics in their Applied Science and Engineering programs (Friedland, 2018). Following the First World War, as soldiers were returning home and many of them aspiring to the engineering trade, the University of Toronto's Bachelor of Engineering program responded to these changing workforce dynamics by expanding its curriculum (Harris, 1976). Subjects such as economics, finance, law, and management were introduced as courses taught by professors from other professional faculties like engineering or law. In fact, for most of the 20th century, these courses became a staple in many engineering programs across Canada. But as enrollments grew, so did the reliance on instructors from outside engineering faculties.

Canadian Business Studies Front and Center

Business studies in newly minted schools across the US followed rapid expansion in the industrial institutional field. As large American enterprises began to crop up, business programs were designed to meet staffing needs of corporate bureaucracies (Muldoon, 2012). Industrialization did indeed exist in the Great White North, but as Russell (2021) points out, the difference in Canadian expansion was the impact of the First World War. Specifically, the context of war had highlighted the need for more formal management training as domestic production shifted into high gear. If Canada was to ever transform its national economy – a key step in pursuit of sovereignty – a truce between business and industrial education was needed.

What gave Canada its first undergraduate business degree program was an understanding that manufacturing was an employable sector requiring specialized knowledge of managing the shop floor. Though it has been long debated about which institution can claim the prize of being first to offer a university-level program in business (Austin, 2000; Taylor & Baskerville, 1994), Queen's University is most often attributed to this honor. In 1919, less than a year from the Armistice, the early days of business education in Canada were set in motion with Queen's University's baccalaureate program. The new program is said to have been a combination of what worked well in three competitor programs: (1) a diploma at the University of Toronto (inspired by the University of Birmingham in England) created in 1901 which obligated students to take courses in English, mathematics, and history; (2) McGill University's diploma course established in 1907 that followed the Wharton approach in its emphasis of descriptive economics and commercial geography; and (3) the University of Western Ontario who gleaned their delivery from the Harvard Business School exemplar and offered courses dealing with corporate finance and stock market activities (Daub & Buchan, 2000).

Once the degree program in commerce got its start at Queen's University, the accretion of undergraduate business studies began at several other institutions including the University of British Columbia in 1929, a full-fledged commerce degree at the University of Alberta in 1926, and an endowed professorship in commerce within the Faculty of Arts and Sciences at Dalhousie University in 1930 (Boothman, 2000a). Entire departments of business and secretarial studies were launched by private religious universities like Saint Mary's in Halifax to match local demand (Ogden & Driscoll, 2000). Even if the development of business education in Canada varied between institutions and was shaped by American and British models, it appeared as though the front door of business education had truly opened in Canada during the early to mid-20th century. As the field legitimized and enrollments grew, the next frontier on the horizon would be a crisis of credentialing business faculty.

Credentialing Crisis: Faculty Qualifications and the PhD in Management

The process of institutionalizing business education in Canada involved key actors over time: select universities mainly in Central Canada (i.e., Queen's University), provincial governments (as the source of most funding), and industry (manufacturing in particular), to name a few. Following new institutional theory that suggests the evolution of an institution involves ideas about legitimacy (Powell & DiMaggio, 1991), processes of institutionalizing the management discipline in Canada are apparent in its history. A history of the business school in Canada – arguably the training ground for Canadian management – involves the legitimacy of business schools. The way in which Canadian programs (and later, business schools) were influenced by the American institutional field seems to suggest that the Canadian success story was at least in part attributed to the growing popularity of business education in the US.

By the 1950s, not only were business degrees in vogue in American higher education, but the schools that housed them had proven instrumental in lending credibility to professionalizing management. Legitimizing management vis-à-vis a university credential seemed analogous to other respected professions like how a family physician receives a medical degree before practicing medicine. The concept of management as a profession in Canada diffused early through the Canadian management education system because, for the most part, faculty had been educated in American universities (Austin, 1998). Not only had Canada 'borrowed' the American model in setting up programs and schools, but the ideological presence of an American-educated professoriate was also becoming quite clear. The problem that Canadian schools were facing was twofold: (1) over some 30 years since the first offering of a baccalaureate program, business schools struggled with a reputation within institutions as not being a 'serious academic discipline'; (2) the profession of management had matured to the point that determining curricula and finding suitable faculty to teach was becoming a challenge.

The Administrative Sciences Association of Canada (ASAC) was founded in 1957 with the intent to help move the field toward action on these issues and more (Coller, 2021). The state of Canadian business schools at this time could not have been more dire. The mission of a serious academic institution (Engwall, 2020) involves the production and mobilization of knowledge. Austin (1998) paints a bleak picture of business scholarship at the time of ASAC's inception: little, if any, emphasis on scholarly activity since only 11.8 percent of professors held a doctorate (compared to the Canadian average of 41.7 percent at the time). This meant the professoriate was overly populated by industry professionals who spent most of their time teaching, determining curricula, and doing institutional service – hardly an emphasis on or expectation of scholarly activity (i.e., research) if even at all. Of those who did hold a doctorate, most were earned outside of Canada – primarily from schools in the US, England, or France (for schools in Quebec).

So, the view from the back of the classroom was clear: business faculty were wholly underqualified to enter 'legitimate academia.' The quality and quantity of research conducted in business schools was to blame (Maher, 1990). The question, however, was simple: what could be done? In just a few years since its founding, ASAC had become a force in business education. It acted as a forum for scholarly research. Meetings were social affairs and thus the temperature of business academia could be felt in conversations over coffee, dinner, or between presentations. From the social aspect of ASAC emerged an important group: directors of small business schools and deans of the established institutions. These were (and remain today) powerful institutional actors, welding influence over the direction of their business school and, in turn, curriculum and program development. Indeed, everyone had a stake in improving their school's practices toward a common standard of 'doing' Canadian business education (Meyer & Rowan, 1977). If nothing else, high-quality programming would garner support across governments to fund the development of qualified faculty which would, in turn, help meet the demand of increasing enrollments.

Currency within the academic community is predicated on research. For the most part, gone are the days of an apprenticeship-based scholar training model (e.g., Plato as protégé to Socrates). Instead, more formal programs have become necessary; the philosophiae doctor (PhD) is accepted as the credential for those trained in research (Cahusac de Caux, 2019). The crisis of faculty qualification appeared to have a potential remedy at the 1959 annual meeting of ASAC when it was proposed that the association "recommends to the Presidents of all Canadian universities that they give urgent and serious consideration to the need for a PhD program in business education" (Larson, 1977, p. 71). It was a question of whether the Canadian school could produce its own spawn of scholars. As our research will show, within five years of this event, the first-ever doctoral program in business – the PhD in management at the University of Western Ontario – had accepted its first freshman class in 1962 (Gwynne-Timothy, 1978).

Storying the Past: Our Approach and Method

History and the Past

The research in this chapter is primarily historical in nature. That is, we are concerned with the potential of history to help us understand the present situation of Canadian doctoral programs in management. While this study involves history from the mid-20th century to present day, we do not explore nor analyze in detail current doctoral programs other than to observe the way that Canadian business schools have evolved in their offer of training management scholars. Our research is not intended as a critique of current PhD offerings; instead, we simply wish to highlight the ways that these programs have developed over time and, through our use of NCA theory (Hartt, 2013a), explore some of the NCAs that appear to have driven Canadian doctoral education development.

We see our work as pluralizing what we know about Canadian management education's past. Austin (2000) contributed a great deal in helping us understand the historical dimension of Canadian schools and how management education developed over time. However, it has been over two decades since the publication of Austin's text, and there has been significant development in the area of historical knowledge of management and organization studies (Clark & Rowlinson, 2004). For example, concerning the Canadian context, work has been underway to address the dearth of research that considers Canadian management thought

(Arseneault et al., 2019; Coller, 2021; McLaren & Mills, 2015; Russell, 2019). In the amodern space (Durepos, 2015) that we wish to occupy in this chapter, our focus in studying the past of Canadian doctoral programs in management is best represented in multiple histories. That is, we are interested in understanding history in the practices in which history-making takes place. What this means is that the story we share herein must only be taken as a version of many histories that could be potentially surfaced about the involved actors (e.g., University of Western Ontario) and their choices (e.g., starting a PhD in management program in 1962).

Non-Corporeal Actant Theory as a Framework

To explore our version of the many possible histories of doctoral business education in Canada, we rely on the theoretical method of NCA theory. Hartt (2013a, 2019) and colleagues (Deal et al., 2019; Hartt et al., 2014, 2020) develop NCA theory to understand how our knowledge of the past is influenced by networks. NCA theory draws from actor–network theory (ANT), ANTi-History (Durepos, 2009; Durepos & Mills, 2012), and critical sensemaking (Helms Mills et al., 2010) and attempts to explain how actor–networks operate and persist regardless of whether a human actor is involved or not. NCA theory offers space for concepts and notions, such as 'rigour' or 'excellence' to operate within actor–networks, influencing the way these networks grow, develop, and change over time as actors make sense of, and are influenced by, non-corporeal elements. Ultimately, NCA theory is one way of explaining how knowledge about a thing first comes to be developed and then understood and accepted as fact.

NCA theory combines the ANTi-History (Durepos & Mills, 2012) view that knowledge of the past is created, rather than discovered by historians with the critical sensemaking framework (Helms Mills et al., 2010) that understands retrospection (the past) as a process that influences how knowledge is enacted in a particular way. These so-called influences are, as Hartt (2013b, p. 19) describes, "reified values, beliefs, concepts, and ideas which have no physical entity (corpus) but interact with the other human or non-human actors/actants of the network." 'Actors' are human (e.g., professors, historians, and colleagues), whereas 'actants' are non-human (e.g., journal article, computer, and a book). For example, we suggest that an NCA can be found in Austin's (2000) *Capitalizing Knowledge*. In the book, Austin showcases early Canadian management education as struggling to differentiate itself as more considerate and caring compared to a more capitalistic narrative in the American context. Factors like the idea of Canada being different, and having a more compassionate approach to business pedagogy, we suggest, may have had an impact on the choice to co-construct a history of management education in Canada with various contributors rather than write the history herself. The NCA in this case would be notion of Canada – as a 'kind' alternative to the American business school experiment – having at least some potential impact on Austin's approach.

In this chapter, we use NCA theory as we craft a story of doctoral business education in Canada. We consider how several NCAs may have played a role in the way that doctoral business education emerged and developed in Canada, ultimately pointing to legitimacy and excellence in particular guide the story.

Materials, Transmedia, and Traces

The material we rely upon to construct our history of doctoral business education in Canada comes from a variety of sources. Initially, we conducted a 'transmedia approach' (Deal & Hartt, 2024) which involves exploring the history of Canadian doctoral programs across multiple platforms and digital formats. We began with what was publicly available on various universities' websites – in particular, the 'about' and 'history' sections. Further, we conducted searches through the Library and Archives Canada website to follow traces (e.g., doctoral dissertations) of actors like Louise Heslop – who was among the first females to graduate from a Canadian doctoral program in business. The annals of the ASAC (including past conference proceedings) were also helpful in determining doctoral student activities within the association and across Canadian business studies field. To supplement what we found in these digital locations, we conducted a 'close reading' (Deal et al., 2018) of Austin (2000) and drew out insights to inform what we found across multiple media and in text.

What resulted from our collection of material was rich, descriptive data. We took note of names of key actors and began to 'follow them around' (Latour, 2005) across texts. For the most part, these individuals are only representative of groups or types. Actants acted as institutions and in ideas. Our efforts found that only a select group of universities in Canada, the US, England, and France acted together to produce a sense of what is 'legitimate' doctoral programming. At another level of our analysis, the AACSB (originally as the American Assembly of Collegiate Schools of Business, now Association to Advance Collegiate Schools of Business but generally referred to by the acronym) was seen as an actor which played a role in the development of PhDs in the US and, later, took a significant role in the pursuit of legitimacy by the Canadian schools. We determined that the most important among the actants are the ideas, values, concepts, and beliefs (i.e., NCAs) which influenced individual deans and university administrators to act in their labor of bringing doctoral programs to fruition in Canada. Specifically, we suggest that legitimacy and excellence are two powerful NCAs. Our analysis and following discussion will help reveal how we made these connections as we traced traces through the past to the present.

204 *Management Education in Canada*

Analysis

Our analysis of the many traces across the data revealed two parts in the story of developing domestic doctoral programs in management. These parts – or story fragments – are revealed in the two tables of doctoral programs, helping us to surface NCAs in the data. The first table shows the part of the story focuses on the 'innovators' – a label that we borrow from the common parlance of technology studies used to describe the diffusion of innovations (Rogers, 1962). By innovators, we mean those early doctoral programs starting in the 1960s–1970s and at institutions that are often esteemed in the domestic market due to their reputation and/or size (Baker, 2014; Davies & Zarifa, 2012). These are presented in Table 9.1.

In the late 1970s and early 1980s, we saw a second tier of Canadian business schools join the project. The HEC group in Montreal is a key feature; Université Laval had already started a program, and the HEC Paris influence is quite visible in Montreal (e.g., the HEC group of programs usually started with faculty from France). From 1976 to 1996, we see this second mover group entering the market.

Another part of the doctoral story begins with the first professional doctoral credential in business (i.e., Doctor of Business Administration – 'DBA') offered at Sherbrooke University that is then emulated by several others. These DBAs tend to focus more on the practical side of management. Rather than a traditional

Table 9.1 'The Innovators' doctoral programs

Institution	Degree	Year of First Admission
University of Western Ontario	PhD	1962
Université Laval	PhD	1968
University of British Columbia	PhD	1969
University of Toronto	PhD	1969
York University	PhD	1972
Concordia University[a]	PhD	1976
HEC Montréal[a]	PhD	1976
McGill University[a]	PhD	1976
Université du Québec à Montréal[a]	PhD	1976
Queen's University	PhD	1981
University of Alberta	PhD	1984
University of Manitoba	PhD	1990
University of Calgary	PhD	1991
McMaster University	PhD	1993
Carleton University	PhD	1996

Notes
[a] = denotes institutions in Quebec that share their doctoral program with HEC Montréal.

Table 9.2 'The Late Majority' doctoral programs

Institution	Degree	Year of First Admission
Université de Sherbrooke	DBA	1998
Saint Mary's University	PhD	2000
Simon Fraser University	PhD	2004
Memorial University	PhD	2007
Athabasca University	DBA	2009
Guelph University	PhD	2009
University of Victoria	PhD	2009
University of Ottawa	PhD	2016
University of Calgary	DBA	2019
Royal Roads University	DBA	2020
Ryerson	PhD	2021
Saint Mary's University	EDBA	2022
Dalhousie	PhD	2023

dissertation, DBA students produce applied research, but most include significant research requirements and produce scholars who (like those from Harvard) pose a problem for AACSB-accredited institutions. For most of its history, the AACSB excluded any credential held by faculty – especially professional doctorates – other than a PhD to count toward the school's accreditation (Elliott, 2013). In turn, for reasons motivated by obtaining (and maintaining) AACSB accreditation, it seems reasonable to believe this rule influenced the subscription of PhD programs versus the DBA. We do point out, however, that this standard from AACSB has since changed as evidenced in their recent accreditation framework that now include DBA programs. We suggest that this group, which continues to grow, would be the 'Late Majority,' a group of institutions exploiting an existing market much like when there was a proliferation of MBA programs in the 1980s (Daniel, 1998). These are presented in Table 9.2.

This overview of the data provides a means to explore the richer stories found on the university websites, university publications, archival materials, and published writings. The overview produces a topline, chronological history of doctoral business programs as they developed in Canada. Next, we explore what lies beneath the surface of said histories.

The Need for PhDs (Tradition as NCA)

One important trace to consider as we begin examining the history of business doctoral programs in Canada is the Ford and Carnegie studies undertaken to review business education in the US. These studies had a marked impact on the situation in Canada beginning in the 1950s through the development of doctoral business programs into the current day. One important outcome of these studies was that business school faculty lacked technical training, and also did not have PhDs, and were therefore not conducting research or insights into how businesses worked and succeeded (McLaren, 2019). The disconnect between the credentials of business faculty and faculty in other parts of the university was one reason for pressure on institutions to develop doctoral business education. The need for credentialed faculty was further enforced by US-based AACSB requirements that sought for programs to be taught by academically qualified instructors, i.e., those with a PhD.

As universities began to recognize undergraduate business schools for their cashflow potential (Parker, 2018), the problem of legitimacy and credentialing became more of a problem in Canada. How could qualified, PhD-credentialed faculty teach and be seen as legitimate, if there were few to no doctoral programs in Canada to produce business PhDs? The need for qualified (PhD) faculty to legitimize the business school within the traditional university system as a whole seems to be one main reason for developing PhD in business programs in Canada.

The first Canadian business doctoral program was started at the University of Western Ontario in 1962, with Universite Laval, the University of British Columbia, and the University of Toronto all following Western's lead by the end of the decade. Tradition, as imported from the US, seems to have been a key part of these doctoral programs, which emulated those at large US institutions. Indeed, many of the new faculty recruits to these innovator PhD programs (e.g., Western, UBC, and University of Toronto) were graduates of doctoral programs at the University of Chicago, University of Southern California – Berkeley, Stanford University, Massachusetts Institute of Technology, and of course, Harvard University. The Canadian programs followed their lead. For example, Western's PhD was designed by alumni of Harvard's DBA and, as such, reproduced Harvard's approach and reputation for rigor. By replicating well-known US programs, the Innovator institutions could draw on a tradition of legitimacy and excellence; a long history of how universities were supposed to work.

The 'Innovator' programs were and continue to be housed within the earliest and largest business and research universities in Canada. The schools which began these programs in Canada are among what was "The U10 Group of Canadian Research Universities." These large institutions today purportedly perform about 80 percent of all the competitive research and, in turn, are awarded the most grants (i.e., government and industry) and house most of the graduate program offerings across the country. We note that this collective has expanded twice and now consists of 15-member institutions ('Group of Fifteen'). These large institutions are important, we suggest, because as influential innovators and first movers, they set the standard for what business-related PhD programs in Canada should look like. And as noted previously, what these doctoral programs looked like were closely related to – and impacted by – what doctoral programs in business in the US looked like. Where the tradition of how universities were supposed to operate influenced the creation of these programs, these programs then became the Canadian tradition in and of themselves – a powerful model of what doctoral business education should be in Canada.

The Importance of PhDs (Legitimacy as NCA)

Despite getting their start within some of the largest and most reputable institutions in Canada, the early PhD programs were small and relatively unsuccessful. By 1971, there were only six total graduates from doctoral business programs in Canada (Boothman, 2000b). Even with tradition dictating that business education must be taught by business PhDs, the uptake of scholars into doctoral programs was low, and institutional support was mixed. According to Boothman (2000b, p. 68), in the 1950s when Western sought to emulate Harvard's DBA, one faculty member (from Arts) opined that "there wasn't enough substance to warrant a degree at this level in management." Eventually, Western received approval to start the first business PhD after abandoning the idea of a DBA. The change from DBA to PhD may represent the desire to emulate the NCA of legitimacy at the university, the PhD as a sign of academic standards.

We suggest that legitimacy continued to be an important NCA as more universities across Canada initiated doctoral business programs of their own. By the late 1970s, five more large and well-respected Canadian universities had PhD programs in business, all in Ontario and Quebec. As the number of programs grew, so too did competition and the need to stand out as a program. The need to be seen as a legitimate choice for doctoral business studies led universities to further entrench the tradition of requiring faculty to be credentialed and engaged in research. This was likely partially impacted by the AACSB, which began having an influence in Canada in the 1960s; although not many business programs joined until the 1980s. We suggest that without enrolling member institutions in Canada, the AACSB had begun to enroll ideas about higher business education in Canada. It has been long practiced that among member schools, there is a requirement that instructors for approximately 70 percent of courses offered be taught by academically qualified persons – and an academically qualified person is broadly constructed as a person with a PhD in the field or a PhD in a related field with publications in the subject taught. Together with advent of business-related research conferences and member bodies, such as the ASAC, the pressure to further legitimize business doctoral education was increasing. As universities considered or began holding AACSB accreditation, the demand for PhDs in business especially in the 1980s greatly increased, and enrollment boomed (Ellis & McCutcheon, 2000). This began a movement to develop more programs and in particular programs which could qualify faculty teaching other functional areas like accounting, for example.

The Growth of PhDs (Replication as NCA)

By the early 1990s, there were 14 PhD programs in business in Canada: 1 in British Columbia, 3 across the prairies, 10 in Ontario and Quebec, and none in Atlantic Canada. By 1991, there were 466 doctoral students in these programs. What had begun as a somewhat sputtering endeavor 25 years prior had transformed into a growth machine as the size of undergraduate business schools exploded across Canada (Austin, 2000), and faculty were sought to teach the new masses. To meet the demand, faculty with PhDs had been recruited from the US or Europe (the UK for English instruction and France for French). But salaries were generally low and teaching loads high and it was not uncommon to see a higher-than-average number of students taught by faculty from other departments. In fact, according to Boothman (2000b, p. 62), about 12 percent of university students enrolled in business programs were taught by just 7 percent of its faculty who were paid about half of the going rate in other programs, departments, and faculties. In terms of gender, yet another layer of complexity to the narrative: the number of women teaching business had grown by 1990, but women were still vastly outnumbered by men. Despite higher enrollments into business PhD programs, only about 50 PhDs in business (or business-related fields) had been awarded in Canada and there remained a demand for new faculty; thus, a demand for new business PhD programs. Universities across Canada betting on continued growth in undergraduate and MBA business programs began to produce their own PhD in business programs, making up the members highlighted in Table 9.2, the late majority.

We suggest that the late majority programs looked to the innovator programs for how to structure their curriculum – just as the innovators had looked primarily to US institutions for how to structure theirs. As institutions in the west and east began to round out Canada's doctoral business offerings, they largely replicated the offerings of the Upper and Lower Canadian innovators. By the late 1990s, these programs had gained legitimacy, built on a tradition of what PhD education looked like at US and European universities, and reproducing the approach and content of the existing programs had largely worked for all new entrants into the market thus far. By the late 1990s, there was a solidly entrenched way of doing doctoral business education. We suggest that this way built on key ideas imported from the US – neoliberalism, self-interest, and the prevailing superiority of maximizing shareholder value through managerialist approaches. That a business doctoral program would take this perspective became largely entrenched as fact as replication of the successful innovator programs took place throughout the 1990s and early 2000s. While there are some notable exceptions, such as the doctoral program at Saint Mary's University which quickly began to differentiate itself from its competitors by offering exposure to alternative, Marxist, and critical perspectives on business, by the mid-2000s, doctoral business education in Canada largely had a specific viewpoint that had been reproduced and entrenched over time with most new programs. We suggest that the replication of successful programs as an NCA has certainly impacted how doctoral business education has developed.

The DBA versus the PhD (Rigor as NCA)

One of the features of the development of doctoral business education in Canada from the 1960s on is the focus on the PhD versus the DBA. We suggest in an earlier section that the focus on the PhD arose out of the NCA of legitimacy; when Western sought to start a doctoral program, it first proposed a DBA program of a type that had proved successful at Harvard. However, the prestige associated with the Harvard name did not give the proposed DBA legitimacy at Western. Instead, a doctoral business program was only approved when it was presented as a PhD-type credential. It was not until 1998 that a DBA was offered in Canada as an alternative to the PhD – at the Universite de Sherbrooke. A second DBA program followed in 2009 at Athabasca University.

The debate between the values of a PhD versus a DBA echoes a long debate in universities: whether one's focus should be on theory or practice. In general, the DBA was designed to be more practical, and the early versions of the DBA in the US trained business practitioners to become professors of business (Pina et al., 2016). However, as business entered the university in greater focus, the needs of tradition and legitimacy seemed to override the need for practice to be a significant focus of doctoral business education in particular. Practice did not denote academic rigor or legitimacy. Again, this seems to have been influenced by the AACSB, which considered a DBA as a practitioner designation rather than academic credential (AACSB, 2021). Schools wishing to become or even remain accredited with AACSB would thus hire faculty with PhDs. Later, the expectation was that these institutions would also offer their own PhD programs too. AACSB changed their definition of what constitutes a 'scholarly academic' between their 2013 and 2020 frameworks, with the result that more schools seem to be (re)considering the DBA. For example, both the University of Calgary and Saint Mary's University have since added a DBA program, and Royal Roads University in British Columbia launched a DBA program as their first doctoral program in business.

While DBAs were initially considered too close to practice to reflect true research rigor, the notion of rigor in business, we suggest, has begun to erode as decolonial and other alternative approaches to knowledge production have increasingly challenged what is traditional and legitimate. As much as tradition and legitimacy were critical in establishing notions of rigorous PhD programs in business in Canada, those same NCAs have begun to take on alternative influence over the past ten years in particular. We suggest that rigor as an NCA was significant in the establishment of the PhD as the preferred credential in Canada, and that it too has begun to take on a new meaning today.

The State of Doctoral Education Today

At the time of writing this chapter, there are approximately 26 PhD or DBA programs producing graduates who staff Canadian business schools from coast to coast. At least two new programs are expected in the next five years – possibly more. The move by AACSB to clearly identify the DBA as a scholarly credential increases the employment potential of those who graduate from this traditionally 'practitioner' degree. The global COVID-19 pandemic has also required many universities to contemplate delivering their programs fully online. However, we suggest that what remains highly impactful as we consider the development of doctoral business education from its outset to the present are the NCAs of tradition, legitimacy, replication, and rigor. Based on our analysis, these four NCAs have significantly influenced how the network of institutions offering doctoral education in Canada has developed and grown over time, and we suggest that they will likely continue to have an impact as we move forward. In the next section, we will discuss these NCAs and the outcome of our analysis in more detail.

Discussion

Our analysis has shown how Canadian doctoral education in business has developed, from the first program in 1961–1962 through to the present. Through the framework of NCA theory, we raised four key NCAs that we feel influenced the development of business doctoral education over time: tradition, legitimacy, replication, and rigor. However, we want to be careful to note that these are just four of many possible NCAs, produced as part of just one of many possible versions of the past. While these stood out to us, we reflect that other NCAs may stand out to others engaged in a similar analysis. That said, we feel that these NCAs help tell the story of how doctoral education in business developed in Canada. By following the traces available to us, we have made sense of the story through these NCAs. Although actors, such as people and institutions, are certainly important to the story, fully tracing the actors involved in this network is far beyond the time and space available in this chapter. Instead, by employing NCAs, we arrive at a story that helps us understand how and why PhD programs in business developed over DBAs in Canada, we make sense of how these PhD programs relied on legitimacy through tradition, we see how replication of the largest and most influential innovator institutions led to the development of similar programs across the country, and we understand the complex role of rigor in the development process through the past to the present.

We suggest that the development of Canadian doctoral education in business is embedded in the tradition of the university system that was/is practiced throughout the west in the early-mid 20th century. The tradition of relying on specialized, expert scholars who most often had high credentials, such as a PhD, to teach incoming lower-level students meant that the new field of 'business' needed new expert scholars. While there was some attempt at disrupting the tradition in the US, and to some degree, in Canada, with the initial promotion of a more practical-based DBA program, tradition endured. The preferred credential became the PhD, opening the need for PhD programs in business.

We suggest that one of the reasons for tradition enduring was the legitimacy that such tradition could confer. In a nascent field, it was important to legitimize the need for scholarly activity related to business and management that was worthy of the highest-level credential. By relying on the tradition of an existing Western system, early Canadian doctoral business programs were able to convey the worthiness of their field as scholarship. Legitimacy was also sought from alignment with accrediting bodies such as the AACSB and from alignment with institutions that had reputational value, such as Harvard. This legitimacy was important because it is clear from the traces that instructors in business programs were considered less legitimate than professors in the rest of the academy. In general, they were expected to teach more, they were paid less, and they were often not included in decision-making processes. The need for legitimacy was crucial in business schools, and this need persisted at the doctoral level.

Legitimacy as drawn from tradition, accrediting bodies, and other institutions points to the third NCA, replication. We suggest that the innovator institutions in Canada largely replicated the delivery of doctoral business education that had been developed in the US and Europe. Faculty from US and European institutions were brought into Canadian institutions to reproduce these programs. By approximating the programs of institutions with strong reputations, the innovator institutions were able to gain legitimacy as first movers in Canada, while drawing on a tradition of what terminal-level university education should look like. Additionally, by justifying their replication by pointing to the AACSB accreditation body, we suggest that the innovator institutions were able to convince other actors of the need for doing Canadian doctoral education in business in a particular way. When late of majority institutions entered the market, we suggest that our traces show they largely replicated existing programs, relying on the existing formula of success, and again pointing to the AACSB accreditation as evidence for why. The late majority institutions largely did what the others were doing, further entrenching a particular way of doing doctoral business education in Canada.

In addition to tradition, legitimacy, and replication, we suggest that the NCA of rigor played a significant role in how doctoral-level business education developed in Canada. Rigor is closely connected with legitimacy in the academy, and as stated, the emerging business faculties needed to convince their colleagues of the value and legitimacy of a more mercantile field. By focusing on rigor; that is, on the import of the rules and conventions of scholarship within the field, Canadian institutions promoting business education could claim legitimacy and value. The focus on rigor brings up the theory/practice debate. When confronted with whether or not business education would be practical (and therefore, less legitimate) or theoretical (and therefore, more rigorous, scholarly, and legitimate), the innovator institutions pursued the scholarly path and endorsed rigor, theory, and the PhD, over practice and the DBA. We suggest that one of the main reasons why the DBA did not take hold in Canada until almost 40 years of doctoral-level business education had passed is because this choice to focus on rigor – to gain legitimacy through tradition – successfully launched doctoral education and was then replicated successfully by other Canadian institutions for decades.

Through our analysis and the above discussion of the four NCAs that we identify, it is possible to see how closely connected each NCA is to each other. The NCAs do not operate in siloes; rather, they impact the development of doctoral business education in Canada as a sort of web, or network. Together, these four NCAs help us make sense of how doctoral-level business education developed from past to present. The powerful nature of these NCAs also helps explain why so many of the PhD and DBA programs currently existing seem to operate in similar ways, offering similar things. We suggest that in their search for legitimacy, individual institutions relied on tradition, replicated one another, and defended their choices by pointing to rigor. We also suggest that the dominant approach to doctoral business education in Canada that emerged through our historical investigation shows the need for programs that are willing to do things differently and explore alternative understandings of powerful discourses such as legitimacy and rigor. This is crucial if business schools in Canada are to challenge the dominant, managerialist paradigms that currently underpin the curriculum of the majority of programs, at the undergraduate, graduate, and doctoral levels across the country. Without doing doctoral-level business education differently, it will be difficult to educate our undergraduate and graduate business students in different ways – ways that challenge powerful norms and assumptions and often act to marginalize alternatives to a neoliberal, vocational, and capitalist understanding of society.

Conclusion

Throughout this chapter, we have sought to surface a history of the development of doctoral programs in business in Canada and bring our version of that development into dialogue with the present. We have relied on the framework of NCA theory to help explore the powerful, non-corporeal notions of tradition, legitimacy, replication, and rigor, and how those four NCAs help us make sense of how and why doctoral-level business education in Canada developed as it has. Overall, we point to an isomorphism among Canadian business doctoral-granting institutions, with the majority of PhD and DBA programs engaging in similar approaches. While we saw a few exceptions to this dominant approach, such as through the programs at York and Saint Mary's University, the pressure to conform to what is accepted as the norm and the temptation to mimic the success of other schools seem to have moved these previously niche programs into the background. The strength of the NCAs of tradition, legitimacy, replication, and rigor persist.

There are many other issues that we could discuss in relation to how doctoral-level business education has developed in Canada from the past to the present. For example, we are concerned to see how new EDBA programs may introduce an opportunity for senior-level practitioners to pay for an expensive, doctoral-level degree based in practice, and how that may change the legitimacy of the field, and/or how we educate students. We find ourselves asking if the aim of doctoral-level education in business remains research and teaching in the academy, or whether it is undergoing a transformation into a more instrumental credential. Despite our efforts as authors, we cling to the values of tradition, legitimacy, replication, and rigor – the NCAs that have helped us understand the development of our own field through time. We wonder what our field would look like if the strength of the NCA-web as described in this chapter begins to weaken and fracture.

That said, we also recognize the potential need for such fracturing. By reflecting on the development of business schools in Canada (Austin, 2000) and specifically on the development of doctoral-level education in business, we see the way that much of our doctoral education follows a dominant paradigmatic norm. The impact of tradition, legitimacy, replication, and rigor, while helping us make sense of our own journeys through doctoral education as academics, also reveals the ways that dominant approaches suffocate alternatives. If we are largely educating our doctoral graduates in the same ways, are we not simply replicating a system that many scholars of business already recognize as problematic or, at the very least, unsustainable? Should we not be challenging the status quo of neoliberalism, the status quo of shareholder value above all else, the status quo of labor exploitation? We do not have the answers for these questions, but we are hopeful that our readers will use this historical consideration of doctoral business education in Canada to reflect on the way in which doctoral-level business education may contribute to reproducing a harmful and marginalizing status quo in Canadian society or, alternatively, may become a productive site from which to develop new possibilities in the future.

References

AACSB. (2021). Business Standards. Retrieved from: www.aacsb.edu/accreditation/standards/business

Arseneault, R., Deal, N. M., & Mills, A. J. (2019). Reading "Canadian" management in context: Development of English and French education. *Journal of Management History, 25*(2), 180–202. https://doi.org/10.1108/JMH-12-2018-0067

Austin, B. (1998). The role of the Administrative Sciences Association of Canada in institutionalizing management education in Canada. *Canadian Journal of Administrative Sciences, 15*(3), 255–266. https://doi.org/10.1111/j.1936-4490.1998.tb00166.x

Austin, B. J. (Ed.). (2000). *Capitalizing knowledge: Essays on the history of business education in Canada.* University of Toronto Press.

Baker, J. (2014). No Ivies, Oxbridge, or grandes écoles: Constructing distinctions in university choice. *British Journal of Sociology of Education, 35*(6), 914–932. https://doi.org/10.1080/01425692.2013.814530

Booth_School. (2021). 100 Years of Pioneering Research. Retrieved from: www.chicagobooth.edu/phd/program-history

Boothman, B. E. C. (2000a). Canadian management education at the millennium. In B. Austin (Ed.), *Capitalizing knowledge: Essays on the history of business education in Canada* (pp. 295–356). University of Toronto Press.

Boothman, B. E. C. (2000b). Culture of utility: The development of business education in Canada. In B. Austin (Ed.), *Capitalizing knowledge: Essays on the history of business education in Canada* (pp. 11–86). University of Toronto Press.

Burrell, G., & Morgan, G. (1979). *Sociological paradigms and organizational analysis.* Heinemann.

Cahusac de Caux, B. (2019). A short history of doctoral studies. In L. Pretorius, L. Macaulay, and B. Cahusac de Caux (Eds.), *Wellbeing in doctoral education* (pp. 9–17). Cham: Springer.

Clark, P., & Rowlinson, M. (2004). The treatment of history in organisation studies: towards an 'historic turn'? *Business History, 46*(3), 331–352. https://doi.org/10.1080/0007679042000219175

Coller, K. E. (2021). *Americanization and the development of management studies in Canada.* [Doctoral dissertation, Saint Mary's University]. SMU Institutional Repository. https://library2.smu.ca/bitstream/handle/01/29673/Coller_Kristene_PHD_2021.pdf?sequence=1

Cummings, S., Bridgman, T., Hassard, J., & Rowlinson, M. (2017). *A new history of management.* Cambridge: Cambridge University Press.

Daniel, C. A. (1998). *MBA: The first century.* Lewisburg, PA: Bucknell University Press.

Daub, M., & Buchan, P. B. (2000). Business education at Queen's, 1889-1988. In B. Austin *Capitalizing knowledge: Essays on the history of business education in Canada* (pp. 101–145). Toronto: University of Toronto Press.

Davies, S., & Zarifa, D. (2012). The stratification of universities: Structural inequality in Canada and the United States. *Research in Social Stratification and Mobility, 30*(2), 143–158.

Deal, N. M., & Hartt, C. M. (2023). A ghost in the machine: The historic caste system of Mexico as a durable actor impacting bias. In J. Helms Mills & A. Thurlow (Eds.), *Race, Ethnicity and Business Storytelling* (pp. 159–174). Singapore: World Scientific Publishing.

Deal, N. M., Hartt, C. M., & Mills, A. J. (2024). *ANTi-History: Theorization, Application, Critique and Dispersion).* Leeds: Emerald.

Deal, N.M., Mills, A.J., & Helms Mills, J. (2018). Amodern and modern warfare in the making of a commercial airline. *Management & Organizational History, 13*(4), 373–396. https://doi.org/10.1080/17449359.2018.1547647

Deal, N. M., Mills, A. J., Helms Mills, J., & Durepos, G. (2019). History in the making: Following the failed attempt of Wolfgang Langewiesche in Pan American Airways history project. In C. M. Hartt (Ed.), *Connecting values to action: non-corporeal actants and choice* (pp. 37–51). Leeds: Emerald.

Durepos, G. (2009). *ANTi-History: Toward an historiographical approach to (re)assembling knowledge of the past.* [Doctoral dissertation, Saint Mary's University]. SMU Institutional Repository. https://library2.smu.ca/bitstream/handle/01/17512/durepos_gabrielle_a_t_phd_2009.PDF?sequence=2&isAllowed=y

Durepos, G. (2015). ANTi-History: Toward amodern histories. In P. G. McLaren, A. J. Mills, and T. G. Weatherbee (Eds.), *The Routledge companion to management and organizational history* (pp. 175–202). Abingdon: Routledge.

Durepos, G., & Mills, A. J. (2012). Actor-network theory, ANTi-History and critical organizational historiography. *Organization, 19*(6), 703–721. https://doi.org/10.1177/1350508411420196

Elliott, C. (2013). The impact of AACSB accreditation: A multiple case study of Canadian university business schools. *Canadian Journal of Administrative Sciences/Revue Canadienne des Sciences de l'Administration, 30*(3), 203–218.

Ellis, R., & McCutcheon, J. (2000). The evolution of management education at a small Canadian university: The school of business and economics at Wilfrid Laurier University. In B. Austin (Ed.), *Capitalizing knowledge: Essays on the history of business education in Canada* (pp. 188–208). Toronto: University of Toronto Press.

Engwall L (Ed.) (2020). *Missions of Universities: Past, present, future.* Cham: Springer.

Friedland, M. L. (2018). *The University of Toronto.* Toronto: University of Toronto Press.

Gwynne-Timothy, J. R. W. (1978). *Western's first century.* London: University of Western Ontario Press.

Harris, R. S. (1976). *A history of higher education in Canada 1663–1960.* Toronto: University of Toronto Press.

Hartt, C. M. (2013a) The non-corporeal actant as a link between actor-network theory and critical sensemaking: A case study of Air Canada. [Doctoral dissertation, Saint Mary's University]. SMU Institutional Repository. https://library2.smu.ca/bitstream/handle/01/24847/hartt_christopher_michael_phd_2013.pdf?sequence=1

Hartt, C. M. (2013b). Actants without actors: Polydimensional discussion of a regional conference. *Tamara – Journal for Critical Organization Inquiry, 11*(3), 15–25.

Hartt, C. M. (Ed.) (2019). *Connecting values to action: Non-corporeal actants and choice.* Leeds: Emerald.

Hartt, C. M., Mills, A. J., Mills, J. H., & Corrigan, L. T. (2014). Sense-making and actor networks: The non-corporeal actant and the making of an Air Canada history. *Management & Organizational History, 9*(3), 288–304. https://doi.org/10.1080/17449359.2014.920260

Hartt, C. M., Mills, A. J., & Helms Mills, J. (2020). The role of non-corporeal actant theory in historical research: A case study of Henry Wallace and the new deal. *Journal of Management History, 26*(1), 60–76. https://doi.org/10.1108/JMH-01-2019-0004

Helms Mills, J., Thurlow, A., & Mills, A. J. (2010). Making sense of sensemaking: The critical sensemaking approach. *Qualitative Research in Organizations and Management: An International Journal, 5*(2), 182–195. https://doi.org/10.1108/17465641011068857

Innis, H. A. (2017). *Essays in Canadian economic history.* Toronto: University of Toronto Press.

Larson, M. S. (1977). *The rise of professionalism: A sociological analysis.* Los Angeles: University of California Press.

Latour, B. (2005). *Reassembling the social: An introduction to actor-network-theory.* Oxford: Oxford University Press.

Maher, P. M. (1990). Business school research: Academics should be concerned. *Canadian Journal of Administrative Sciences, 7*(1), 16–20. https://doi.org/10.1111/j.1936-4490.1990.tb00524.x

McLaren, P. G. (2019). Stop blaming Gordon and Howell: Unpacking the complex history behind the research-based model of education. *Academy of Management Learning & Education, 18*(1), 43–58. https://doi.org/10.5465/amle.2017.0311

Meyer, J. W., & Rowan, B. (1977). Institutionalized organizations: Formal structure as myth and ceremony. *American Journal of Sociology, 83*(2), 340–363. www.jstor.org/stable/pdf/2778293.pdf

Muldoon, J. (2012). The Hawthorne legacy: A reassessment of the impact of the Hawthorne studies on management scholarship, 1930–1958. *Journal of Management History, 18*(1), 105–119. https://doi.org/10.1108/17511341211188682

Neatby, H. (1978). *Queen's University: Volume I, 1841–1917: And Not to Yield.* Montreal/Kingston: McGill-Queen's Press-MQUP.

Ogden, H. J., & Driscoll, C. (2000). Business studies at Saint Mary's University: Progress with a human touch. In B. Austin (Ed.), *Capitalizing knowledge: Essays on the history of business education in Canada* (pp. 239–251). Toronto: University of Toronto Press.

Parker, M. (2018). *Shut down the business school: What's wrong with management education.* London: Pluto Press.

Pina, A. A., Maclennan, H. L., Moran, K. A., & Hafford, P. F. (2016). The DBA vs. Ph. D. in US business and management programs: Different by degrees? *Journal for Excellence in Business & Education, 4*(1), 6–19. www.jebejournal.com/index.php/jebe/article/view/63

Powell, W. W., & DiMaggio, P. J. (Eds.). (1991). *The new institutionalism in organizational analysis.* Chicago: University of Chicago Press.

Richardson, A. J., & Kilfoyle, E. (2012). Merging the profession: A historical perspective on accounting association mergers in Canada. *Accounting Perspectives, 11*(2), 77–109.

Römgens, I., Scoupe, R., & Beausaert, S. (2020). Unraveling the concept of employability, bringing together research on employability in higher education and the workplace. *Studies in Higher Education, 45*(12), 2588–2603.

Rogers, E. M. (1962). *Diffusion of innovations.* New York: Free Press.

Russell, J. (2018). *Making managers in Canada, 1945–1995: Companies, community colleges, and universities.* London: Routledge.

Russell, J. (2019). Finding a turn in Canadian management through archival sources. *Journal of Management History, 25*(4), 550–564. https://doi.org/10.1108/JMH-02-2018-0020

Russell, J. (2021). *Canada, a working history.* Toronto: Dundurn Press.

Spender, J. C. (2005). Speaking about management education: Some history of the search for academic legitimacy and the ownership and control of management knowledge. *Management Decision, 43*(10), 1282–1292.

Śliwa, M., & Kellard, N. (2021). *The research impact agenda: Navigating the impact of impact*. London: Routledge.

Taylor, G. D., & Baskerville, P. A. (1994). *A concise history of business in Canada*. Oxford: Oxford University Press.

Wren, D. A., & Bedeian, A. G. (2024). The evolution of management thought (9th ed.). Hoboken, NJ: Wiley.

10 Gendered Experiences

A Dialogic Co-Creation with One of the First Female PhD in Business Graduates in Canada

Kristin S. Williams and Louise Heslop

Introduction

Meeting Professor Louise Heslop was a fortunate accident. While researching the history of doctoral training in Canada as part of a larger project investigating the history of management education, a colleague of mine came across some of the earliest dissertation records. The University of Western Ontario (now referred to as Ivey) admitted their first PhD students in Business in 1962; the first PhD programme in Business in Canada. The first woman to earn a PhD in Business from an American University was Ursula Batchelder Stone (1929), from the University of Chicago (Chicago Booth School of Business) which launched their programme in 1920 (The University of Chicago Booth School of Business, 2004). Professor Heslop was the first woman to graduate from her programme with a PhD in Business in 1977, with a focus on Marketing (Ivey PhD Program, personal correspondence, October 19, 2021). Confirming with Ivey's PhD Program, Professor Heslop is likely one of the first, if not the first female graduates in Canada.

When I started to delve into Professor Heslop's career, I was quite frankly amazed. Not only by what she had accomplished as a brilliant scholar and academic, but I was also perplexed as to why she was ignored by Ivey as an important, pioneering graduate. I could not reconcile the attention that the University of Chicago had given Ursula Batchelder Stone (with a splashy profile, prominent on their website) with the lack of attention the University of Western Ontario had given Louise Heslop. Clearly, Ursula Stone is a point of pride for Chicago Booth. This lack of recognition certainly fuelled my desire to see Professor Heslop more broadly recognized for her trailblazing status. As I soon learned, it is not unusual for a university to privilege some archaeological and archival projects over others (Skowronek & Lewis, 2010), but this seemed like an inexcusable oversight. Indeed, this is true of my own university, where I now reside as a historian in residence and have uncovered not only gaps in policy but also in resources and planning, which has contributed to a failure to recognize notable historical actors.[1]

DOI: 10.4324/9781003612612-11

Contextual Literature Review

New historical accounts of isolated management interests are emerging (Randy Evans et al., 2013). This chapter contributes a novel biographical account of the developing history of management education in Canada and specifically the neglected story of a female trailblazer (Louise Heslop) who faced numerous gendered obstacles, including the fight for pay equity in business academia and fully waged maternity leave. In becoming one of the first PhD graduates in Business in Canada, Professor Heslop's story also highlights the overlooked role of home economics in providing women with a path to study and work in business, thus challenging our ideas of what constitutes the history of management education in Canada.

When I went looking for other accounts of early female contributors to marketing thought, there were but a few related articles. One charts the development of marketing thought and the evolving interest in the consumer, which is an area of particular interest to Professor Heslop (Zuckerman & Carsky, 1990). Zuckerman and Carsky (1990) credit the emergence of the discipline to home economics and cite the roots of consumerism to the relationship between the household and the marketplace and the homemaker as the decision-maker in a commercial setting. I see this as a significant omission in contemporary management educational thought, and we will elaborate on this further in the chapter. Home economics was a new field in the early twentieth century. An early thinker in the field was Martha Van Rensselaer (1864–1932). She taught in the School of Home Economics at Cornell University and published broadly to general audiences and women's journals (others include Christine Frederick, Sarah Splint and Katherine Fisher, see (Zuckerman, 2009)). Additionally, students of marketing history may enjoy reading *Pioneers in Marketing: A Collection of Biographical Essays* (Jones, 2012) which traces agricultural marketing, market research, teaching advertising in business schools, micromarketing, marketing systems and more.

I would also be remiss if I did not briefly contextualize this chapter in the glass ceiling literature. Women remain underrepresented in the professorate (van Anders, 2004). Since the 1970s when Professor Heslop completed her PhD, more women have entered academia, but despite this increase, there remain systemic barriers and a lack of equal representation (van Anders, 2004). Research attributes this gap to the "incongruous, gendered bureaucratic structures" and calls for interventionist strategies that address "organizational structure, culture and practice" and the "hegemonic masculine ideas that inform decisions" (Bird, 2011, pp. 203–204). More contemporary research has revealed that navigating motherhood has become no less easy for academic mothers and the pandemic has reaffirmed the dominant care role of women (Wagner et al., 2022).

Professor Heslop entered a career in academia when the dominant and assumed future path for women was to get married and have children (Beyer et al., 1996). At most, it might be acceptable for women to work at a local community college as long as it does not disrupt the career of the husband whose ambitions would take precedence (Beyer et al., 1996). Professor Heslop never doubted in her ability to have both a career and a family (and succeed in both), but she faced many gendered obstacles set by masculinist institutional norms of academia (Cyr & Horner, Reich, 1996).

Methodological Approach

Professor Heslop and I corresponded for several weeks and ultimately set up a time to chat virtually in February of 2022 – she from her home just outside of Ottawa and me from mine in Halifax. We selected a set of questions to foster a conversation on the topics that most interested me, namely her experiences as one of the first female PhD students in Business in Canada as well as her education and career path. I wanted to know: if she felt supported in her studies? Did she feel comfortable with all male peers and mentors? What gendered effects did she experience?

This chapter features highlights from our conversation. Professor Heslop was given free and unfettered editorial control, and thus, this chapter is really co-authored and co-created. Our 3-hour interview generated over 200 pages of verbatim transcripts. I then set out to draft the ensuing conversation by clarifying the critical questions, connecting the text to these answers and arranging it in a logical flow. Our draft went back and forth, and the edits focused on (1) Professor's Heslop's lived experiences, (2) preserving her voice and personality throughout, (3) keeping it deeply personal, (4) finding moments of interest for readers, (5) making explicit the "gendered moments" and (6) adding context markers and associated reading to help the reader contextualize the insights shared.

Though the process began as a typical interview with agreed-upon questions, it grew into a tight collaboration. As we reflected on this approach, we realized that we had embraced the principles of feminist phenomenological theory with both a focus on both lived and gendered experience (Butler, 1988). Our method was also aided by a dialogic, re-storying approach (Cunliffe, 2002; Grant et al., 2015) and a colloquial-styled mode of writing, akin to an interactive interview (Ellis et al., 2011).

In Conversation with Louise Heslop

Remarks of Professor Heslop will appear by the initials LH, whereas my comments will appear by the initials KW. For unspoken thoughts of mine that I wish to express to the reader directly, you will find these in italics.

> *I start with a set of questions related to her background and then continue with her early education leading up to the PhD.*

KW: Tell me a little about your background and upbringing and how these factors might have led you in the direction of your PhD in Business.

LH: As with most life choices, it was a combination of family, experiences in school, personal interests and capabilities and the help of many people along the way. I would have to say that I had what could be called a privileged upbringing. My father had an unusual background, making dramatic life choices that led from his leaving home in a small town when he was a young teen through many diverse jobs but eventually pursuing skilled training and a university engineering degree, leading to a job in industry management. My mother was the eldest child in a large working-class family but chose not to marry young and rather worked until she was 32, and unlike her siblings, left home with *this guy* with a university degree. I was the youngest of four and hung around with my brothers for many years as a child – a real tomboy. I enjoyed being with my dad and liked many of the same things – how things worked, fishing, sciences, math, reading the *Globe and Mail* and learning. I was a very good student in school and was quite successful, graduating elementary school at the age of 12. My older sister and I attended a Catholic high school for girls where I had only women teachers, which was good for me given my younger age. My friends included international students with shared interests in politics and world affairs.

KW: What was your prior education and experience leading up the PhD?

LH: Well, I have an unusual background for someone studying business at the PhD level. My first degree was in Home Economics. I have a bachelor's degree in Home Economics and an MSc degree with a thesis on causes of consumer indebtedness. Now, one of the things that's useful to understand about a degree in Home Economics is that it isn't what you might think it is. The degree had a foundation of about 16 courses mostly in the physical sciences, as well as the social sciences and the humanities. The major field areas of the Home Economics (foods and nutrition, clothing and textile sciences, housing, child and family studies) drew on these foundation courses, i.e., the degree was an applied physical and social sciences programme.

KW: How did you decide what to study?

LH: I wanted to pursue something in science and math as a university degree. My father was an engineer, and I thought I'd like that field. When I expressed an interest in engineering, my father strongly discouraged that direction; not because he didn't think I could succeed in an engineering degree programme (he believed his daughters, just like his sons, had the abilities to do anything they wanted), but because he was in industry (in the 1960s), he knew what I would face trying to get a job. He told me I would be happy for four years and never get a job. And he was probably right for the times. This was probably my first real hint about barriers experienced by women. My sister was already at the University of Guelph studying in the clothing and textiles major in the Home Economics programme, so the idea was that I would go there as well. The programme's orientation to sciences, specifically chemistry, biology and physics, was of interest. I particularly enjoyed nutrition because it was science-based. However, I discovered [while there] my interest also in the social sciences – what motivated people to behave as they do, as individuals and in groups.

It appears that the field of Home Economics is somewhat of a lost history to that of Business or Management Education. There is an interesting book I would recommend by Sara Stage and Virginia Bramble Vincenti (1997) that explores some of the links between the disciplines and outlines the barriers women encountered in college and university and subsequently in careers when attempting to achieve legitimacy and advancement. Another book by Carolyn Goldstein (2012) traces the origins of the Home Economics movement, beginning at the turn of the century, as a way to train women to be effective "home" managers.

KW: What other experiences contributed to your formative years?

LH: Every summer during my undergraduate degree, I trained at St. Michael's Hospital in Toronto as a dietetic intern to be professionally accredited as a dietitian. However, what I observed was that the dietetic profession at the time seemed little concerned about the human side of people's decisions about what they ate. I felt the human connection to nutrition was missing. My interest in pursuing the nutrition field declined at that point. However, I've continued to be interested in nutrition sciences and consumer food choices in the marketplace.

KW: Were you exposed to management as a subject?

LH: In my fourth year, I decided to double major in both nutrition and what was later called family studies and, in that area, is where I was first exposed to management as a subject. I was really interested in what people do and the science behind their choices and how they live. I had taken courses in sociology and psychology, so my interests were starting to crystallize. This is ultimately why I stayed on to do a master's on a topic related to consumer behaviour.

KW: Where did your graduate studies take you?

LH: During my master's degree, I was working with the local family services agency. The agency offered debt counselling, and my master's thesis research involved interviews with families about how they found themselves overwhelmed with debt that they could no longer manage. For some context, this was before universal health care, and one of the major findings of that research was that the debt spiral often began with significant health care bills.

For context, the Canada Health Act of 1984 introduced a national system of publicly funded health care, which was free at point of service, "portable, accessible, and universal" (Canada's Health Care System, Government of Canada, 2019). Though profound health inequities persist in Canada, Medicare remains one of the few examples of universal health care coverage globally.

KW: What happened after your master's degree?
LH: Once I completed my thesis, I was offered a teaching position at Guelph. I taught for about five years, mostly in subjects related to areas of consumer products and marketplace activities, and I also continued to do research. I was very interested in consumer behaviour and continuing my understanding of that field. Perhaps surprisingly, I had taken a marketing course at the undergraduate level as part of Home Economics, and I was starting to see synergies across the fields of interest to me. By this point, the College had completely revised its curriculum and changed its structure and programme name. I was now teaching in the newly formed Department of Consumer Studies which had hired a Chair for the department from the University of Toronto's business faculty, Dr. Richard (Dick) Vosburgh. Dick was a very supportive mentor and encouraged me to explore PhD options.

I think it interesting to note here that a degree in Home Economics in the 1960s provided a broad range of foundational training in everything from pure and applied sciences to consumer behaviour and marketing. Arguably this training was even more liberal and comprehensive than most business school undergraduate programs of today.

KW: What led you to a PhD with a focus on Marketing?
LH: I remember telling Dick Vosburgh at one point, I had been looking in the home economics literature about consumer behaviour and I said that I saw something amazing. There's so much more in the business literature, and of course, he had such a laugh. I can understand now why he found that funny, but at that point, I had never explored that literature [in Marketing]. I realized that what I really needed was a PhD in Marketing with a focus on consumer behaviour. The University of Western Ontario was the only well-established PhD Business

programme in Canada. It was an early programme (first PhD awarded in 1964), had an excellent reputation and was close to where I lived.

I now turn my questions to the Professor Heslop's PhD journey.

KW: What can you tell me about the entering the PhD programme at what many know now to be the Ivey programme at Western?

LH: The PhD was not a large programme and sometimes only took one or two students each year. The year that I entered, they admitted five, which was a large group for them. When I inquired about getting admission to the programme, I was first told "you don't have an MBA" [...], they said, "we always take in people with an MBA [...]; (at a minimum), you would have to complete courses equivalent to the first year of an MBA with outstanding grades to be considered." So, that's what I did – I completed the necessary courses part-time while I was still on the faculty at Guelph. I did some of these at Guelph and others at York [University].

I interject here, because it seems to me that the foundation that Professor Heslop had was in many ways stronger than her peers, but she was still required to take courses that duplicated the education she received in her undergraduate and master's degree. Not to mention, she was likely the only student to have done a thesis, since MBA programs do not require this. So, I put my thoughts to her to see what she says.

KW: It seems to me that you were over-qualified in many ways and one of the few if not the only student to complete a thesis, so how did you feel about this?

LH: And I had been teaching for several years as well! However, I did want a strong foundation in all the areas of business. But yes, there was considerable reluctance to consider my application. I didn't know it at the time, but there had not been a woman accepted into their PhD programme. However, my credentials were strong. I scored in the 90th percentile on the GMAT, and my business course grades were excellent, so they had to take me seriously, and they did offer me admission. However, I was told subsequently that when my candidacy was being considered, a particular faculty member had said, "all she's fit to manage is a kitchen."

KW: How did you handle that with so much grace?

LH: I certainly learned a lot about attitudes to women in the business school at Western, but I didn't really think it presented an obstacle I couldn't deal with nor something I needed to directly confront. I had a very supportive husband and family and lots of female role models and supporters, including my mother and my sister, and many female teachers and colleagues at Guelph. My education primarily in an all-female environment was good for me because there was no question for me as to what women could do and what I could do. I had had the opportunity through my schooling to excel without ever considering what impact that might have on males. Women doing things, accomplishing things and being at the top of the class was nothing new to me. And I had enough experience with boys, including hanging with my brothers for much of my childhood, not to be intimidated in interacting with them. Confidence was not an issue for me. I went in with the right frame of mind, which is, of course, "I'm going to work really hard, and I'm going to do well." Even in teaching [at Ivey], when 80% of the MBA class was male, it didn't occur to me that I should or would have any problem with that! But I also knew I wasn't going to change attitudes to women during my few years there with the established, senior male faculty members.

KW: What else can you tell me about the entry into the programme?

LH: Well, I was told later, by one of the other students in my cohort, who was also in marketing, that he had been told the only reason he was accepted into the programme was because they wanted to admit two people in marketing and they wanted me to come, so they had to take him. Not surprisingly, I was told the opposite. I was told, "we accepted you because we really wanted the other guy, and we wanted two people [in marketing]." My attitude was "whatever, I am going to be fine."

KW: And you had set your sights on marketing because you had made this connection between consumer psychology, marketing and business. Can you unpack how you made that connection?

LH: I was basically trying to find out why people did what they did in the marketplace, which led me to the marketing literature. Understanding business was not difficult for me, but I came at it with a different perspective. My interests were primarily in how to ensure the best experience for customers and the well-being of consumers in the marketplace. I recall being referred to by one faculty member as their "pinko" PhD student – which has nothing to do with being female but rather meaning being a "socialist" because I was interested in the consumer and the broader society perspective, rather than only that of business. Some faculty seem to think that was somewhat subversive in a business context. However, my perspective on marketing is that it is an exchange relationship. You need to understand the value package and the reasonableness of that value to the consumer in the short and long run, as individuals and as a society. As a business, if you are not doing that, then the relationships you are trying to build just won't happen in a sustainable way.

For US and Canadian historical women leaders, it was not unusual to paint strong female figures, who we might call feminists today, as socialists. The ideas and terms were often conflated and used to both target and attack women for occupying roles outside of gender norms. See for instance (Williams, 2022; Williams & Mills, 2017, 2018).

KW: How did these ideas about marketing line up with what you were taught?

LH: I don't think there was any particular business or marketing orientation in what I was taught that suggested business should not have a positive role in the marketplace, but I don't recall any specific concern for the social impact of business. However, the exploitive side of marketing is almost always the first impressions held by most people, and there isn't always a good effort to counterbalance that perspective in the classroom. I remember a textbook I saw in marketing one year. The cover depicted a collection of fishing lures. This just drove me crazy. I wrote the publisher, and I emailed the author. I said, "how can you do this?" I would never put such a textbook in front of my students. Too many of them think that way already – that marketers' goal is to lure people and hook them, like fish. They think marketing is just trying to trick people into buying stuff they don't need. I don't believe responsible business can think that way, and it isn't a sustainable approach. I always included this perspective in my marketing teaching over the years.

KW: Do you think you subscribed to feminist ideas at the time?

LH: Yes, I would certainly say I was firmly subscribed to feminist attitudes. I clearly saw the attitudes of many in the business school at Western – off-handed remarks made by senior faculty about my (presumed) capabilities or my appearance. I wasn't prepared to fight a battle with them as a PhD student – you're pretty vulnerable in many ways. I did see the barriers, but I was perfectly capable of accomplishing what I wanted. My background gave me considerable resilience and commitment to my chosen path, and my personal support system in family and friends was strong. My fellow PhD students were completely supportive. The faculty member on whom I would rely for support in completing my PhD, i.e., my supervisor, never gave me any reason to doubt his belief in my ability to succeed. So, bottom line, at Western, the faculty attitudes were minor issues in terms of affecting my success and were not worth fighting about – not a "hill to die on." I just got on with completing my degree and moving on with my plans for my career and for my life together with my husband. I remember being appalled when a bank manager told me my husband would have to co-sign for my education loan because he was responsible for my debt! I literally stared him down, and he gave up that position pretty quickly. I would say I didn't

Gendered Experiences 227

face the challenges many women faced because I had resources. In that respect, I'd say I was privileged. But I did recognize that barriers existed and still do.

KW: Tell me more about those early days and getting settled into the programme at Ivey.

LH: Well, let me say of course, that I was married by this time. I was leaving my home to go to London from Guelph, and I would stay there all week. So, you might ask, "how did your husband feel about that?"

KW: How did he feel?

LH: It was not an issue that created any concerns between us. He was totally supportive. He was doing his master's when I was teaching, and he had started working when I started the PhD. We were trading off who was employed and who was studying for a few years. He was very busy with his job. He knew that I wanted a career as a university academic. The PhD degree was a requirement for doing that. He's a great partner and totally subscribed to sharing the household and child-rearing. He was my birthing coach, went through two different birthing courses with me, and [he was] in the delivery room when our daughters were born in the early years of such practice. By the way, he's an engineer!

KW: Tell me more about the programme.

LH: That first year, it was intense with five courses in each term across most areas of business, but the next year involved special field studies, which for me was focused on marketing. By the end of 2nd year, there was no reason for me to be in London often. I started my PhD in 1973, and by January 1976, I was back in the classroom at Guelph with my dissertation data analysis well underway. And then I finished within that year, and I went back to teaching. I had submitted the final draft dissertation to my committee by December of 1976 with my defence shortly after, and the PhD degree was conferred the following spring, in 1977.

KW: What were the relationships like with your peers in the programme?

LH: There were five of us who started that year – as I recall, one in accounting, one in information systems, another in what he called human resource accounting, two of us in marketing. Four of us were married, and two had young children. I really enjoyed the relationships with them. The kind of interactions we had in the hallway, over coffee and among ourselves as a group were intense timewise and very supportive. I really enjoyed them and have very positive feelings about that experience [as a cohort].

KW: And what about your relationship with faculty?

LH: The younger faculty were much more accepting of me as "an anomaly," but I did get remarks. Lord knows what faculty members said about me when I wasn't there, right? Some faculty members would refer to me as "my girl" or "the girl," and occasionally there were comments made about my appearance or possibly causing difficulties being female among the all-male students. Such remarks were one of the reasons I decided not to stay there when I finished even though there were suggestions about my doing so. There was one first-year course in which early in the fall term, all the students had talk to every faculty member who was teaching us and ask about what books we should read in business, philosophy, history etc. I was quite concerned with meeting with one particularly difficult very senior faculty member who had considerable stature and control in the programme – if he didn't think you should succeed, [then] you weren't going to get through first year. So, I went to talk to him, and before I got the question out of my mouth, he said, "I don't know why you are here. You obviously won't succeed." Now, I didn't enter into an argument [with him]. I just simply said, "well, some people think I can, so we will just have to see." Another time, in class, this same professor was assigning the books we were to read for the next class, and he said everyone should read this one particular book except me "because there's unsuitable language in there." I was certainly taken aback a bit because he was so blatant about his attitude toward women as delicate, needing to be sheltered from the world. It was quite obvious to me the kind of obstacles women, and particularly myself, could face there. Very subtle, and yet Ivey has a history that extends decades after I graduated. When Ivey finally began hiring women faculty with PhDs, they developed a reputation for a glass ceiling approach to women in their faculty. Many of the women they did hire – very bright and accomplished women – were not given tenure or were not promoted and many left. The problem was certainly there when I was there and it persisted, but it is not a situation in business schools that is unique to Ivey.

As recently as 2020, an external investigation found that women who teach at Ivey's business school face systemic discrimination when applying for tenure or promotion (Richmond, 2020). In 2019, the American Association of Collegiate Schools of Business (AACSB), an accreditation providing institution to schools of business reported that schools of business have a persistent glass ceiling with women earning less, progressing more slowing and holding fewer leadership positions (AACSB, 2019).

KW: What was the book that you were not supposed to read?
LH: Saul Alinsky's Rules for Radicals (1971). Of course, I read it. He's very insightful about the use of tactics by those who could be termed the underdog or "the little guy" in confronting powerful opponents.

KW: Can you tell me a little more about the structure of the program and how you navigated it?

LH: The first year was a set of general foundations courses across most areas of business. The five of us took the same courses in seminar-style classes every day of the week in the first year. There was a tremendous workload of reading assignments for those seminars. So, I stayed in London for the week and came home on weekends. At the end of the first year, there was a written and an oral comprehensive examination across all the subjects with all the faculty present for the oral defence. At the end of the fall term of that first year, there was a practice comprehensive exam. At the beginning of the winter term, all of us [students] were told to solicit feedback from each of the faculty members about how we had done in the practice exam. I received positive feedback from the faculty members I initially visited, but it took until March before I had the courage to go back to the professor who had said "you'll never succeed." When I did, he said, "I don't know why you are here. You're doing fine. Get out." Again, I decided not to argue with him. I just took the win. The second year involved the Special Fields course with classes in one's area of concentration. We also had a comprehensive examination at the end of the Special Fields course. Besides the course work, we learned to write and had the opportunity to teach cases with evaluations of our abilities – so, case teaching was part of the PhD learning process. I appreciated the concern for teaching ability that was built into the program. By the end of the second year, I had also developed and defended my dissertation proposal and had begun data collection.

KW: Was there ever any talk about the fact that you might be the first female PhD graduate in the country, certainly at Western?

LH: Not at all, except for one comment someone made to me when I was close to completion. I was told that the Dean had apparently been perhaps bragging a bit at a meeting of the Deans, "hey, we're going to have the first woman PhD in business in Canada."

KW: Can you tell me about your dissertation?

LH: I had an idea for my dissertation topic before I started the PhD based on my experience serving as a member of an advertising industry review board. While I was on the faculty at Guelph, I served on the Advertising Standards Council of Canada, an industry self-regulatory group. I served on that Board for several years. The Board was comprised mainly of advertising industry and media people with a consumer representative and me as an academic. The Council developed codes of advertising practice which were upheld by the media, thus giving the standards enforcement process considerable power. At the time I was there, there was a set of standards for general advertising and a separate set of standards for advertising to children. I wanted to know if anybody knew how the advertising techniques that were being regulated by the industry were affecting children and what were the purchasing outcomes within the context of family purchasing dynamics. Was there research and evidence to support these decisions regarding what was in the standards and did the requirements in the standards help moderate any problematic effects on children? At the time, there was very little research. Theories about child development were just beginning to be explored by marketing and child development researchers. The topic was a very good fit for my interests and background.

If you would like to read Professor Heslop's thesis or a paper she had published on the research, please see (Louise A. Heslop & Ryans, 1980; Louise Annette Heslop, 1977).

KW: Did you have support in the direction of your research?

LH: I will say first that I did have outside support for the research from the industry, particularly Bob Oliver who was the President of the Advertising Standards Council at the time. I had a very good relationship with him while I served on the Council. He was interested in the research because of his leading role in advertising industry self-regulation, and he facilitated my access to the advertisements from the advertisers themselves that I used in my research. This was crucial support to facilitating the research itself. I also received a modest scholarship from the Canadian Advertising Foundation, which was helpful with some research expenses. However, I should note that there was no industry control or vetting of the research results. From the PhD perspective, I did receive scholarship support through the School of Business, so it was recognized that I was doing well. The marketing group also chose me to go to the American Marketing Association Doctoral Consortium, which was a fantastic opportunity to meet other doctoral students who would be my colleagues in the profession in years to come. One of the great things about going to Western was that I found the person in marketing who supported my research interests, Adrian Ryans. He had completed his PhD at Stanford University and had a strong knowledge of research. In many ways, he was a model for me of how to supervise PhD students in terms of providing support and direction. Basically, he just let me do what I wanted and was interested in and provided supportive feedback and direction as needed, rather than controlling the topic and the process. I already knew what I wanted to do and had research experience. He just basically said, "that looks like a great topic. You'll do that." Unfortunately, he left when I had just finished second year and went back to join the faculty at Stanford.

In Professor Heslop's thesis acknowledgments, she had this to say about Professor Ryan:

> He was extremely patient and generous in sharing his time and discussing ideas about this project in particular and about research in general. He was what every doctoral student needs – a source of inspiration and good counsel. I can only repay him by endeavouring to offer similar aid to my own students.
>
> *I have to confess, I too was similarly supported and encouraged, and I think it can make such a difference for women pursuing PhD studies to have excellent supervision.*

KW: What did you do when Professor Ryan left?

LH: Though he went back to Stanford, he continued to advise me. I think he understood that it would not be easy for me to find anyone else in marketing at Western who could pick me up as a PhD student at that stage. I had my data around the time he left, and we had discussed a plan for the analysis, so I proceeded on my own with the analysis and the writing. I would send him chapter drafts – hard copy by mail, given the times we are talking about – and after a few months, he would send back lengthy commentaries [on my several drafts]. He was also helpful when it came to the data analysis in a general sense. He said, "I've had some discussions with colleagues here [at Stanford] about the analysis approach, and the general consensus is that regular regression analysis won't work with your (binary) dependent variable." He said "I don't know what will work. Good luck." Today, there are well-developed procedures for doing that kind of analysis, but this was the mid-1970s and there simply weren't. It took me about 6 months of study and inquiry of various people, and eventually I was able to find an approach that did work through talking to an econometrician. But that is the fun thing about doing a PhD. There are always some wrinkles. I had lots of wrinkles. My whole committee was replaced more than once as people went on leave and were replaced, and each new person took a long time reading the document, and all, of course, had opinions about what needed changing and how complex it all was. Adrian just stayed with me as a co-supervisor (the head of the PhD programme was the resident supervisor) through it all, and [he] was there at my dissertation defence.

KW: Overall, how did you find the PhD programme?

LH: Comfortably challenging, but not difficult. In many ways, I had a better background than some of my peers, particularly in reading and conducting research. I received an excellent grounding in the business and marketing fields. I also gained a lot of confidence as an academic in business.

KW: And after the programme, you had made up your mind to not stay at Western, can you expand on why?

LH: I recognized that this was not a place I wanted to be a faculty member. The attitude to me as a woman was not helpful. I had no support systems there. It was all back at Guelph. I was offered an appointment at Guelph following the PhD as an Assistant Professor in a tenure-track position. My husband and I also had plans for where and how we wanted to live. We bought a farm shortly before I graduated and started our family shortly after.

I now transition our conversation to her post PhD experience.

KW: Please tell me what happened after you finished your PhD.

LH: I graduated in the Spring convocation, and that July I became pregnant. That was the plan. I had my PhD, and I had a good teaching job, so the timing was right. We planned the pregnancy so that I would have the baby in April. The second one we planned also, and she was born at the beginning of May. I'm a good trouper and very lucky! For the first pregnancy, I had to negotiate hard around maternity leave.

KW: What was that like?

LH: Well, the university had little experience with female faculty applying for maternity leave. They simply said, "you can go away until the beginning of September; you can have the 3–4 months and you can collect unemployment insurance." We had a faculty association, but no union, and the faculty association did not have any ability to deal with this issue. When I got the university's response, I said, "no, it is not good enough." And then they came back and said, "apply for unemployment insurance and we'll make up the difference." Again, I said, "that's not good enough." Then, eventually, they came back with "OK, never mind, we'll just pay your full salary for the four-month leave period." I said I was satisfied with that offer. Now, that may have sounded quick and easy, but it certainly wasn't. You had to push back until a fair arrangement was reached. I wasn't costing the University anything. They didn't have to replace me in the classroom. The potential impact was on my research output since I was dealing with a newborn in my research term. The resulting gap in research productivity when having and raising young children wasn't taken into account at the time and is often a problem facing women faculty still today.

According to the Canadian Labour Congress, maternity leave was introduced in Canada in 1971 as a limited 15 weeks of paid leave, or what is now referred to as unemployment insurance. The labour movement has continued to push for expanded benefits including better pay and longer leave. Professor Heslop might well have been one of the first (if not the first) to push for expanded benefits in an academic environment.

KW: What other kinds of gender barriers did you encounter?

LH: When I came back to Guelph with my completed degree and was offered a position as an assistant professor, the Dean brought me a salary offer, and I said, "that's not enough. My peers are getting this (higher amount), and that's what I want." My Dean was impressed. This had never happened before. Female faculty generally accepted what was offered. But someone had to say no, and I knew what my peers were making, and I could see no reason why I shouldn't receive the same. So, the Dean went to the President and got the salary I'd requested approved.

KW: You were very brave!

LH: I guess so, but by now I was getting it. There's no way I was accepting less than my male peers.

KW: Those are two very significant gender equity issues, paid maternity leave and pay equity in the 1970s. Did you think at the time that "I am doing this for myself, but others will benefit?"

LH: Yes. It was the first time the university did either of those things, and I did understand that this was ground-breaking and that's a good thing. I felt that they would only get good women if they did this. Most of the faculty when I was coming through the Home Economics programme were unmarried women. They were forced to decide between advancing their education and making a home. I didn't want to make that choice. I was going to have both. That was important to me and also to my husband, and we were going to have a small farm business, as well. I guess you could say we were ambitious, but these were important life goals to both of us.

I know that Professor Heslop ultimately does leave Guelph, so I prompt her to tell me what came next in her career.

KW: What came next?

LH: About 7 years later, we moved to Ottawa. My husband's job had been lost in a corporate buyout. He had several opportunities that we considered regarding the suitability to both our careers and where and how we wanted to live. He did find a good match fairly quickly in Ottawa in a position for him at Agriculture Canada as a research engineer. So, I began looking for an academic position in a business school or for a position in the government as a social science researcher. I contacted Stan Shapiro, who was Dean of the School of Management at McGill at the time and had already been an excellent mentor for me and very supportive. I worked with him on several projects, and he advised me when I was moving to Ottawa which business school to consider. I interviewed at Carleton, and I was a good fit for their needs. One of the most senior faculty in marketing at the time, Nick Papadopoulos,[2] and I shared an area of research interest in country images held by consumers and how these affected marketplace choices. I had already completed research with colleagues at Guelph with funding from Social Sciences and Humanities Research Council of Canada (SSHRC) on how products were perceived by consumers based on the producing country's image.[3] I had a good base of research funding and experience, so Carleton's School of Business was a good place for me. When I started there, Carleton didn't have a strong research focus and [the business school] was not a separate entity, [but rather] a school within the Faculty of Social Sciences. I also received an offer of to be a researcher in a new division of Statistics Canada. I took the Associate Professor position at Carleton with a 2-year leave under an Executive Interchange Agreement to have the research experience at Statistics Canada. I believe I may have been one of, if not the first woman with a PhD at the school at that time.

KW: This was early to mid-1980s?

LH: Yes, we moved to Ottawa in 1983 with our two pre-school daughters and bought a 100-acre farm and continued a beef cattle operation we had started while I was at the University of Guelph.

KW: What else was unique about your time at Carleton in those early years?

LH: The school was young and in a strong period of growth and was hiring many young faculty members dedicated to advancing research but also willing to put a lot of effort into building the school. There was a strong comradery and a strong work ethic among the faculty. We basically built that school [and] it was very close-knit… very tight relationships, really purposeful [with] a vision of where [we] wanted to go, together. During a particular period of culture shift, I served as director of the school, the first woman in that position for the school. In 1990, I was promoted to Full Professor, the first such promotion in the school. There were, I believe, two other full professors in the school, but they had been hired in at that rank.

KW: What about teaching at Carleton?

LH: I taught consumer behaviour, which was very big gap in the teaching area coverage that they needed to fill, and [I taught] Introduction to Marketing. It was a perfect fit with my interests and teaching experience. As the school grew in enrolment, I developed courses in Business Marketing, at the undergraduate level, and graduate courses in technology marketing and business research methods. I also liked

	to teach consumer, business and government relations. Working at the Advertising Standards Council at Guelph gave me an understanding of how responsible business self-regulation could work.
KW:	It seems to me that you really like the intersection of policy, ethics, consumers and value.
LH:	Yes, yes! And research of course. I especially liked teaching research methods, and I did teach it at the graduate level and introduced my undergraduate students to it in the consumer behaviour course. I loved working with [students] on that…watching and helping them craft their research question and their research approach, see the data come through the analysis process and often they'd excitedly say, "oh, look, this is what I had hypothesized!" Or helping them when they could not find a predicted result and saying, "Let's see what we can make of that." "What else might you have done?" or "What would you suggest from these results?" – in other words, what have you learned?
KW:	I don't want to sound predictable, but I am interested in what it was like for you to be a working mother. Can you tell me about that?
LH:	Well, it was very busy. It was very, very busy. And we were operating a farm, as well. This affected the household task distribution, as you might expect. We had a very egalitarian marriage. Lorne was very engaged with the children, but he had to do most of the farm work on top of his job. I helped where I could and gained a great deal of knowledge and skills in farm life, but basically did more of the traditional household chores and childcare. And you don't always think that you are doing it well. Like many women, I have an imposter complex! Someone is going to figure out that I'm not really that good at what I do – and not just in my profession. I had very little experience with children when I was growing up because I was the youngest. So, when I had children of my own, you'll love this, I said, well "I'll just reason with them, explain why, and they will cooperate. I'm sure that will work well."

At this point I must confess that Professor Heslop and I are laughing and commiserating sympathetically with these very difficult pressures placed on working moms and how much of the work of becoming a mom is "learning while doing." Professor Heslop continues.

LH:	I didn't know what I was doing! Not a clue! Despite reading lots of books about birthing, feeding, raising children – reading is what I do. But, despite my limitations, they are wonderful, wonderful daughters and brilliant women, so capable, smart, generous, accomplished, dedicated and not surprisingly, overly busy! – so, my husband and I must have done something right.

KW: I am sure you did great! What were some of the other challenges you experienced as a working mom?

LH: Finding good childcare was extremely difficult, but I did find a wonderful woman who would come into our home when the children were very little. We still call her Aunt Shirley. However, given the daily farm chores, I would take on most of the household and childcare, and my husband did more of the animal care and fieldwork, so it was busy. [After I got the kids off to bed with stories read] I would put in another 3–4 hours of work.

KW: I am curious if you felt that you got specific assignments at work that you thought were gendered?

LH: Not really, that I recall. I was certainly involved in considerable committee work. On occasion, I might point out the lack of diversity on a major committee. When I was Associate Dean (Research) for Social Sciences, a university restructuring committee was appointed by the President. Originally, it had three members, but I raised the point with senior administration that the committee consisted solely of older white men and [then] (of course, be careful what you wish for!), I was asked to join the committee. The committee was a very useful learning experience for me on university dynamics. When the report went forward from the committee to the President and was released for comment before going to Senate for approval, there was considerable resistance from some departments in Social Sciences and from the Faculty of Arts and my own Dean. The President was hesitant to proceed. I was very committed to the report. It made sense for advancing the University but required a major shift for those two Faculties. I gave the President a book on change leadership, which he did read, and I advised him to do some careful predicting of the likely outcome, i.e., "count the votes at Senate." The report passed in Senate and was implemented.

I did observe the dearth of women in senior leadership positions at Carleton. The School of Business was growing quickly during this period and hired several excellent women. There was quite a change in dynamics in the school, and the proportion of women in the Business School at Carleton was definitely higher than most other business schools. It made a difference to their level of impact. I do give tremendous credit to these very strong and competent early female leaders – for example, in the School of Business, to Lorraine Dyke[4] who in 1992 developed and led the Centre for Research and Education on Women and Work and the Management Development Program for Women, a certificate programme for women in early-stage career who were looking to advance and needed management skills. She insisted that all faculty teaching in that programme were women, so the experience in the classroom was all female because of the impact it would have in empowering the women in the programme. It was an excellent certificate programme. However, when it went to the Senate for approval, there was a lot of push back from Senate members, who were, as you would expect, mostly male. One senate member made the comment that women faculty in the school were "just flaunting their credentials for gain" because we received a stipend for teaching in that programme. Then came the question, "why don't they have a management development program for men?" It reflected a lack of understanding of the difference between equality and equity.

KW: It seems to me that you didn't allow too many things to get in your way. I try to see myself in your place and I don't know that I would have been as brave as you were in terms of asking for pay equity or asking for paid maternity leave or being selective about service proposals. It seems to me that you were very comfortable and really empowered.

LH: Yes, I was. I think that the [reason] partly comes from the experiences [that I had], in my early years, the good support I did receive at critical times and from the right people, and there were issues of timing – there is always some luck involved and lots of hard work. I felt comfortable in [and with] power. I could do it. There was no question that I could do it, though, I did recognize the inequities in the system.

KW: You've had the opportunity to supervise your own PhD students. You've had other young women come up and be educated. How did you support them?

LH: I really liked working with graduate students. It is a very personal relationship and very inspiring. You can make quite a positive difference in their career and life. I had about 30 research master's and PhD students. I like working with all students, but with PhD students, you really do get to know them, and you get to try to help them make their world work. You can be there to provide support for their degree advancement but also, as they launch their careers. I had a model in mind from my own PhD supervisor that I found worked for me. There is quite a bit of variance in directiveness of faculty supervisors. Some faculty are very directive and only take students willing to work in their own research topic area. That's not been my approach. Graduate student supervision is a big commitment, [but] over the years I've taken on a lot of students who were not in my research area at all. Part of the reason I do it is because I do feel the PhD path is so difficult and long, and their having a passion for their research area is critical to the student's success.

KW: What do you think the role of a supervisor should be? How do you supervise?

LH: It's as a facilitator and guide. I know how to do research, [and] if I can possibly help with developing their research capabilities and skills, then I will go and learn about their specific research topic area. It's part of the skill set that I can bring. I can get up to speed on the topic area pretty quickly. I can find key research and sort through it faster than a PhD student to help with what's useful and to find the important conceptual and research issues. So, I can help them understand what a research dissertation looks like, understand the intellectual leaps that are needed for their success, and how to advance the process and overcome the obstacles. That's where I can be useful to them.

KW: What about young women faculty coming up through the ranks?

LW: I do think that there are still gendered issues with new women faculty and advancing their careers. There is lots of research that shows major differences in career advancement pathways for men and women, differences still on how they negotiate, how they are rated and commented on by students on teaching evaluations, the willingness of senior colleagues to work with them on research projects, what access they have to research resources, the impact of family commitments on their work time, what demands are made of them. They are often expected to do more on the service side. They are tapped all the time, especially if there are any gender-issue-based committees. It is the same for Indigenous colleagues and those from diverse backgrounds. They are expected to "represent" the whole community – that's crazy. When they're trying to get into their first teaching post and doing all the work to prep the courses, and also trying to get their research off the ground and publish and then somebody says, "I bet we can ask 'them/her' to do this, this, and this." For women, the assumption is that she'll want to be seen to be a team-player and a contributor and it will help with her tenure and promotion, but it's only true to a point, and then it isn't true at all. So, I talk to my younger colleagues and my PhD students, both male and female and ask them to carefully make these choices. It's important to make your contributions because you have lots to offer and there is so much to learn, and you need to know the environment you are working in to make [that] contribution. It's important, but don't take everything that administration might want to throw your way. Over the last few years of my career, there were several new faculty members joining the marketing area, and [my feeling was] let's give them a low teaching load and I will carry the committee work [or the overloads] that would normally be done. It won't hurt my career. And that's fine. It is difficult being a new faculty member. There are a lot of demands, and then business schools are subject to more than most units because it is not only inside the university but also outside the university that they need to be engaged. Business schools are expected to be so much more to organizations. I do notice a considerable culture shift among both women and men for more work-life balance, but it certainly isn't easy to get that balance right.

I have but one final question.

KW: How has your experience been over the course of your career, as a woman with a PhD in Business?

LH: I think you can probably sense that I loved it and overall, feel very positive about it. There were many challenges, but hey, that's how you grow! I know I did make some mistakes and probably, if I'd had fewer outside responsibilities, I might have taken more opportunities, but I think I usually made the right decisions for me and those who are important to me. My experience at Western in the PhD programme, even though it had its bumps, gave me considerable insight on the real obstacles for women, but it also prepared me so I could say no to the lower salary, no to the inadequate maternity leave offers. I have said no to university presidents here at Carleton. I remember faculty members at different times saying, "don't do battle, Louise, you can't win against the university." But I did, and I did win, because I thought and still do think my colleagues, my School and the universities I have worked in were better off with the outcomes. I am very grateful for the great career I've have had, and I'm grateful to those who helped along the way – there were many among my colleagues and mentors, not least of all, in my family. I continue to try to contribute because I'm learning. I'm still learning. That's where the joy is!

Conclusion

My conversation with Louise Heslop was enlightening and so much fun. It was a thrill to co-create this chapter with her and to use an approach in which we could fully explore her lived experience. I am in awe of her confidence and the many gender barriers that she broke. She may be Canada's first female PhD in Business, but it would also seem that she has many other triumphs to celebrate, including being likely the first in the country to negotiate for long-term, fairly waged maternity leave, as well as a forerunner in the fight for pay equity. Her long career has allowed her to see the Sprott Business School come into being, to develop a flourishing research programme and to mentor many students and colleagues. I have no doubt that she had some luck and some great supporters, but it is also clear that she was tenacious in pursuing her goals, confident in her abilities and keen to break any barrier she encountered.

Discrete historical accounts are emerging in the management history literature, and in this case, it was a pleasure to work with Professor Heslop to help author a historical account of her own past, so very worthy of inclusion in our Canadian management education history. Perhaps the most interesting aspect of our approach is that it allowed Professor Heslop to activate her own sensemaking regarding her gendered experiences as we co-wrote and co-edited the piece. Another interesting insight was the role of home economics as an educational path for women to study and work in business. The field of home economics is likely a lost history of women's early study of business and provided a robust and comprehensive foundation for further study. This also speaks to some possible neglect of what constitutes the history of management education in Canada.

In this chapter, my goal was for you to get to know Louise Heslop and for her to receive broader recognition for the trailblazer she is. I also wanted to share a gendered perspective within the context of our understanding of the history of management education. I think it is particularly important when talking about the history of management education in Canada to consider some of the neglected stories, figures and discourses they reveal about gendered experiences. Selfishly, I also wanted for you, dear reader, to be inspired. I hope that you are.

Notes

1 At the time I wrote this chapter, I was Historian in Residence with Dalhousie's Faculty of Management, whereas now I am located at Acadia University.
2 Nicolas Papadopoulos is Distinguished Research Professor of Marketing and International Business at the Sprott School of Business, Carleton University.
3 This is an area of consumer decision-making and considers what attributes people look at when they make buying decisions and how they assess quality.
4 Dr. Lorraine Dyke is the current Vice President, Finance and Administration, Carleton University, and Professor in the Sprott School of Business.

References

Association to Advance Collegiate Schools of Business (AACSB). (2019, Mar 1). *The business school's glass ceiling*. AACSB. www.aacsb.edu/insights/articles/2019/03/the-business-schools-glass-ceiling

Alinsky, S. D. (1989). *Rules for Radicals: A Practical Primer for Realistic Radicals*. (Vintage Books ed.). Vintage Books.

Beyer, J. M., Roberts, K. H., & Von Glinow, M. A. (1996). Leaders in their field: Making a difference. In D. Cyr & B. Reich (Eds.), *Scaling the ivory tower: Stories from women in business school facultieshe ivory tower: Stories from women in business school faculties* (pp. 181–189). Greenwood Publishing Group.

Bird, S. R. (2011). Unsettling universities' incongruous, gendered bureaucratic structures: A case-study approach. *Gender, Work and Organization*, *18*(2), 202–230. https://doi.org/10.1111/j.1468-0432.2009.00510.x

Butler, J. (1988). Performative acts and gender constitution: An essay in phenomenology and feminist theory. *Theatre Journal*, *40*(4), 519. https://doi.org/10.2307/3207893

Canada's Health Care System. (2019, Sept 17). *Government of Canada.* www.canada.ca/en/health-canada/services/health-care-system/reports-publications/health-care-system/canada.html

Cunliffe, A. L. (2002). Social poetics as management inquiry: A dialogical approach. *Journal of Management Inquiry*, *11*(2), 128–146. https://doi.org/10.1177/1059260201 1002006

Cyr, D. J., & Reich, B. (1996). Conclusion: A personal quest. In *Scaling the ivory tower: Stories from women in business school faculties* (pp. 191–195). Greenwood Publishing Group.

Ellis, C., Adams, T. E., & Bochner, A. P. (2011, January). History of autoethnography. *Forum: Qualitative Social Research*, *12*(1), 345–357, Art. 10.

Ellis, C., & Bochner, A. P. (2003). Autoethnography, personal narrative, reflexivity: Researcher as subject. In N. K. Denzin & Y. S. Lincoln (Eds.), *Collecting and interpreting qualitative materials* (2nd ed., pp. 199–258). Sage Publications.

Goldstein, C. M.. (2012). Creating consumers: Home economists in twentieth century America. Chaple Hill: The University of North Carolina Press.

Grant, A., Leigh-Phippard, H., & Short, N. P. (2015). Re-storying narrative identity: A dialogical study of mental health recovery and survival. *Journal of Psychiatric and Mental Health Nursing*, *22*, 278–286. https://doi.org/10.1111/jpm.12188

Heslop, L. A. (1977). *An experimental study of the effects of premium advertising on cereal choices by parents and children.* Western University.

Heslop, L. A., & Ryans, A. B. (1980). A second look at children and the advertising of premiums. *Journal of Consumer Research*, *6*(4), 414. https://doi.org/10.1086/208784

Jones, D. G. Brian (Donald Gordon Brian) (2012). *Pioneers in Marketing: A Collection of Biographical Essays*. Routledge.

Randy Evans, W., Pane Haden, S. S., Clayton, R. W., & Novicevic, M. M. (2013). History-of-management-thought about social responsibility. *Journal of Management History*, *19*(1), 8–32. https://doi.org/10.1108/17511341311286150

Richmond, R. (2020, Feb 12). Ivey Business School, ex-professor resolve discrimination case as two more speak out. London Free Press. https://lfpress.com/news/local-news/probe-finds-women-faculty-discriminated-against-at-western-universitys-ivey-business-school

Skowronek, R. K., & Lewis, K. E. (2010). Beneath the ivory tower: The archaeology of academia. *Beneath the Ivory Tower: The Archaeology of Academia*, *82*(3), 1–341. https://doi.org/10.1080/00221546.2011.11777208

Stage, S., & Vincenti, V. B. (1997). *Rethinking home economics: Women and the history of a profession.* Cornell University Press.

The University of Chicago Booth School of Business. (2004). *100 years of pioneering research.* Chacago Booth, The University of Chicago. www.chicagobooth.edu/phd/program-history

van Anders, S. M. (2004). Why the academic pipeline leaks: Fewer men than women perceive barriers to becoming professors. *Sex Roles*, *51*(9–10), 511–521. https://doi.org/10.1007/s11199-004-5461-9

Wagner, K., Pennell, S. M., Eilert, M., & Lim, S. R. (2022). Academic mothers with disabilities: Navigating academia and parenthood during COVID-19. *Gender, Work and Organization, 29*(1), 342–352. https://doi.org/10.1111/gwao.12751

Williams, K. S. (2022). *Historical female management theorists: Frances Perkins, Hallie Flanagan, Madeleine Parent, Viola Desmond.* Emerald Publishing.

Williams, K. S., & Mills, A. J. (2017). Frances Perkins: Gender, context and history in the neglect of a management theorist. *Journal of Management History, 23*(1), 32–50. https://doi.org/10.1108/JMH-09-2016-0055

Williams, K. S., & Mills, A. J. (2018). Hallie Flanagan and the federal theater project: A critical undoing of management history. *Journal of Management History, 24*(3), 282–299. https://doi.org/10.1108/JMH-11-2017-0059

Zuckerman, M. E. (2009). A great influence still further multiplied: Martha Van Rensselaer and the Home-Making Department of the Delineator. In *Proceedings of the Conference on Historical Analysis and Research in Marketing*, Vol. 14.

Zuckerman, M. E., & Carsky, M. L. (1990). Contribution of women to US marketing thought: The consumers' perspective, 1900–1940. *Journal of the Academy of Marketing Science, 18*(4), 313–318.

Index

Note 1: Entries in **bold** refer to tables, entries in *italics* refer to figures.
Note 2: Entries refer to Canada unless otherwise indicated.

AACSB 130, 203; accreditation 205, 207, 211; influence 207, 209; requirements 206, 207
Academy of Management Journal 69, 71, 72, 76, 106
accounting courses 198
Act Respecting French 103
actor-network theory (ANT) 202
Administrative Sciences Association of Canada (ASAC) 1, 66; articles accepted 67, 71; articles written in French 81; beginning 200; commitment to French inclusion 108; conference 67–71, 75; conferences as bilingual 77; conference contributors **83-5**; conference locations 68, **86-7**; conference themes 68–9, **86-7**; divisions 67; as forum for research 200; funding support 70; growing pains 69–71, 77; presidents 67, 70, 77, 80; submitting papers 69
Advertising Standards Council of Canada 229, 230
African Nova Scotians 176
Africentric knowledge systems 157–8
American conventions, adopting 78
American publications/journals 71, 72, 73
American texts, Canadianized 20, 21, 22–3
Anglocentric character of management 107
Anglocentrism in French-speaking Universities 106–8

anti-Black racism, combating 156
ANTi-History 66–7, 202
apartheid laws 166
Applied Science and Engineering programs 198
Austin, Barbara 1, 93, 102, 103, 196, 202

baccalaureate program 199
Bachelor of Management program 45, 50, 51
Bantu languages 158
Biko, Stephen 166
bilingualism 99
Black Consciousness Movement 166
Black, Indigenous, and Persons of Color (BIPOC) economic activity, neglect of 176
Black migration into Canada 156
Black underrepresentation 156
book market 20
bookkeeping courses 197, 198
borders and boundaries 42–4
brand awareness and identity 129, 130
"Building Collaborative Capacity" 189
business, basic parameters 123
business histories 93–4
business education: absence of French perspectives 98–102; curriculum components 127–9; early curricula 197–8; French 100–2; and Indigenous knowledge intersection 150; in Quebec, evolution of 99–102; start of 95–7

244 *Index*

business needs and teaching methods gap 82
business practices, socio-cultural differences 17
business scholarship, international bodies of 130
business schools: cashflow potential 206; competetiveness 72; curriculum 71; drawing on extra-national resources (mainly US) 21, 69, 70; history of 197–201; lack of Canadian faculty 70, 206; legitimacy 199–200; over-reliance on US models 70; reputation 200; role of 120–2, 123; sense of history 35; state of 200; *see also* management education
Business Schools Association of Canada (BSAC) 121, 122, 130
business theory and usable knowledge 122–6, *125*, *132*

calls to action 151, 167
Canada: population 119, 156; regions of 98
Canadian Consortium of Management Schools (CCMS) 121
Canadian Federation of Business School Deans (CFBSD) 120–1; publications of 120–1; revolt against 121
Canadian Federation of Deans Management and Administration Sciences (CFDMAS) 70, 120
Canadian identity 80, 81–2
Canadian International Development Agency (CIDA) 121; fund mismanagement 121
Canadian Journal of Administrative Sciences (CJAS) 67, 74, 79, 80
Canadian journals 105, 106
capitalism and globalization 117
Capitalizing Knowledge (book) 1, 93, 196, 102, 103, 202
case study Dalhousie University 36-61: documents used 41–4, 56; internal reports 41; intertextual analysis framework **46**, **47**, **49–50**; interviews 41; methodology 40–1; narrative participant accounts 41–4; participants 55; social linguistic analysis 41–4, **42–4**; tensions between schools 45; timeline 56–61
Catholic Church and education in Quebec 100

Center for International Business 59
ceremony, Western and Indigenous 145
Ch'nook Indigenous Business Education initiative 150
collaboration theory 190
Collective Fingers Theory 160
colonization 98, 183; legacy of 141, 151
commercial colleges 96, 197, 198
competence 133–4, *134*; components of 133; managerial 134
conference articles: content and context 75; context-free 75–7; devaluation of Canadian sources 74–5; editor decisions 79; omitting geographical references 75, 76–7; peer reviews 78; reliance on American sources 74; written in French 77
consumer behaviour 119, 222, 223, 225, 234
consumerism 219
corporate citizenship responsibilities 128
corporate identity 145
COVID-19 pandemic, effects of 118
Credit Unions 188
culture uniqueness 183
cultures, combining 92
curriculum for globalization strategy 135

Dalhousie Census Report 184
Dalhousie Faculty Association 39
Dalhousie, Lord 179, 180
Dalhousie Report on racism 179–80
Dalhousie University: anti-Blackness 176, 179–80; connections to slavery 180; funding 38, 52; history 38; inclusive excellence 181–2; strategic plan 181–3
Dalhousie University Faculty of Management 35, 36, 37–9; candidate recruitment and retention 191–3; cross-cultural events 193; four schools of 37, 38–9, 60; history 53, 54; integrations 37; MBA-Leadership program steeped in Indigenous and Afrocentric values 177, 189–91; mini cases 185–91; presidents 38, 39; stories of change 191–3
deans 49; depicted 48; list of 61; power of 48; targets of criticism 48, 49
decolonial work 144
digitization, large scale 118–19
diploma as separate from degree 97

Index   245

diversity metrics 186–7
Doctor of Business Administration (DBA) 204–5, **205**, 209, 212; vs PhD 209; change from PhD 207
doctoral business education *see* PhDs"doing management" 51–3

École des Haute Études Commerciales de Montréal (HEC Montréal) 93, 101, 107, 204
École Supérieur de Commerce de Paris 93
economies, interdependence of 116
economy, early 95
Elders 144
engineering programs 198
English and French Canada tensions 102–3
environmentalist 143
Equitable Admissions Policy 187
equity, diversity, inclusion, accessibility and decolonization (EDIAD) 177, 192
Eurocentric views undermining Indigenous knowledge 167
exchange programs 121, 122

Faculty of Administrative Studies 58, 59
Faculty of Graduate Studies, Dalhousie 57
Faculty of Management Promise Scholars Program 177, 188, 189
First Nations University of Canada 150
foreign direct investment (FDI) 117
forgiveness 165–6, 167
French business scholars disadvantaged 105–6, 108
French Canada 104
French culture 98–9
French language; of instruction 104; placement of 92; speakers 104; underrepresented 104
French representation across universities 103–4
French society in Quebec 99
French socio-cultural context 92
funding agencies 79, 80

gendered bureaucratic structures 219
gendered experience 218–239; attitudes to women 224, 228; gendered obstacles 219, 222; maternity leave 219; pay equity 219

glass ceiling 219, 228
global competence model 133–4
global competitiveness 119
globalization: and capitalism 117; consequences of 117; definition 116; economics and sociology 116; efficiency 116; incorporating 129–31; power and legitimacy 116; and value chain 118–20
Google Scholar 107–8
gross domestic product (GDP) 117

"Halifax School" 1, 67
Harvard Law School 94
health care 223
Heslop, Professor Louise 218; on advertising 230; children 235; declines to argue 226, 228, 229; degree 221; dissertation 229; family 221; farm business 233; feminist ideas 226; gender barriers 232, 233; husband 226, 227, 233; industry support 230; interests 222; interview 220–39; marriage 235; maternity leave 232; pay equity 233; peers 227; PhD journey 224, 227; post PhD 232; research 230, 231; schooling 225; supporters 224–5, 226, 231; supporting others 237; teaching 223, 227, 229, 234–5; training 222–3; upbringing 221; as working mother 235–6
histories of business 93–4
home economics 219, 240; degree 223
human resource management (HRM) practices 17, 119
human resource professionals, need for 119
humanistic management 168

identity boundaries 44–5
identity components 40, 52–3
identity development 14
identity, interdisciplinary 36
identity regulation 40, 52–3
identity work 40, 53
immigrants to Halifax 178, 180
In.Business programme 140–1, 144, 149
income inequality 117
Indigenomics 143
Indigenous business development 150
Indigenous "cousins" 141

Indigenous cultures, dream catchers 141
Indigenous knowledge, oppression of 167, 169
Indigenous students marginalized and dehumanized 167
Indigenous view of leadership 144
Indigenous view, seven key teachings 143, 148–9
Indigenous/Western thought 142
Indigenous youth, connections to traditions 141
industrialization, transition to 95
injustices, perpetuating 182
innovator institutions 212
innovator programs 206, 208
Innovators' doctoral programs **204**
Institute of Environmental Studies 58
institutional barriers 156
interdependency 129, 160, 169
International Federation of Scholarly Association of Management (IFSAM) 130, 131
Internet and publishing 19
Intertextual Analysis 41, **46**, 51; conventions 46, 47, 48, 49; of formal documents 46, **47**; metamorphization 46, 47, 50; organizational artifacts 46, 47, 50; of participant narratives 48, **49–50**; social identities 46, 47, 49

Journal of Management 72
journals, Canadian 67, 74, 79, 80, 105, 106
journals in English 106; *Academy of Management Journal* 69, 71, 72, 76, 106; American 71, 72, 73
journals in French 77, 108–9
journals impacting factors and indices 105

Kenneth C Rowe Management Building 42, 60
knowledge 131–2, *134*; as information 12; mobilization 105; as transmitters of cultural content 13; usable 132, 133, *134*; as a way of thinking 12

'Late Majority' doctoral programs 205, **205**, 208
leadership 146–7; definition 146; traits and behaviours 146; Western and Indigenous views 144, 146–7

leadership studies 146, 181
League of Nations 10
learning by doing 144
Lord Dalhousie Report 176, 179, 180, 182; recommendations 177, 183
Lord Nelson Report 185, 186, 188

management: as an academic field 36; Anglocentric character of 107; concept of 36; fads and fashions 16; as ideology 15–17; and leadership 125; and organization studies (MOS) 93, 109
management education: neglect of French 92, 93; strawman in 45, 50; unmet needs 36; U.S.-centric 18
management knowledge: in Global South 107; as universal and western 17–18
management studies 78–9; influenced by US values and interests 78; seen as universal 76, 82
management teaching, cultural differences 17
management textbooks 20, 21; Canadianized 9; homogenous nature of 18, 19, 23; narrow domain of 16; reflecting gender binaries 23; US-centric 9, 21, 22, 23
management theory, Americanization of 65, 66
management training and welcoming environments 184–5
Management Without Borders course 45, 47, 50, 51, 61
managerial thought and practice, focus on Western ways 157
managers, idealized 15
Mandela, Nelson 159, 165, 166, 167
Marine Affairs Program 60
Maritime School of Social Work 57, 59
market surveys 19
marketing: exploitive side 226; history 219
Master of Environment Studies program 59
Master of Information Management 61
Master of Library Service 60
MBA programs 38, 120, 121, 128–9; grounded in Indigenous and Afrocentric values 177, 189–91
McGill University 97, 100, 121, 199
medicine wheel 147–8

mentoring 79, 144, 192
migration into Canada 156
Mi'kma'ki, territory 138; leadership symbol *139*
Mi'kmaq people 138, 150, 190; Grand Council 189; laws 190; needs of 182; post-colonial effects 183; treatment of 182
Mi'kmaw knowledge keeper 140
model of society 122, *123*
Montreal business schools 101
Mount Allison University 97
multinational corporations (MNCs) 117, 118

"Netukulimk" 190
non-corporeal actant theory 202–3
non-corporeal actants (NCAs) 212, 213; legitimacy 207, 211; replication 208–9, 211; rigor 209, 211; tradition 205–7, 210, 212
Nova Scotia community 182; black community of 176, 177
Nova Scotia government 39

Obama, President Barack 159
Open Educational Resources 22
Open Texts 22
Organization for Economic Co-operation and Development (OECD) 116
organizational rules 147–8

PhDs 201; built on US ideas 206, 208; change from DBA 207; courses by university **204, 205**; history of 203–5, 210–11; importance of 207; instructors recruited from US and Europe 208; need for 70, 201, 205–7; programs 70, 79, 80, 201, 207, 208–9; today 210; vs DBA 209
population of Canada 119, 156
power: as a form of domination 167; opportunity imbalance 116
productivity 119
program design 126–7, *126*
Promise Scholars Program 177, 188, 189
publishing houses 18, 19; American, British 20; in Canada 19, 20; international with subsidiaries in Canada 20
publishing industry, changing structure 18–19, 23

publishing market 18
Purdy Crawford Chair in Aboriginal Business 150

Quebec 98; Catholic Church and education 100; French culture in 99; French society in 99; modernizing 100, 101; referendum for separation 1–3
Québécois society 99, 103–4
Queen's University 97–8, 150, 197, 199; business program 97
Quiet Revolution in Quebec 99–101

racial segregation 166
racism 166, 183–4
ready-to-work graduates 39
research, importance of 201
research publications in French 107
rituals in management context 145
Rowe School of Business (RSB) 37, 38, 42, 43, 49
Rules for Radicals (book) 228

Saint Mary's University 208
Sankofa 190
School of Information Management (SIM) 37, 42, 43
School of Library Service 58
School of Public Administration (SPA) 37, 38, 42, 43, 58
School for Resource and Environmental Studies (SRES) 37, 43, 45
scientific knowledge as universal 65
SCImago index 105
security apparatus 122
self-identity 53
sense of belonging 192
settlement agreement 150
settling in Canada 95
sexist remarks 226, 228
Sharing Circle 190
skill fusion 134
skill theory 133
skills, personal, interpersonal, group, organizational 133, *134*
slave compensation money 180
slave trade beneficiaries 180, 182, 184
slave trade money 179, 180
slavery, legacy of 177
smudging ceremony 141
social capital 143

social identities 46
Social Linguistic Analysis 40
Social Sciences and Humanities Research Council (SSHRC) 70, 234
social unrest 117
South Africa: democratic elections 166; executions 166; fight against apartheid 166; "homelands" 166; as rainbow nation 167; reconciliation 166; reparation 167; Soweto school children 166; transformation 165–6; violence in 166
stenography courses 197
students, financial burden 22
Symons Report 69, 79, 82

Teaching Tolerance Anti-Bias Framework 179
technological expertise 131, 132
"textbook problem" 10–11
textbooks 18, 19–20; always out of date 12–13; cost of 19, 21–2; collective understanding 10; content 12, 23; function of 11–13; future of 21–2; ignoring BIPOC contributions 182, 184; imparting ideology and information 15; inculcate values and identities 13; influence on students 9–10; and the market 18–19; as pathways and gatekeepers 12; as perpetuation of social ideologies 12, 15–16, 24; production, niche areas 23; research 10–11; resistance to change 16; in schools 10, 11; socio-political nature 9, 10, 11–12, 23; as tools 13; ubiquity of 11
traditional knowledge practices 144
transnational mobility, people and capital 117
Truth and Reconciliation 151, 167, 190
Truth and Reconciliation Commission (TRC) South Africa 165, 166–7
Tutu, Archbishop Desmond 159, 160, 165, 166, 167; granddaughter 160
Two-Eyed Seeing 178, 189, 190

U10 Group of Canadian Research Universities (now Fifteen) 206
Ubuntu philosophy 158–62; application of 170; collective ownership 160, 164; and common good 164–5; decolonizing Western knowledge 165; equivalent words 159; and ethical thinking 164; for leadership and management 161–5; meaning 159, 160; for pedagogical change 167–9; seeing a business as a community 163; underlying principle 160, 168–9; values 160, 161, 162; valuing each individual 161, 163, 170
Ubuntu: Shaping the Current Workplace (book) 162
Unama'ki College 150
unconscious bias training 187
Underground Railroad Movement to free slaves 178
United Nations Sustainable Development Goals UNSDGs) 185, 186, 187
Universal Design for Learning 187
Université de Laval 107, 204
Université du Québec 101, 107
University of Toronto 97, 197, 198, 199
University of Western Ontario (UWO) 97, 120, 199, 201, 206, 218
Upper Canada 95
usable knowledge 132, 133, *134*

value 118
value allocation 127
value and wealth 124, *124*
value assessments 127
value chain (VC) 118, 119; and globalization 118–20; manipulating 118
value creation 123, 127
value enhancement 125, 126, 127
value exchange 127
value transaction 123
Vroom-Yetton's decision model 76

Ward, Jeff (Dancing Son) 140, 142, 144, 146, 148, 151
wealth 142–3; creation 125, 127; distribution mechanisms 123; economic terms 142–3; ignores environmental harm 142–3; Indigenous view of 143; Western profit-centric view 143
Wharton School of Finance and Economy 93, 96–7
women's advancement 238
women's work, acceptable 220
worker lay-offs 117
workers, subordination of 15
working from home 118
workplace rituals 145

Printed in the United States
by Baker & Taylor Publisher Services